I0709119

THE HORSE MASTERS

THE PRIDDEN SAGA: BOOK FIVE

J. M. TIBBOTT

Copyright ©2022 by J. M. Tibbott
All Rights Reserved

No part of this publication may be reproduced or transmitted in any form or by any means, electronic or mechanical, including photocopy, recording or any information storage and retrieval system without the written permission of the author and publisher, except by a reviewer who may quote brief passages in a review.

The author expressly prohibits any entity from using this publication for purposes of training artificial intelligence (AI) technologies to generate text, including without limitation technologies that are capable of generating works in the same style or genre as this publication. The author reserves all rights to license uses of this work for generative AI training and development of machine learning languages models.
Disclaimer:

All characters in this book are fictitious, and any resemblance to actual persons, living or dead, is purely coincidental.

Cover Art by Deranged Doctor Designs

Editor: Laura LaRocca

ISBN: 978-1-7390189-0-0

Printed in United States of America

Published by JMT Publishing, Canada
www.jmtpublishing.com
Second Edition, 2023

THE HORSE MASTERS

THE PRIDDEN SAGA: BOOK FIVE

J. M. TIBBOTT

DEDICATION

To the man who always believed in me, and,
who is always missed

Robert Kleiber.

I remember.

J. M. TIBBOTT

ACKNOWLEDGEMENTS

A special and very appreciative thanks to my critiquing partners and my wonderful Beta readers … your help has always contributed to me to let my readers know what I was up to, and to curb my tendency to become overly wordy.

A huge amount of appreciation to my friend Marilyn Temmer who helped me keep focused through a difficult year, who listened, when I slept instead of writing, and raised an eyebrow when I preferred chocolate to writing.

A special thanks to the wonderful Ed Greenwood, who acted as a mentor, and steered me back on track when my focus slipped to some bright and shiny object to the side of my path.

Much appreciation to my wonderful readers who kept requesting the next volume.

A special thanks to Irene Carr who has continually helped me promote this series, and who I discovered is a fabulous salesperson.

To my Editor who constantly guides me to improve, and critiques lovingly, with a rock-hard hand. She keeps me focused on constant honing of my writing skills.

To my sister, an ocean away, who practices tough love in her critiquing.

To all my other friends who supported me and purchased books, and to those, both near and far, whose suggestions helped whenever I was stuck for an answer.

J. M. TIBBOTT

MAP OF PRIDDEN

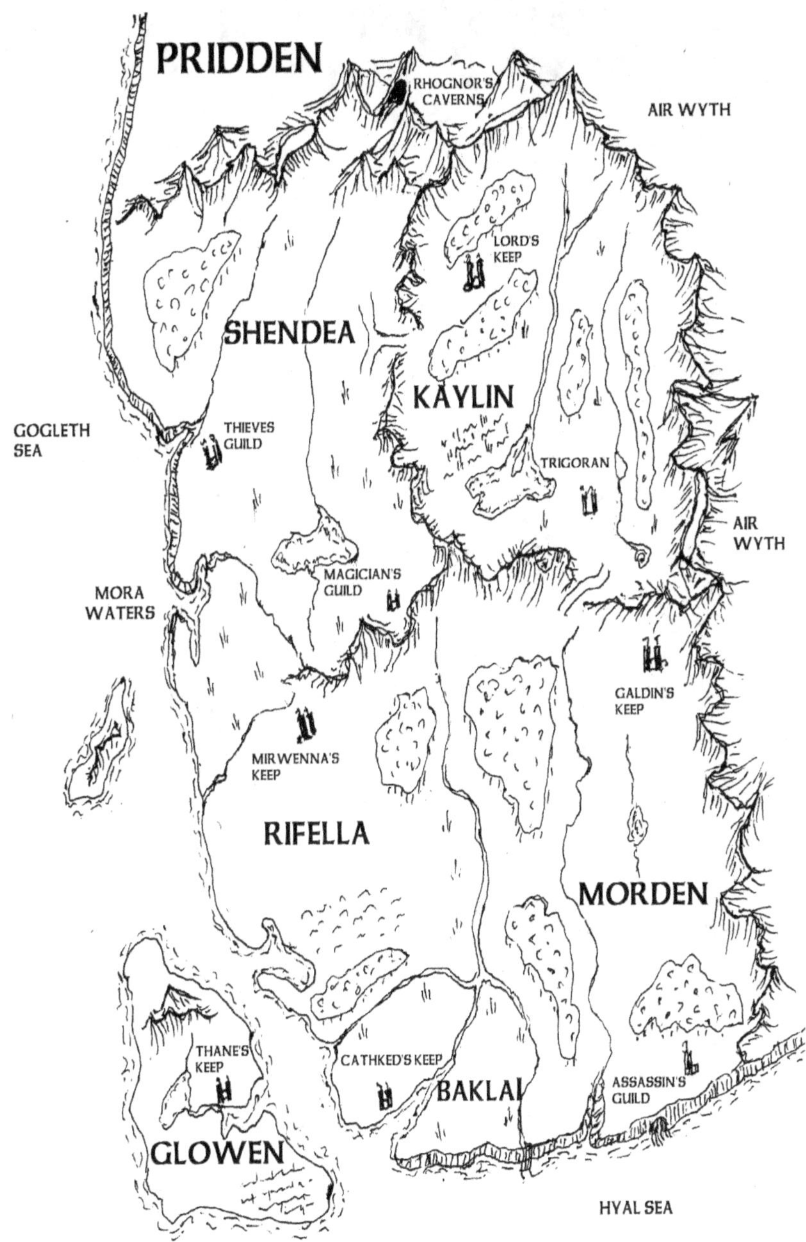

MAP OF BAKLAI

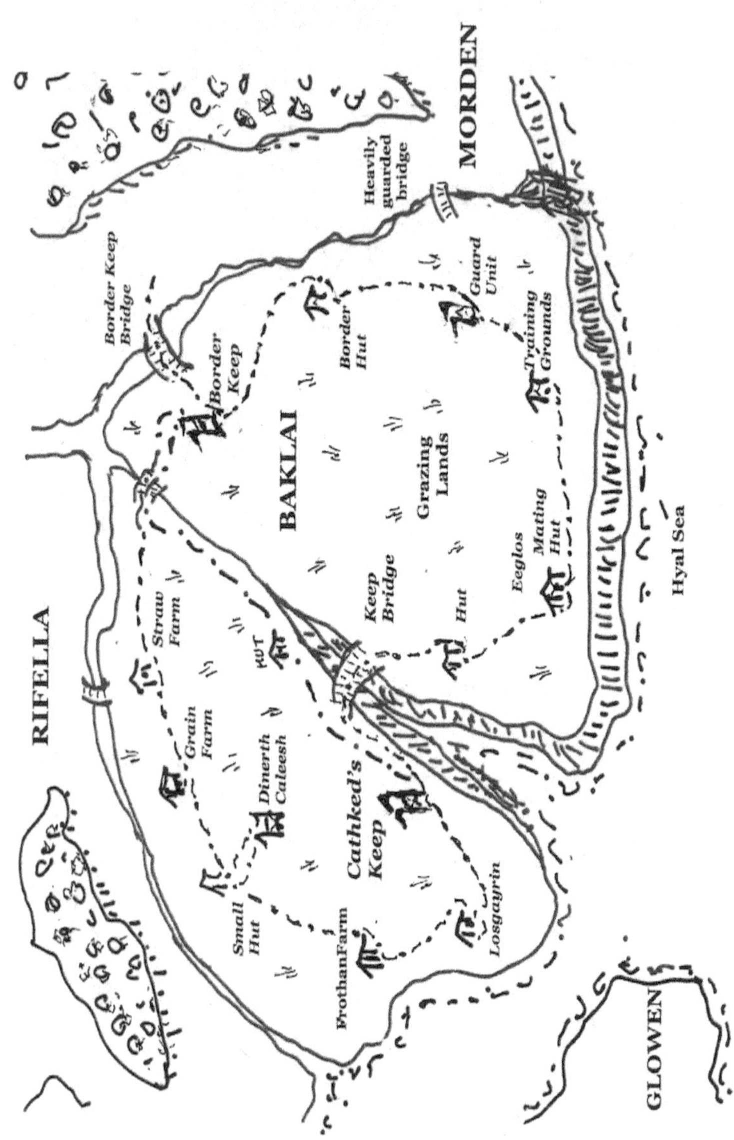

WHAT HAS HAPPENED SO FAR

Kat, a solitary but brilliant video game designer, is thrust into the unfamiliar world of Pridden, while on sabbatical, and her world is turned upside down. Offered a chance by Eduardo, the ruling Lord of Kaylin, to return home if she will help save his subjects from the winds of war, Kat must decide what risks she will take and what restrictions she is willing to accept. Beset by bizarre and ferocious creatures, narrow-minded social mores, seductively erotic men, and with no idea who is friend or foe, she must wend her way through a minefield of challenges, the biggest being capture by Assassins for transport to the foul Thane Galdin of Morden. After her rescue by Eduardo's men and other sympathetic inhabitants of Kaylin, she persuades at least two people with enough power to support her in her quest to return home.

❋❋❋

With the help of an adorable pyrock, a creature who can convey messages instantly to any area of Pridden, the journey continues, as Kat picks her way among the spiritual healers of Shendea.

In this next land, she encounters heart-stopping confrontations with a ferocious cathnog and violent strangers. Still tasked with Eduardo of Kaylin's request to help Pridden avoid a devastating war, but without clear instructions, she is escorted by her mysterious guide, Mouse, and the glorious, but invisible big cat, Shade. With her tendency to blunder through peculiar customs, how will she keep her word to Eduardo and return safely to her own world?

She is astonished by a Thieves' Guild who do not steal and Magicians' Guild who demonstrate no magic, and she learns to sidestep the wiles of the alluring Rifellans. Despite these difficult tasks, Kat is able to gain the trust and support of two residents of Shendea to help her return to her own world.

❋❋❋

When she enters Rifella, Kat, with only her guide, Mouse, and her pyrock, Wink, is often mistaken for a red-headed, royal-born Rifellan. The inhabitants she encounters are strong, fine-looking men and women who are surprisingly welcoming. Rifella is a harsh land, filled with many new dangerous creatures, and often grim terrain, but Kat is entranced by the beauty she encounters when she faces some delightful new animals.

Drawn to Liandock, the intensely attractive Metal-Master whom she encountered in Kaylin, returns, and Kat requests his help when she will need it to return to her own world.

If she can help Rifella's ruler and her heir, discover the oppositions within the land of Rifella, she may gain additional help. Mouse and Wink are integral in helping Kat escape from the terrifying Assassins and further foil Thane Galdin's intent to capture her.

❋❋❋

Sailing to Glowen, Kat is felled by seasickness. When they arrive, they meet the Thane and his advisors. The Glowens are people with yellow-gold skin, pitch black hair, and eyes that Kat refers to as wolf eyes. The Glowens are the most sensual people of all the lands, and, as such, they think nothing of demonstrating their sexual attraction to all, male or female. Kat, nonplussed by this attention, is uncomfortable, and worries they will not accept her refusals.

As she and Mouse travel around the island, they are attacked by vicious, almost prehistoric types of birds. When Kat visits the exotic flower gardens, she is pushed into the sea below, and then rescued by an enormous creature with massive teeth, who dives below the surface and takes her to an underwater cave. Here, Kat meets the Shahees, a shape-shifting, androgynous race, who are curious about her and the abilities they suspect she has. Kat is sworn to secrecy about them, and they teach her how to foil all outside attempts to penetrate her thoughts.

The Sha-hee return her to the surface, where she again meets up with Mouse. Kat flaunts Glowen customs and places herself in danger and has to call on the Thane for his help.

When she visits a vineyard and eats Orenberry grapes, she is poisoned. The cure? The placement of hundreds of pollinators, which resemble spiders, on her body.

The criminal Emrys, Wine Merchant of Glowen, threatens to kill her, he is sure she discovers his secret of providing forbidden wine to the Mordens of the north. Emrys was recruited by the Assassins to discover the true secret of Glowen. Kat is helped by the Shahee, who she knows, are the real secret.

After obtaining an agreement of help from the Thane, she and Mouse set sail for Baklai.

CHAPTER 1

The ship rounded the land's end of the main harbor of Glowen and slipped into the Mora Waters. The crew extended the boom to swing the mainsail out to the port side of the vessel. Swiftly, they swung the huge jib from the mizzenmast to the starboard side.

With the wind blowing from aft of the ship, the sails billowed out like the wings of a massive seabird, carrying the crew and passengers south toward the Teeki Dow fjord of Baklai. With only the foremast square-rigged, the slender length of the ship sliced the water with a mild rolling motion.

Kat thought all would be well while they were still sheltered by the main harbor, but the slight motion kept her fighting to repel nausea. She thought about her horse stored in the hold. *Do horses get seasick?* As a precaution on her own behalf, she moved toward the rail. *Where's Mouse? I need red leaf tea.*

As if she had conjured it, a hand appeared in front of her, holding a canteen. "My lady, you appear to require help. May I offer you some red leaf tea?"

She took the container and sipped. "My thanks." Her unruly stomach quieted, and she handed the canteen back to the man. He appeared to be Rifellan, except for the odd turban-like head covering. She intended to ask his name but someone called her, and she glanced toward the stairway descending to the lower deck.

Mouse appeared from the entrance. "Kat, your tea."

"Just in time. Luckily, I received a sip from this man's…"

She turned to indicate the turbaned man behind her. *Gone. Odd.*

Mouse approached her and handed her a drink.

She thanked him and took additional and grateful swallows. "A man gave me a few sips of his tea, and it helped, but he's not on deck anymore. I guess he needed to feel better down below."

Mouse frowned. "Who was he?"

"I don't know. Some Rifellan, but not clothed in leathers."

Mouse shrugged. "A Rifellan. I know you favor Rifellans, but even so, it might not be wise to accept drinks from strangers."

"I wouldn't normally, but I was quite nauseous and I could smell it was red leaf tea."

"I think it wise to be careful, Kat. I almost forgot to bring you your tea. However, I find I am still somewhat weary, and I plan to sleep until the evening meal. I arranged with the captain of this vessel to obtain a small but separate cabin for myself. I thought for us to share the same one would be most improper."

"Perhaps it might." Mouse was usually correct, and if he thought sharing a cabin was improper, it probably was. "I also need more sleep. I'll meet you in the mess hall when the crew advise us that the evening meal is ready."

"Excellent, Kat, and I will find our assigned table."

She returned to her cabin and glanced at Wink, who slept soundly in her cage, snoring softly. She removed her outer leathers and sighing with pleasure she rolled into her cot.

❋❋❋

A loud bell woke Kat. Rumblings from her stomach demanded food. She left her bed, stretched, and yawned. She donned her leathers, and paused at the small mirror over the dresser to run her fingers through her hair. Satisfied with her appearance, she headed from her cabin toward food. Kat was delighted that their cabins were on the same deck as the mess hall. This meant less descending or ascending ladders from one deck to the next. She faced fewer potential falls in unsteady seas this way. She moved along the passageway, bracing herself against the walls to compensate for the swaying of the boat.

As she walked unsteadily toward the mess hall, Kat mulled over her last meeting with Garren pen Darryn of Glowen. He fascinated her. She checked the veil covering her thoughts, which allowed her to revisit memories securely. *Garren had power. But what kind?*

When she rounded a corner, she collided with a warm body. It was the man who had given her tea earlier.

"My apologies, my Lady. I am so intent on eating I did not pay attention."

Kat laughed. "I'm also focused on food."

He asked her to what Rifellan royal family she belonged.

She laughed again. "I am not Rifellan, although I'm told I resemble their royal families." She double-checked her mind veil. "Thank you for the tea earlier."

"I am pleased I helped."

Kat gazed up at him. "You appear to be Rifellan, but I never encountered such headgear before." *Did I see a hint of brown eyes and black brows?*

Some odd thought rippled across his face. "Please pardon me. I am Ssestin, and am no Rifellan warrior, just a simple scribe. I am on my way to visit my sibling, who is a guard near the border of Morden."

She still peered at his head.

"Ah yes. As to my head covering, during the last red rash onset, I fell seriously ill. Eventually I recovered, thanks to an apprentice healer. However, I no longer possess hair on my head, and rather than bear embarrassment in public, I discovered this wrapped head gear via a nomad from Morden."

"You have dealt with your challenge in a unique way." She beamed at him. "I am Kat and am journeying through Pridden with my guide."

They arrived at the entrance to mess hall, and Ssestin stopped abruptly, and turned to leave.

"I thought you planned to dine?"

"I do, but I believe I left my voucher in my cabin. Hopefully, we will share a meal on the morrow."

Kat stared at him, puzzled. "That would be fine." She glanced curiously at him as he vanished swiftly down the hallway.

How odd. I detected no Rifellan pheromones from him.

After pausing for a moment to watch Ssestin vanish toward his cabin, Kat turned and entered the mess hall. Mouse waved at her from a table for four.

He raised an eyebrow at Kat. "Who was the man you spoke to at the entrance? I notice he did not enter the hall with you."

"He was the one who gave me some red leaf tea earlier. We met each other in the passageway and spoke briefly. He is a scribe from Rifella."

"His resemblance to a Rifellan is not clear. What is he named?"

"He called himself Ssestin."

Mouse's eyes widened. "Did you say Ssestin?"

"Yes. Why? "

"Then the man cannot be Rifellan. Ssestin is a Morden

name, and the style is most often one used by those from the Assassins' Guild."

Kat raised her eyebrows. "That explains something odd I saw. When we collided with each other, I was sure I had seen the blue color of his eyes turn to brown and his blond eyebrows become black."

Mouse nodded. "I have heard they use illusions to disguise themselves at times."

"But why would a Morden Assassin be traveling from Glowen?"

Mouse gazed at her silently for a moment. "One explanation is that the Assassins were aware of a Glowen secret and attempted to discover the truth about it." He rubbed his eyebrow. "How did he explain having black hair instead of blond?"

"Black hair? What makes you think he had black hair? Didn't you see the weird turban he wore?"

"If he is from Morden, his hair would be black. But I did not see him clearly, Kat. His face was concealed in the shadows of the passageway." Mouse rubbed his jawline. "He called it a turban?"

"No, but I know of similar head coverings in my world, and that is the name for them."

Mouse remained silent, but continued to frown.

Kate peered at him. "What?"

Mouse twisted his face in a scowl. "I am discomforted by the appearance of this man at this time."

"Why does this worry you, Mouse? He's just a lone man traveling from Glowen."

Mouse shook his head. "Assassins rarely leave Morden unless they have a commissioned project. They are not lightly known as part of that Guild."

"He didn't appear to desire to be in our company for long. Surely he can't be of danger to us."

"I am not convinced that his appearance does not predict danger—especially for you."

Kat snorted. "Why me? I'm not important to the Assassins."

"Morden's Thane is a peculiar man, and he might well be anxious to foil Eduardo's plan to ease relationships between the various lands." He stared intently at her. "You have a growing reputation for discovering areas of challenge."

Why is Mouse worried about me?

CHAPTER 2

Ssestin's day had begun with a mild challenge due to the ship's motion. Then he had seen the woman with hair of fiery red bending over the rail. He had assumed she was Rifellan and unused to the motion of the vessel, so he had offered her his tea.

He paid little attention to her mumbled thanks, and had returned to his cabin to relax. Once abed, he turned his thoughts again to Morden.

He was anxious to be home among his fellow Assassins, and had worried for the safety of his Guild Master, Ssarff. Galdin's continual requests of Ssarff were becoming increasingly onerous.

Remembering, Ssestin curled his lip. *Requests*? He sniffed. *Galdin ordered.* Ssestin was uneasy about Ssarff. Galdin must be enraged that no secret could be learned in Glowen. Did Ssarff bear the brunt of this rage? Surely Galdin's hold on the people of Morden was weakening. *Is our Guild strong enough to oppose him? Will the Thane's armed guards support us?*

When the bell rang to announce the evening meal, he headed for the mess hall. The red leaf tea worked well, and he was ready for food.

Buried in his thoughts, he collided with the red-headed woman. He stared at her eyes—one glowed emerald green and the other displayed the color of his favorite chestnut horse.

Her face lit up as she laughed. *Most attractive.* He examined her more closely, and discovered her mind closed to him. He wondered at the time if Rifellan royalty possessed the ability to shield their thoughts from others. He was curious to know if the blurring of his features, to show blonde eyebrows and blue eyes was holding? His abilities were not as strong as those of Ssarff, and he normally accessed others' minds to strengthen his illusions.

Then in the mess hall, he saw the man known as Mouse, and escaped just in time.

He entered his cabin, closed the door as he leaned against it, and breathed a sigh of relief. Thankfully, Mouse had not seen him. The small man served Galdin, and, Ssestin suspected, also acted as the guide that Kat mentioned.

She must be the woman whom Galdin was desperate to bring to his Keep. Ssestin had sensed a form of power emanating from her. She exuded great strength of character, and he understood why Galdin's little servant had been so ineffective in bringing her to the Thane's presence. *She intrigues me. I do not want Galdin to possess her.* He decided to remain in his cabin for the duration of the voyage, but would set off for Morden once the vessel docked in Baklai.

He hoped Ssarff would not accept a fee again from the Thane of Morden to bring Kat to him. Galdin would not have any plans for her well-being.

We should not deliver her to the Thane.

Chapter 3

When she first sat down with Mouse, Kat wondered at the two extra chairs. "Who's joining us?"

"They are Rifellans. He, apparently, is a guard, returning home after a quarter path assignment in Glowen. His mate was with him. Both are pleased to leave this assignment and return to their familiar residence here on Baklai." Mouse chuckled. "Rifellans are serious warriors, and living a life of excess is challenging to them. You found the Glowens trying, so you can imagine how difficult it would have been for them."

Kat grinned at him. "I most certainly can relate to their experiences."

Mouse glanced toward the entrance to the mess, and raised his hand to the couple about to enter. "Here they are."

The Rifellans returned his greeting and headed toward their table, the warrior clasping Mouse's hand in the weird handshake Rifellan males extended to each other. Kat had consistently failed to replicate the gesture. "Mouse, forgive our tardiness. We were on deck, enjoying our departure from Glowen."

The man was tall and exuded strength. He was definitely a warrior, with a long scar running from his brow down his right cheek. His hair was blonde, much darker than that of Liandock, and his blue eyes reminded Kat of the clear skies of Greece. She experienced a stirring within her, from his strong Rifellan pheromones. *Oh, oh, need karri-san tea.*

Mouse introduced Kat to the Rifellan couple. "Kat this is Eestred, who is bond mate to Makinti. He is the Praetor to Thane Cathked. Eestred, Makinti, this is Lady Kat, who journeys here on behalf of Lord Eduardo."

Kat smiled broadly at the two. "Makinti, I know of you. My friends Bardu and Irina mentioned you to me when we met in Kaylin. But what were you both doing in Glowen?"

"Our Thane is fond of Orenberry wine, and sent us to arrange for deliveries for the next path."

They sat and Mouse called a steward and indicated they were ready to receive their meals.

Eestred turned to Kat. "Lady Kat, although the Glowens are strange in their ways, we do enjoy visiting the vineyards and the wineries. It is a small break from our duties with Thane Cathked."

"Is he difficult to deal with?"

"Not for us. We are his hired guards. But to many, he is a very strong and demanding man. Exacting burdens rest on his shoulders. Sharing a border with Morden is not an easy task. Unfortunately, unlike us, he does not allow himself the time for breaks of any length."

Kat grimaced. "I suspect this will be an interesting visit, and I look forward to comparing my journey to Glowen with your insights. I should mention, Eestred, I am not formal, and would appreciate being referred to as Kat, not Lady Kat."

"I will do as you ask." She smiled. "However, I must warn you, Thane Cathked is a strong-minded man and demands we all follow the formal rules. I do apologize if I must use the Lady honorific in his company."

Mouse grinned at Kat. "You may be required to rein in your normal compulsions. Annoying a Thane such as Cathked would not be wise."

She glared at him. "I am well aware you will no doubt remind me constantly if I stray from what you consider wise."

Makinti and Eestred glanced at both her and Mouse, and then at each other.

They burst out laughing.

Kat turned her frown on them. "What is so amusing?"

Eestred patted Kat's arm. "We find your relationship with your guide more like that of an acrimonious bonding of two people who have spent far too much time in each other's company."

Mollified, Kat assured her they were not bonded.

Their food and Kat's tea arrived, and she breathed a sigh of relief as all four applied themselves to their meals in silence. *I want to pay attention to his warnings, but Mouse can be damned difficult at times.* Kat, annoyed that her guide did not give her credit for the changes she had achieved, snorted to herself. She was convinced she was a more easygoing person than the woman who, after being caught in that storm in the Virgins, found herself in Eduardo's Keep

As they parted, Eestred suggested she and Kat meet on deck on the morrow. "I would love to discuss Glowen with you, and we can enjoy a mid-turn meal and then continue our discussion. Makinti has reports to prepare for the Thane." She grinned. "He and I always enjoy a shared bond meal in our cabin on the final eve on board."

"I would enjoy that."

Eestred continued. "The four of us can meet again on the following turn for our morning meal."

"I will see you on deck on the morrow."

They parted, and Kat headed down the passageway to her cabin. Once there, she withdrew Wink from her cage, fed her, and spent a few moments cuddling the little pyrock. The small creature dropped off to sleep, and Kat returned her to her cage. "You really aren't much of a cuddle bunny, are you?"

Wink only emitted a soft snore.

❋❋❋

The following morning, Kat showered, ate a hasty breakfast, and went up on deck. She gazed around, but Ssestin was nowhere to be seen. *I wonder if he realizes we're convinced he's from Morden?*

When Eestred arrived on deck, they found chairs and spent a delightful day comparing their notes on Glowen. Kat was careful to keep her thoughts concealed behind her mindveil, but the Rifellan woman never referred to a supposed secret of the Glowens. She did mention the blud wine scandal, but the Rifellans only consumed Orenberry wine in their land, so it did not affect them.

When at last they parted, Kat grinned at her friend. "Have a wonderful bonding eve."

"My thanks, Kat." She gazed at her, a thoughtful expression on her face. "I believe you need a bond mate of your own. My friend Irina has a sibling who would be perfect for you."

Kat's face heated. *Liandock.*

Eestred's thoughtful expression changed to one of puzzlement, but she shrugged, and they parted for the evening.

Kat left the deck to join Mouse for her own evening meal in the ship's mess.

❋❋❋

When Kat woke, the rocking of the ship was much reduced. She had packed all her belonging the previous evening after returning from her meal with Mouse. She dressed for the day, fed Wink, and set off down the passageway to join Mouse and her Rifellan friends for the morning meal.

Mouse was already seated, and the other two followed into the mess hall. Once they all sat, the steward brought their meals and filled their mugs with a pleasant and aromatic tea.

"The ship's not heaving about so much. Are we in that long fjord in Baklai?"

"Yes, it's called the Teeki Dow, and the waters are very protected here." Makinti seemed relaxed and happy, and glanced at his bond mate affectionately.

Kat grinned at the pair of them. "I trust you had a fine meal the previous eve?"

Eestred beamed. "We did indeed."

When they completed their meals, a young Baklai man rushed into the mess hall, and hurried over. "Lady Kat. Lady Kat. Your horse. She is killed."

Kat rose in horror. "What?"

"I am sorrowed to tell you. Your horse is dead."

"Oh no." The ice cold of her stone stabbed at her chest. Kat rushed from the mess hall toward the ladders, down past the crew deck and the food storage deck to the level where animals were held. Below that were only the bilges, filled with ballast.

Why? What? Who killed her?

CHAPTER 4

Stunned, Kat collapsed on a hay bale, staring at the pool of blood surrounding her faithful horse. Although she had never said the name out loud, she thought of the mare as Fiona. This had been her mother's name—a good Celtic name meaning fair one. The beautiful horse had white stockings on her forelegs, and had borne Kat on her journey through Pridden with patience and strength. A bond had grown between them, and when she groomed her, the animal's soft breath had felt warm against her skin.

There would no longer be soft breaths. Kat's heart felt as cold and lifeless as the body which lay discarded among the stalks of straw that covered the boards of the stall. *Why?*

A hand rested on her shoulder, and she turned to discover Mouse offering her tea. "We must disembark this vessel. The crew need to remove the animal from their boat, as the Baklai are waiting to deal with her."

Kat nodded and rose, almost stumbling with grief. "What must I do?"

"Healer Caleth is here to take us to Thane Cathked's keep."

She followed Mouse up the ladders to the upper deck. As they descended the gangplank, Makinti and Eestred stood on the dock, waiting for them with another male who was clad in a light blue robe.

Eestred stepped forward, took Kat's hand and patted it. "We are so sorry to hear about your animal. When anyone has journeyed so far with a horse, a strong bond is formed.

We know you will be much affected by this loss." She waved a hand toward the man in blue. "This is Healer Caleth, who is assigned to Thane Cathked's keep. He will guide you there."

The healer greeted them both and arranged for their luggage to be loaded on a cart. Leading Mouse's horse and the baggage animal, they proceeded from the dock to Thane Cathked's magnificent stone edifice. Inside the main gate, their horses were led into stalls within a stable, and two young males transported their bags to their rooms.

Caleth helped Kat from the cart. "I will take you to your room, Lady Kat, and will arrange for a light refreshment to be delivered to you."

Kat gazed up at him. "Thank you, but I would prefer no refreshment at this time. I need to spend time alone."

"I understand Lady Kat. You have suffered a great loss. I will ask my mate, Layleene, to meet with you after the midturn meal."

Kat shook her head. "No."

Mouse took her hand. "Kat, he is the Healer for Baklai. He will be able to help you deal with this."

"You don't understand."

"You are correct. I do not understand. I have seen you experience loss of a number of people during our journey, and yet you rarely shed tears. However, for your horse, you appear to experience grief beyond expectation."

Kat shook his hand off her. "You don't understand, Mouse. People have the ability to make choices. If they pick one that ends their lives, that is the freedom they have to make their own decisions. Animals have no such ability. It is for their lack of freedom from our choices, that I grieve."

Mouse raised his eyebrows and leaned toward Caleth. "I will leave her to your ministrations." He turned to Makinti and Eestred and suggested they have tea together.

The three walked toward the dining hall, although Mouse looked back at Kat, a worried expression on his face.

❋❋❋

After Caleth left, Kat set up the permanent cage for Wink. Before transferring the small creature from her travel cage, she held the furry body in her hand and brought it to her cheek. She held the pyrock to her and sobbed.

Wink shook her body to free herself of Kat's tears, reached out a tiny tongue, licked Kat on the cheek, and peeped as if in sympathy. Kat gazed at her. "I'm sorry. I guess I made you all wet." She fed the wee creature and placed her in her cage. Wink gave herself a few perfunctory licks and circled three times before tucking her head under her wing. Within seconds light snores issued from the cage

With Wink bedded down, Kat gazed around her quarters. Compared to the keeps she had visited in the other lands, Cathked's stronghold was austere. The hallway was plain and serviceable. Her room held a modest wardrobe, a simple table with two chairs, a small desk, and a bed that resembled a cot. The bedclothes were white, and the curtains utilitarian, without ruffles or pleasant patterns.

Kat sighed at the lack of adornment, but withdrew her writing materials and sat down to record the happenings since leaving Glowen. She began by writing of her meeting with Ssestin, and pondered Mouse's suggestion that he was an Assassin from Morden. Penning question marks beside his name, she completed recording the discovery of the death of her horse and the meeting with Healer Caleth. At last, laying her pen down, she relaxed her body and breathed deeply. Kat sensed she had reached the point where she could relate all that had happened through a game design without re-experiencing an overwhelming sense of loss. But now there were more questions.

She rose from her seat and tugged the tassel in the corner. When the young apprentice appeared, she ordered tea. She also asked that he request that Mouse join her in her room. He departed immediately down the hall. A short time later, a knock summoned her to the door.

Mouse stood, balancing a tray with mugs and a pot of steaming liquid, on one hand. "I met the server, and he suggested I bring the tea with me."

"Thank you." Kat inhaled a great breath and released it slowly. "I realize much of my grief came from the shock of losing my faithful horse. I know she is in a place of endless meadows and maybe even with your Caleesh." She did her best to smile to assure him of her acceptance of the loss of her horse. "Now I need your counseling."

He entered and placed the tray on the table and sat in the chair opposite her. "You know I will always be willing to help."

"I've put much thought into the occurrences of the past few turns, and I cannot yet find sense in what has happened." She stared at Mouse. "Why would someone want to kill my horse? And who would do such a thing?"

"I have puzzled over this as well, but I am unable to arrive at an answer. This carries no logic for me, Kat."

"Do you think Ssestin, the man you consider an Assassin, was to blame?" *No. My stone was warm around him.*

"I am sure Assassins are able to perform such deeds, but I cannot see why he would do this."

"It had to be someone on board, and one whose presence among the animals would cause no questions from the crew." She rubbed her brow. "Do you think it would be easy to replace my horse with another from the Baklai? If not, do you suspect this was intended to delay our journey?"

"I thought of that as well, but I am unable to see what or whom it would benefit."

A knock at the door startled Kat, and she rose and opened it.

Healer Caleth waited at the entrance. "Lady Kat." He glanced at Mouse at the table. "Ah, Sire Mouse, how fortunate you are here as well. Thane Cathked has requested that you both join him for the evening meal in his quarters." He started for the door and turned. "If you would order your mid-turn meal shortly, my bond mate, Layleene, will visit you afterwards. She is a healer apprentice and will help prepare you for your interview with Thane Cathked."

As she closed the door, Kat turned to her guide and shrugged. "The healer is a very formal man. I assume he follows Cathked's rules." Kat noticed Mouse's hesitation. "I know what you were going to say. Obviously, knowing the Thane's predilection for formality, I will not omit his title in front of him." *Why does Mouse always suspect me of breaking rules? I don't break them, I bend them, like Dad once told me.*

"I know you better than that. What I was about to say is that I suggest you make sure you use the Thane's title in front of all the Baklai. They have very specific ideas on protocol."

"I wonder if the Thane is anything like Haydar?"

"If he is, then all should be well. Although you and Haydar did not communicate in the beginning, the two of you eventually did solve your problems." Mouse tugged at his ear. "Are you planning to eat?"

"No. I am more weary than hungry. I'll have a brief nap instead. We will see each other when Layleene visits me."

“A rest will probably be beneficial. This turn has been challenging, and I suspect you wish some solitude.” He gazed at her for a moment or two, then turned and left her room.

Kat sighed. *Challenging for sure. Poor Fiona.*

CHAPTER 5

A knock at Kat's door woke her from her nap. "Who is it?"

"I am Layleene, Lady Kat. My mate, Caleth, advised that you would be expecting me."

"Yes, he did." She rose from her bed and unlocked the door for the apprentice healer. "Please enter, and forgive my appearance. I needed a nap more than a mid-turn meal."

The healer smiled. "I am aware of the circumstances which confronted you on arrival." She reached out and patted Kat's hand. "Would you order tea for us, and I will enlighten you as to how Thane Cathked operates his land." She cleared her throat. "Our Thane is rigid in his protocols, and your meetings with him will be smoother if you are aware of how he conducts all his business within Baklai."

Kat walked over to the tassel in the corner of the room, tugged it, sat at the small table, and invited Layleene to join her.

"I gather your Thane is a most formal man."

"He is indeed. Baklai is an odd land. Their primary assets are their horses, and the Baklai themselves insist on training them."

A knock indicated their tea had arrived, and after she had poured for both of them, Layleene continued. "To maintain their control on their horses, they sell only geldings and a few mares who are fed certain plants to make them infertile."

"Unbelievable." Kat gaped at the healer. "So, the horses in all the other lands are unable to breed?"

"Correct. You traveled with your mare for nearly three seasons. Did you never wonder why she did not come into estrus?"

"I never thought about it." Kat shook her head. "How extraordinary. I am beginning to see why your Thane is so controlling in his dealings with his people. He has created a situation where the rest of Pridden will always need to purchase horses from the Baklai. If a horse they own dies a natural death, they will need to purchase another from the Thane."

"Lady Kat, as I said, Baklai is an odd land."

"Oh Layleene, I am not a formal person. Please forget the Lady bit. Call me Kat."

"I will refer to you as Kat in private, because those of us from Shendea are also less formal. However, when we are with any persons from Baklai, and especially Thane Cathked, I must use the honorific."

"It sounds like I am about to enter a minefield. You better tell me how I need to act, particularly since I wish to request a horse for the rest of my travels."

"Your expression puzzles me. Our mines are underground, not in fields."

Rats. How to explain? "My apologies. We use this expression on my world because we possess weapons that explode and we place them in fields to prevent enemies from attacking us."

Layleene raised both brows in apparent shock. "Your world sounds quite violent."

"Only sometimes." Kat coughed. "What should I be aware of about your Thane?"

"When you enter his private dining hall, the Thane will be at one end of the table, with Lady Kerdinon at the other. His important male associates will be seated on either side of him, with their bond mates on either side of Lady Kerdinon. She is the Thane's mate. You will always find that in public, males and females sit apart."

"Odd. Why?"

"Thane Cathked is more comfortable surrounded by males and is convinced females should be assigned their own specific duties."

Kat opened her mouth. Her face grew hot.

Layleene held up her hand. "There is more." She swallowed. "In the Thane's presence, females do not speak unless invited to do so."

"What?" Kat narrowed her eyes. The healer had to be exaggerating. "So how am I going to request a new horse?"

"You should ask your guide, since he is male, to make the request for you."

Kat growled. "I don't believe this." She wanted to scream in rage.

"Please Kat. You must tread carefully in Baklai until you are accepted by the Thane and his advisors."

"You're telling me he is going to attempt to control me through the use of one horse?" *If I were a dragon, I'd be belching fire right now.*

"When it comes to horses, Thane Cathked is all powerful. His Horse Master is an advisor only. The Thane has the final word on the sale and disbursement of these valuable animals. Since his rules brought the protection of the Rifellans and created a stable economy for all Baklai, his people support him without question."

Kat rose. "Layleene we must meet with Mouse, my guide, immediately. It's vital he knows about the potential challenges facing me."

"I agree." Layleene rose and followed Kat out the door

to Mouse's quarters, where they knocked and were admitted.

As Mouse opened the door Kat marched in the room, spat out what the healer had told her and waited for his reaction, her nostrils still flared, and she breathed heavily.

Mouse's eyes grew bigger and he raised his eyebrows as the story unfolded. "I did not know this about the Thane or about Baklai. I have never visited this land before, and these rules are quite unknown to me." He rubbed his chin. "Please sit, both of you. We need to spend time deciding how to achieve our desires, without arousing the Thane's ire. Kat, I suspect this will be most difficult for you. Throughout our journey, I have been aware you chafe when you believe others are attempting to control you or your actions."

Kat did not sit as he requested. "I come from a world, Mouse, where women spent many yea…er paths fighting for equality with the males of our world. To now be viewed as less than important is…is… unacceptable." Her voice rose, and she thumped her fist on the table.

Mouse gave a long deep sigh. "Kat, we are in a land belonging to the Baklai, and when you enter another land, you must accept their rules. You are in need of a horse. To obtain one, I suggest you do all you can to be amenable to these people, and definitely to Thane Cathked. Is not the need of a horse worth accepting his way of life?"

Kat glared at him. Unfortunately, he was correct. She folded her arms, strode around his room, and planted herself in the middle. "To get a new horse, I suppose I can swallow my pride. You must be aware, I'm not happy about this." She sniffed loudly. "But I will try to pretend I am." *My father would suggest I find a way to turn the rules into situations that benefit me.*

"I hope you can. Remember Kat, you made an agreement

with Lord Eduardo that requires you to work with the people in each land."

Kat exhaled. Guilt forced her to agree.

Her eyes still wide, Layleene rose to her feet. "I should leave you both. You have issues to resolve." She almost scuttled to the door. "I will return in time to escort both of you to Thane Cathked's dining hall. I will first report to Caleth about our conversation, and you will both have time to prepare. Kat, I suggest you wear your leathers. Our Thane is familiar with this mode of dress by Rifellan females, whom I believe he reluctantly views as warriors. Plus, the leathers convey a serious attitude toward traveling via horseback. Remember, do not request a new horse from him." She faced the two of them, reluctance in every fiber of her stance. "Sire Mouse, I ask that you request this from the Thane on behalf of the Lady Kat." She left before either of them had time to reply.

Mouse opened his mouth to speak, but no sound issued from him.

Kat scowled at him. "I knew she was going to ask that of you. The only reason I agree is that I need a horse. If doing this will manipulate them into granting my wish, I will allow you to do the asking."

Mouse swallowed. "I will ask on your behalf, Kat. I find this difficult to do, when I know how capable you are."

"At least you know I am." She scowled. "I will return to my quarters and prepare myself for the dinner. Since you won't be beside me, I'll need to rely on Layleene to catch me in any social challenges. Cathked better be sympathetic to me."

She left Mouse's room for her own quarters. Fists clenched, back rigid, Kat strode briskly down the hallway.

I will solve this myself eventually--no matter who is responsible.

CHAPTER 6

When she arrived at her room, Kat forced herself to have a cold shower to cool her temper. Her mood improved as she thought about it, because she believed Mouse would be able to intercede on her behalf. *He's diplomatic. He'll get me a horse.*

Wink squeaked for food but wiggled free when Kat tried to cuddle her. She shrugged, fed her, returned the pyrock to her cage.

She dressed and got ready for the evening meal with Cathked.

A knock came at the door and she opened it. Layleene smiled. "Excellent. You resemble a royal Rifellan warrior perfectly. I am sure the Thane will be impressed." They left Kat's quarters and stopped to collect Mouse, and the three proceeded to Cathked's private area, without speaking. Kat tucked her thumbs in her hand, her favorite ritual for good luck.

The guards admitted them, and Layleene led them into the dining hall, where her mate, Caleth, waited. He guided them to their seats.

Kat followed Laylene's lead when she bowed her head to the Thane before seating herself.

The Thane acknowledged them with a nod. He was taller than most Baklai, about five foot ten. He was handsome, his skin a rich dark brown, similar to a well-worn saddle, and his black hair covered his head in untamed shaggy curls. He wore a loose robin's egg blue shirt, laced up the front. The lines between his eyes were cut deep and furrowed and told of many turns of concern for the safety of his people. The Thaneship did not lie lightly upon the shoulders of this man, and in the way his dark eyes bored into her, Kat expected little in the way of sympathy from him.

From his appearance, Kat assumed Laylene's description of him was valid, and he filled the room with his powerful presence.

He was robustly built, and despite his shorter stature, she suspected he would hold his own in a fight with most Rifellans. However, Rifellans took their physical power for granted, with easy acceptance. Kat felt sure that because of his Morden neighbors, Cathked always needed to demonstrate his capabilities. He was a man, she sensed, who reigned over his land with an iron will.

He stood and Kat saw he wore Rifellan leather leggings. *Interesting*. He acknowledged first Mouse and next her, demonstrating, no doubt, his belief in the superiority of men. He welcomed them both to Baklai and sat down without further comment.

The servers brought the meals and later drinks. Aware of his preference toward men, she was surprised that, unexpectedly, they served the women first. She raised an eyebrow at Mouse, who ignored her, his face blank.

Layleene, seated beside her, patted her hand, and whispered information about the members around the table. "On his left, is Makinti, Praetor of the guards in Baklai, whom I believe you met previously. Next to Makinti you can see my mate, Caleth, and next to him is your guide, Mouse."

"Interesting. Your Thane seats all those from other lands on his left."

"You are most observant, Kat. I paid no attention to this

before." She smiled. "To the Thane's right is Penabon, who is Horse Master in Baklai. Both he and the Thane are equally strong in their thoughts about Baklai horses. Seated next to Penabon is Hunter Master Galakis."

"What is a Hunter Master? I never heard the term before."

"I will explain later. At this end is Thane Cathked's bond mate, Kerdinon. This end is set up with the mates of the males seated with the Thane. On Kerdinon's right are the mates of Penabon and Galakis. On the left are Eestred, whom you also know, then us. All of us on the left, as you so cleverly pointed out, are from other lands."

"You warned me Baklai is formal. My mind is filled with questions. Can we meet for a morning meal on the morrow?"

"Indeed." Layleene stopped and turned toward Cathked, who had clapped his hands for the servers to clear the remnants of the meal, and replace the drinks.

He turned his attention to Mouse. "Sire Mouse, I believe you are about to make a request of us." His strong baritone voice resonated in the hall.

Mouse stood and bowed his head. "My thanks, Thane Cathked, for giving us the chance to request assistance from you. As you may be aware, My Lady Kat's fine horse was cruelly murdered on board the ship we travelled in from Glowen. She needs a replacement horse from Baklai, and I have Lord Eduardo's assurance that he will cover payment of a new animal."

"We suspected you would make this request of us, and my Horse Master and my councillors discussed this at length. We decided to decline your request."

Kat's heart hammered, and she blinked in surprise, stifling a gasp. *Why?*

Mouse bowed again. "My pardon for asking, Thane Cathked, but Lady Kat has always taken excellent care of her horse, and this unfortunate incident was beyond her control."

"We do not doubt she treated the animal well. Haydar in Kaylin would never have consented to allow her a horse if he thought otherwise. However, she herself, must be the reason the horse died. Thus, we cannot risk another to be in similar danger at this time."

Mouse's mouth opened. He made no sound. He glanced back at Kat and shook his head, his forehead wrinkled.

Kat had to bite her tongue to keep herself from yelling at the Thane. *That's stupid? How can I be the reason the horse died?*

Makinti stood and addressed Cathked. "My Thane, Lady Kat intends to travel through the northern section of Baklai, and we will be able to observe how she and Sire Mouse fare in this time. Perhaps, my Thane, you might be willing to revisit this decision when they return to the Keep?"

"That is possible Praetor, but at this time, our decision is final." He stood, and motioning to his mate, left the hall. The rest of the table followed suit.

Glaring at their departing backs, Kat rose, digging her fingernails in the wood of her chair. Clenching her teeth, her spine rigid, she stalked after Mouse back to their rooms.

When they reached his room, Mouse opened his door and waved at Kat to enter. Nostrils flared, back stiff, and her eyes burning, she waved him ahead of her and reluctantly followed. She clutched at a chair to prevent herself from smashing things, pressing her lips in a thin line to stop from screaming and expressing the vilest words she could think of to describe Cathked.

Without speaking, Mouse tugged the tassel in the corner, and when the young apprentice appeared at the door, he requested a sedative tea.

Kat, still clutching the chair, panted short but deep breaths.

They waited in silence until the drink arrived, at which point Mouse poured her a large mug. “Kat, it is important you maintain your silence.”

“Maintain my silence? Are you mad?”

He swallowed. “I am well aware you are incensed with the decision by the Thane.”

“Incensed? I’m not incensed. I’m ready to tear him limb from limb.” She slammed her fist on the table. “I want you to sit down and write a note for me to Eduardo to ask him to intervene. Right now!”

Mouse gazed at her his face twisted in horror. “We cannot do that. Baklai horses are needed by all of Pridden. Eduardo would never interfere in another land’s rules—particularly those of Baklai.”

Kat curled her lip. “Eduardo is a Lord. Cathked is only a Thane.”

“That is true, but Eduardo would not appreciate you requesting he do this for you. Please sit down and drink some of this tea. It will calm you.”

“I don’t want to be calm.” She did sit, however.

“Drink, and breathe slowly.” He held out his hand in a pleading gesture. “Kat. You promised to pay attention to my advice.”

Kat drank the tea, and, staring at Mouse’s face, twisted up in worried lines, breathed in and out slowly.

“Are you beginning to feel a little calmer?”

“Yes. But I’m still furious.”

“At least we can thank Makinti that the decision is likely to be reconsidered when we return to the Keep after our visit through northern Baklai.” Mouse grinned. “When we are in the north, we will encounter some small animals known as hissars. Though they are only about the size of your boradai in Shendea, they are so fierce, even Rifellans avoid them."

She scowled at him. "What's your point?"

Mouse grinned again. "While we are in Baklai, I would strongly request you act less like a hissar, and more like the Lady Kat."

Kat couldn't help grinning back at him. *Poor Mouse, he's not to blame.* "I'm sorry for screeching at you. I wasn't mad at you."

"I was aware of that."

Kat stared at him intently. She knew Mouse didn't really understand. She remembered a discussion she'd had with her father about situations that others controlled.

❋❋❋

She recalled that time vividly and could picture it in her mind. Her father was an important member of a middle Eastern diplomatic corps, and they moved from post to post until shortly after her twelfth birthday. Since he was a diplomat, they lived in Washington when he was stationed in the United States. Both she and her brother had been born during a previous posting in that country. They had the opportunity to live within the consulate but chose not to, because her father believed her mother should not be forced to wear the Hijab. Her mother agreed, although when they were posted back to his country of birth, she did her best to be well covered with loose clothing.

Kat asked her father why he told her not to accept constricting rules that made no sense, and yet made sure her mother wore loose clothing when they were in the Middle East. "That's illogical, Daddy."

He explained that since these rules were part of the culture and ancient religion of his homeland, that dressing this way was a polite way of acknowledging this about his country. As she grew older, he explained that he often did things with which he did not agree. He followed some rules simply to ensure the safety of his family. Thus, Kat grew up not entirely trusting any government, because so many rules seemed flawed. Naturally her father had rules for the family, but if she objected, he at least explained the need for them. She accepted many things when she lived with her parents, because she did trust them, and only began questioning most rules once she was on her own.

❋❋❋

Those memories made such a strong impression on Kat when she was young. She knew that Mouse could not understand why she resisted being controlled by others. It was one of the main reasons she missed her home. She knew how to avoid or at least side-step most of the rules there.

Mouse frowned and stroked his chin. "We need to plan how we will handle this initially. On the morrow, we should visit the market and purchase two smaller bags to hold the bare necessities for our initial trip. We might be able to send some items directly to Eduardo's Keep for when we return to Kaylin."

Kat thought a while. "You make sense. I'm not happy about this, but I guess we're lucky we have the baggage animal to rely on." She sighed. "Thank you. I'm feeling better, particularly now I think I've got a solution to the problem."

Mouse raised his eyebrows. "Solution? What are you planning?"

"I remembered something today." She rubbed her brow and let out a long breath. "Others may try to control me, but often I can find a way to wrest it back. For example, I will still have a horse, even if it's a baggage animal. So, I do have some control."

"Kat, I must admit I am proud you kept your temper in check. Our travels have covered many turns, and I know you well enough that I thought you were about to explode." He smiled. "But you did not."

"Well, yes." She shrugged. "I'm going to my room and I'll start sorting things so that I only pack the minimum items I'll need. I'm meeting Layleene for the morning meal, and I'll ask her to show me the best baggage to purchase."

Mouse bid her a good night at the door to his room, and Kat set off down the hall.

Damn Cathked. He alone made the decision, not his councillors.

CHAPTER 7

The following morrow, Kat wakened to the sound of Wink cheeping for food. She slid from her bed, and fed the little creature, who gulped the treats as if ravenous. "You," Kat frowned at the pyrock, "are not starving. From the size of your belly, you need more exercise."

Wink cheeped at Kat, as if her protests were completely innocent. Once fed, and returned to her cage, she turned around three times and immediately fell asleep.

Kat shook her head. Wink was too small to hug. She missed holding Breen, her boradai, or Shade. her beautiful black panther from Shendea. Thinking about pets, a pang of longing hit her for the soft lop-eared rabbit she'd raised as a young teenager When Kat was been placed in foster care, the rabbit disappeared. Where to, either no one knew or would tell her.

Back home, she had Nick's kids to snuggle with when she babysat a few times a year.

She imagined herself cuddling with Liandock, and shook her head abruptly. *Stop. You can't afford to get involved. He can't go with you when you leave.*

She left her room and headed for Mouse's quarters. When she arrived, she rapped on the wooden barrier.

He poked his head out the door.

"Mouse, do you want to join Layleene and me for a morning meal?"

He nodded a yes, and they set off for the communal dining hall. As they entered, Kat saw Layleene wave a hand for them to join her at a table for four.

Once seated and meals ordered, Kat plied the healer with questions. "You told me you would explain the term, Hunter Master."

"I did indeed. You are familiar with the goddess Caleesh, to whom most of Pridden pay homage?"

Kat nodded. "Yes, except I believe the Mordens worship a snake goddess."

"You are correct. They worship Ssayleese. Although I am aware of rumors that many of the southern Mordens are also proponents of Caleesh."

Kat raised her eyebrows in surprise, and glanced at Mouse. "You know quite a bit about the Mordens. Is this true?"

"Indeed. I am aware of a number of those in the south who prefer Caleesh to Ssayleese."

The serving woman arrived with their food and beverages, and once she tasted her meal, Kat's assessment of the Keep did not change. While the food was filling, it was modest, not nearly as luxurious as the food in Cathked's personal dining hall.

Kat turned back to the Healer. "You were talking about the Hunter Master."

"The Baklai believe Caleesh is mated to the god Calanta, who all refer to as the Hunter God. He is a warrior of great power, who rides a magnificent horse, which, legend has, the ancient Baklai bred. He is so forceful a figure in Baklai spiritual ways, that our people call our Thane, Hunter Cathked."

"Surely, Layleene, they don't think Cathked is a god, do they?"

"Well, the people of Baklai ascribe to him god-like qualities, which also accounts for his power in this land."

Kat grimaced. "No wonder he's so controlling. Do you think he believes he's a god?"

"I do not believe so, but the Thane is extremely intelligent. I believe he makes use of his people's beliefs."

Mouse piped up. "I suspect you are correct. Cathked is an astute leader. Where does Galakis fit in this situation?"

Layleene smiled at him. "He is Hunter Master to Thane Cathked, and answers all his questions about spiritual practices. He is also the Thane's representative at the Matings of Horses."

Mouse rubbed his brow. "So, it appears that Galakis is in a position of much influence."

"He is, and" --she turned to Kat-- "his mate, Grayseen, whom you met at the evening meal, holds a similar position of power among the women of Baklai."

Kat held up her hand. "Wait a minute. You said the Matings of Horses? You made this sound as if it's a ceremony."

"It is. My mate, Caleth, is invited as a Healer, in case one is needed. But he is not allowed to tell me what occurs. No female is ever invited to a mating."

Kat shook her head. "Baklai males certainly do their best to keep all the control of this land in their hands. I can't imagine how you can live under such restrictions."

Layleene held up her hands. "Kat, you do not understand how males and females relate to each other in Baklai."

Mouse, curiosity stamped all over his face, leaned toward her. "I never travelled in Baklai before, and am not aware of any unusual relationships between them. Can you explain?"

"This is not easy to explain until you meet both groups in their respective areas of expertise." She turned to Kat. "During your first journey from the Keep, when you pass the bridge over the northern branch of the Farralawn River, which connects Baklai to Rifella, you will find a road leading to Dinerth Caleesh."

"What is Dinerth Caleesh?"

"The Dinerth is the spiritual meeting place for women and is dedicated to the goddess Caleesh. The women of Baklai meet there a minimum of four times per path. They come to discuss all manner of items which fall within their guardianship."

"Can I visit this place?"

"Yes. I am officially inviting you to attend a ceremony at Dinerth Caleesh with me."

Mouse raised an eyebrow at her words. "I suspect I would not be allowed to attend?"

"Forgive me, Sire Mouse, but no males are ever allowed to attend."

Mouse blinked. "No males? Ever?" He rubbed his chin. "Hm. I am not surprised."

"Layleene, how interesting." Kat found herself intrigued. *Is this how the women get revenge on the men?* "I would be honored to be your guest at Dinerth Caleesh. I would love to experience how the females of Baklai conduct themselves."

"I do believe you will appreciate the ceremony." She rose from her seat. "Now, let us be off to the market to purchase the new luggage you need."

They all left the table and followed her through the hallways to the market, which although located out of doors, was still within the protective outer walls of the Keep.

Impressed by the walkways filled with luscious green bushes severely trimmed to represent horses prancing and galloping along the paths, Kat's mind was a jumble of thought, absorbing all the information the Healer gave her. *Can I somehow find a way to view the Mating of Horses? It must be really different to be so wrapped in secrecy.*

The market they entered was vastly different from the basic amenities of the inner Keep. The area, alive with conversation and laughter, most of which came from females, chattering about families and offspring and decoration of homes, astounded Kat. Surrounding her were stalls replete with a rainbow of wildly colored flowers, fabrics both delicate and sturdy, and the aromas exuding from these stalls were entrancing. The few male shoppers seemed more serious, and they appeared to be involved in the business of bargaining for and discussing of horses, and all things horse related.

The three wandered through the various sections, before both Layleene and Kat paused to examine the beautifully carved wooden toys for children. The color of the wood, the skill of the carving, and the final polished sheen of the various creations, had Layleene crooning over them. Kat found herself compelled to touch the exquisite toys, smiling as she did so.

Layleene purchased a small wooden cart, pulled by a beautifully fashioned horse. She also added a gallivanting foal to her order. "I am blessed with two progeny and my youngest male will spend hours playing with the cart, while the other, who is an artistic young female, will place this on a shelf in her room and will spend much time gazing at the carving. She is not someone who carves, but she is a talented painter. In a few more paths, I will send her to Shendea to apprentice to our renowned Master Weaver, Godrith."

"I was able to tour his studio in Shendea, and I thought him an amazing weaver. The colors and patterns of his tapestries are breath-taking." Kat glanced at the Healer. "I didn't know he also taught painting."

"Master Godrith is talented in many artistic styles."

"Won't you miss your daughter?"

Layleene smiled. "Daughter? Kat you resemble Rifellan royalty so much, and you use many of their terms. Are you sure you are not Rifellan?"

"I drink karri-san tea."

The Healer grinned. "Ah."

Mouse who had been following them past the many stalls, a bored expression on his face, interrupted. "Kat, you and Layleene are both enjoying spending time at this market. I would appreciate if we can find the luggage stalls, and I can obtain what I need." He sighed. "Shopping is not my favorite pastime."

Layleene hid a smile. "My apologies, Sire Mouse. You are not alone in this. My own mate finds shopping tedious. The leather goods stall is in the next aisle."

Mouse breathed an apparent sigh of relief as they headed along the pathway to the next aisle.

At the first leather goods stall, Mouse found exactly what he needed for the next part of their journey, and he handed over a chit for his new bag.

"The luggage is small, Mouse. Are you sure it will be sufficient for you?"

He aimed a dry grin at Kat. "I am not a female." He handed her a chit to cover the cost of a bag of her choosing, thanked Layleene for her help, and walked in the direction of the inner Keep.

With chit in hand, Kat examined the options for a new bag. "I can't understand how he will manage with such a small piece of luggage. I sorted my clothing last evening, and I will need something larger." She found one that would be easy for her to carry, and turned to Layleene. "Is the country we will be traveling through dangerous?"

"No. Why do you ask?"

"I must decide which of my weapons to leave here and which I will need to carry."

"Do you possess a long bow?"

Kat nodded.

"The only creatures are the hissars that attack without warning, and they are reasonably small. A long bow is sufficient to deal with them."

"Thank you. I can carry my dagger on my belt."

"I would advise you not to expose the dagger when you are around Baklai males. They consider weapons not appropriate for women." Layleene grinned. "They do not realize that most females carry knives."

"Thank you. I also own a spring bow, but have not made use of it since I got my long bow, so I will send it to Wynneth in Kaylin to keep it for me."

She picked up the luggage she liked, and paid with the chit Mouse had given her. "Layleene, might we stop somewhere in the market to enjoy tea and a snack?"

"Excellent idea. Shopping always requires a tea and a snack." She laughed.

❋❋❋

After relishing her first cup of karri-san tea in a while, Kat rose. "This has been fun. My thanks, Layleene. I must return to my room and pack what I will need for the journey to north Baklai. Mouse intends we should leave after our morning meal on the morrow."

The Healer rose, and the two women headed back to the residential area of the Keep, arm in arm.

I adore healers. I hope the Baklai women are as delightful.

CHAPTER 8

When she arrived at her room, Kat yawned, so she delayed the final sorting and packing of belongings for a nap instead. Although it was time for a mid-turn meal, she was not hungry, and sleep called to her. She was astonished how much sleep she seemed to need, but assumed it was because of the stress of losing her horse and worrying about replacing it.

As she sank on the bed and pulled up a light cover, her eyelids grew heavier and she drifted off.

❋❋❋

A knock woke her. "Who's there?"

"Mouse. Did you find an appropriate piece of luggage?"

"Yes." She rose and walked over to open the door. "Come in. I think I may need some help."

She stood aside as Mouse entered. "What sort of help?"

"You mentioned sending some items on to Lord Eduardo's Keep. I'm not entirely certain what I will need before we return to Kaylin, and which items I will need for our upcoming journey."

She pointed at piles of clothing and other purchases stacked on the desk and a small table. "Layleene suggested I will not need the spring bow, so I will send this to Wynneth in Kaylin. However, I've got two sets of Rifellan leathers and a set of armor. Plus, I received the rust brown robe that you ordered on my behalf. I obviously cannot take all this on our journey on the morrow, and I suspect some of my things can be sent to Kaylin. What are your thoughts?"

Mouse surveyed the piles. "Hmm. I doubt you will need the armor in Baklai, but you will definitely need it in Morden. I suggest you take Rifellan leathers and your robe with you now. Put the second set of leathers aside to be sent to Kaylin. For both Baklai and Morden, you will only need two sets of boots, and any other footwear can be shipped as well."

Kat moved the items as he spoke, to the various piles. "Anything else?"

"Yes, send all cold weather wear, any formal wear, and extra shirts and pants to Kaylin. It is also unlikely you will need any bathing gear."

Kat surveyed the three piles. "Wow. Mouse you helped me perfectly. I had no idea I was dragging around so much stuff."

"Kat, the lands we visited thus far required a greater variety of clothing, so you did not bring too much."

"My thanks for your help. It's almost time for the evening meal. Shall we head to the dining hall now?"

"I would appreciate eating. Because I overindulged at the morning meal, I skipped the mid-turn one, and am now hungry."

"Me too." Kat hung her clothes for the morrow in the closet, sealed the smaller luggage, and followed the waiting Mouse from her quarters. She closed the door firmly behind her, and walked beside him as they headed for the dining lounge.

At the entrance, Kat paused to sniff the delicious aromas of roasting meats and baked breads. Mouse walked toward Eestred and Makinti, seated at a table for four, and she quickly caught up with him.

Kat joined them and sat, eager to order her meal from the waiting attendant. When all four had conveyed their orders for food and beverages, she eyed Eestred curiously. "I was under the impression you two live in your own accommodations attached to the Keep. Do you normally eat in this hall?"

"No, but we wanted to catch you before you left on the morrow." She put her hand on her bond mate's arm. "Makinti has a request."

"What do you need, Makinti?"

"As Praetor, I visit the guard installations on a regular basis, and I am heading for the guards' Border Keep across the left Farralawn River from Morden. I thought because of the challenges you encountered; I might accompany you on my first visit. While there are some resting huts for the first night, you would need to camp the second one. With no full-time baggage horse, that could be difficult. Instead, I can invite you both to stay at the Border Keep for one night."

"We would love to have you join us on the journey. Do you agree, Mouse?"

"I do. You are correct, Makinti. Using the baggage horse as Kat's mount, will slow us down, and we cannot carry camping gear."

Kat thoroughly enjoyed the well-spiced meal and remarked on the difference between some of the other meals at the Keep. "Most of what we've eaten has been rather bland, but this one's delicious."

Eestred smiled at her. "We are nearing the end of the end of the fourth quarter, and our Head of House will shortly be examining the bounty produced immediately after the fourth quarter rains. Within a few turns, our supplies will be replenished, and the variety of food will again be plentiful."

The serving woman, arrived with their meals, and silence reigned as they ate.

Once they finished their meals, Makinti rose from his

seat. "We must retire because getting an early start is important. I will meet you both at the stable immediately after your morning meal."

The other three stood, and Eestred hugged Kat. "Have a safe journey, and I will meet you at Dinerth Caleesh."

Kat smiled and nodded. "I look forward to that."

She and Mouse left the hall and headed back to their rooms.

He paused outside his door. "Kat, pack your bag tonight and order our morning meals to be delivered to your rooms. Let me know when they arrive, and I will join you. Make sure your larger bag is packed with the items to be delivered to Kaylin. Our smaller bags, we will need to carry to the stable ourselves."

"Fine. I do not have much work to do, as everything is in piles. I'll call you on the morrow."

Kat waved at him, as she entered her quarters. Once inside, she began the task of packing the small bag with items for her journey and placing most of the rest, destined for Kaylin, in the larger one. She left her amor and the leather leggings hanging in the closet, together with one pair of boots.

Finally, she fed the squeaking Wink, placed the little creature in the travel cage, and tucked the more permanent one in her Kaylin bag. Once she was packed, she prepared for bed.

After a quick shower, she slipped beneath the covers and stretched her arms over her head. The cot-like bed was surprisingly comfortable, and she closed her eyes, her body ready for sleep. *I'm glad Makinti will be with us. Nothing can go wrong with a Rifellan guard at our side.*

CHAPTER 9

Mouse's preparations for sleep completed, he opened the window to allow air circulation, and, yawning, climbed into bed.

Maintaining his cover became more difficult each day. Baklai might prove the most difficult of all the lands. Kat's rage at Cathked's rules did not last as long as he expected. She appeared to be changing, but without the ability to sense any of her thoughts, he was at a disadvantage. He believed, without a doubt, she possessed abilities unknown to him. *Do people from her world have the same talents?*

Galdin would want her delivered to him soon, but Mouse's resistance to avoid his bidding increased daily. He did not want Kat delivered to the man. He needed to consult with Eduardo and obtain his help in keeping Kat from entering Morden.

His eyes closed, and sleep beckoned, when something fluttered at his cheek. He reached out and captured something small in his hand. When he sat up to discover a messenger moth within the confines of his palm, he groaned. *Oh no, Galdin. Curses.*

He raised the moth to his ear and Galdin's voice, arrogant and demanding, issued from the tiny creature. "I am incensed with your failure to bring the woman to me. You are merely across the border in Baklai, and the assignment should be easy for you. I demand you inform me of what plans you have for completing your task."

The moth fluttered and died -- its mission complete.

Mouse gulped. He rose and retrieved the bag containing additional moths, extracted one, and brought it to his lips. "Master, controlling this woman has been the most difficult undertaking you have ever honored me with. Baklai is proving more onerous than any other land. Unfortunately, some unknown person killed the woman's horse, and the Baklai refuse to grant her another. In addition, the Rifellan warriors are everywhere. Believe me, one must tread with care around Rifellans, but I give my word to you I will do my best, despite these enormous challenges, to complete my mission for you. Your loyal servant, Mouse."

He took the moth to the window and threw the creature upward. The moth fluttered off in the direction of Morden.

Mouse shook his head and returned to his bed. *Sleep? After such an order?* He settled himself comfortably under the comforter, and reached mentally for a calming state. His mind would not quiet.

The danger to Kat was enormous. If Galdin could gather her in his clutches, he would force her to bring Eduardo to him. Galdin was convinced that if he consumed the beating, living heart of another, he would absorb the powers of that being. The Thane had hissed that at him when they met in that cold stone tower, when he first ordered Mouse to bring the woman to him. He shivered in remembrance of that ice-cold wind and those fathomless black eyes. Galdin's studies of necromancy affected his mind to the degree where he would accept no other explanation. He seemed to descend further into madness, ever since the death of his parent, Gritch. Most Mordens suspected that Galdin murdered Gritch to protect his female parent from a life of brutality and pain. Mouse suspected this to be true, and almost felt a touch of empathy for the man. No longer did Galdin appear to be in control of his actions or his faculties. His subjects were beginning to doubt his power.

The people of Morden feared him rather than supported him. The only circumstances working for the man were his fiercely loyal personal guards. Mouse felt deeply that Galdin needed to be replaced. *But by who and when? Was this possibility what the Thane feared most?*

Mouse desperately needed to keep Kat away from Galdin. Traveling through Pridden with her, despite the problems of guiding her through the potential minefields of customs in the various lands, had proved enchanting in its own way. Kat, as a strong woman, intelligent, capable, but irreverent, intrigued him. *If I could have met her as myself, instead of as Mouse, where would I be now?* He sighed and again tried to clear his mind to obtain the sleep he needed.

He closed his eyes. *Eduardo, we need to save her...*

CHAPTER 10

The following morning, Kat rose from her bed and prepared to depart the Keep. After she dressed, fed Wink, and tugged the tassel to summon the apprentice, she set her new small bag on the bed beside her long bow. She tucked her diplo bag into her backpack, and, with Wink's cage attached, deposited it beside the smaller bag.

At the sound of a knock, she opened the door and ordered meals for both her and Mouse. "Please, when you bring the meals, would you summon Sire Mouse to join me here?"

The young man agreed.

As Kat waited for the food to arrive, she remembered a perfect addition for her word list. *Collywobbles.* A lovely word her mother used when Kat was young if anyone in the family developed an upset stomach.

Kat pulled her diplo bag from her backpack, took out her word list, and added collywobbles to the page. She gazed at the list in her hands and, surprised, she saw she had not added a word for some time. She smiled to herself. An excellent word, so she sighed with satisfaction, and returned the list to the bag, which she placed again in her backpack.

A rap, and Kat jumped up to let the apprentice in.

Mouse stood at the door with a tray in his hands. "I decided I would deliver this myself."

Kat grinned. "Are you attempting to gain employment with the Keep as an apprentice?"

He shrugged. "An apprentice might be a less onerous position than as a guide to a woman who manages to create irritating situations."

She glared at him. "I don't create them."

Mouse stared at her, as he raised a questioning eyebrow.

"I don't create situations, Mouse."

"Perhaps not knowingly." He grinned. "My pardon, I was being facetious."

They moved to the small table, and Kat, frowning, distributed the mugs and plates. They seated themselves and began to eat.

She ate the Baklai version of journeyklim, but made a face at the rather bland and tasteless food. It was filling, however, so she consumed the entire bowl.

"Mouse, what a shame you dismissed the apprentice, I intended to ask him to have my biggest baggage delivered to Kaylin."

"I am glad you did not have the opportunity, because I believe we should wait until we return to the Keep. We might just discover we need some other item to carry."

"You make sense." She stood. "We've finished our food, and we should make our way to the stables because Makinti is waiting for us." She eased the straps of her backpack over her shoulders, and slung her quiver across her chest. With her long bow and her small bag in her left hand, she turned to Mouse. "I'm ready."

He opened the door, his own luggage and map bag in his hands, and stopped. An apprentice stood with hand raised to tap on the door.

They stood aside and waited for the young man to remove the tray containing their empty plates and cups so Kat could close and lock her door behind them.

Mouse led the way down the hall as they strolled toward the outer door of the Keep.

Kat gawked at the wooden walls. "The Baklai show a preference for an uncluttered way of life. Everything about this Keep is plain and unadorned. What a massive change from the embellishments of the Glowens."

"I suspect these are the desires of the males. The females at Thane Cathked's dinner wore colorful clothing."

They exited the inner portion of the Keep and walked to the stables. Makinti and Eestred were trading a passionate kiss as Mouse approached them. Eestred patted her mate on the cheek and wished him a safe journey.

Kat watched them and smiled. *Ah. Love.*

As Eestred walked toward the inner Keep, she turned back and called out to them. "Sire Mouse, may you and Lady Kat enjoy a safe journey. And Kat, I will meet with you in Dinerth Caleesh."

"I look forward to our meeting, and with Makinti accompanying us, our journey is guaranteed to be a safe one."

Makinti entered the stables and brought their horses from the stalls. "Your unique saddle appears to fit the baggage horse well, Kat, so you should not be too uncomfortable during your ride. I tightened the cinch to allow for the less bulky animal."

"Thank you. I thought I would be required to do this myself, based on the fact I'll be judged on how I take care of the baggage horse."

"Only the Thane receives extra privileges in Baklai, with one exception. Rifellan guards are considered so valuable in the protection of Baklai horses, we are accorded similar benefits. As traveling companions on this part of your journey, you too will be given our concessions. Once we part ways, however, you will no longer receive these advantages."

"I sensed I was safer traveling with you, but I did not

expect anything more. How wonderful." Kat turned to the horse, strapped her long bow to the attachment on the right side, and her bag on the rear of the saddle. She bent to pick up a stool to make mounting the horse easier, when Makinti grabbed her around her waist and tossed her upward. "Oh my. You surprised me. My thanks."

She studied Mouse as he put a foot in the stirrup and hauled himself into place. Continually surprised to discover how easy he made it appear, Kat considered he seemed as strong in many ways as Makinti. She shrugged and picked up her reins.

Makinti told her to follow him and suggested Mouse take up the rear. When they agreed, the Rifellan set off on the pathway along the shoreline of the Farralawn River, flowing on their right. On either side of the path grew fields of grain. The breeze rippled through the golden strands and created the hiss of waves on a sandy shore.

Kat closed her eyes and imagined she was at sea. Pridden's star was fully risen, and the warmth, tempered by the breezes, lulled her, and her thoughts drifted. She remembered Haydar as arrogant and controlling. Maybe he was a typical Baklai after all.

Kat's stomach growled, but luckily Makinti had halted at a clearing off to the right. "We should stop here and use the noon-turn food prepared by the Keep. Past those rocks, is a clear pool formed by the Farralawn, so we can water our horses. Before we leave, re-fill your canteens, and you will have plenty of water for the rest of this turn."

All three dismounted, and led their animals to the pool to allow them to drink. Once they drank their fill, Mouse led his horse to the rock area and tied the reins to a small tree. Makinti and Kat followed suit, and they all sat on nearby logs to consume their meals.

Kat, full of curiosity, finished her sandwich. "Makinti, where will we spend the night?"

He smiled at her. "As I mentioned the previous turn, we will make use of the resting hut. When we arrive, we will have to unsaddle our own horses and tend to them, making sure they are well settled until the morrow. After you finish caring for your animal, take your saddle to your room in the hut."

Kat frowned. "Why?"

He laughed. "Nothing serious. This will protect them from the weather, and some small rodents who exhibit a preference for chewing on leather."

Kat relaxed and nodded.

Each took time to fill their canteens and picked up the packing from their meals.

As Mouse walked to his horse to place the debris in his saddle bag, he stopped and motioned with his hand to the others. "Hissar." His voice was a hoarse whisper.

Makinti hissed at them. "Hurry. Mount your animals and ride from here as fast as possible."

Kat, her stone like a block of ice between her breasts, hurried to her horse, untied the reins, and fear enabled her to scramble up to the saddle, glancing along the path as she did so. Expecting something huge and vicious, she was surprised at the sight of only a fat, furry animal about the size of a house cat. *That tiny thing's a hissar?*

Makinti yelled and cantered his horse to the road. He turned left, away from the direction of the resting hut. The creature growled, hissed, and sped after him almost as fast as the horse.

Mouse yelled to Kat. "Quick. Ride as fast as you can to

your right. Makinti has created a diversion for us."

Kat cantered after Mouse, wondering what was so dangerous about such a small animal.

She assumed they traveled about five hundred yards when Mouse slowed to a stop.

"Why are you so afraid of such a tiny animal?"

"That tiny animal is a hissar, and I do not believe we gave you a proper warning about them. Their eyesight is pathetic, but their hearing and their sense of smell is unparalleled. They can bring an adult horse down by biting at the tendons above the fetlock. Hissars have enormous teeth and can run as fast as most horses, although they do tire quickly. But they can rip out the tendons in at least two legs of horse in less time than it takes to say 'hissar.' When their victim goes down, two or three of those foul creatures can disembowel a horse within minutes."

"If they can run as fast as a horse, how could a person on foot escape them?"

"Without protection, they cannot. Have you seen that most Rifellan guards wear the gee-leg pieces of their armor in Baklai when traveling to the west of the Farralawn River? Many, use similar pieces to cover the legs of their horses. At least with that protection, a Rifellan warrior can use their swords to their advantage."

"Why didn't Makinti wear these now?"

"From what I have been told, finding a hissar this close to the Farralawn is most unusual."

The sound of hoofbeats reached them, and they glanced down the trail. Makinti rode up holding a very dead hissar in one hand. "I had no choice. I had to kill the creature."

Kat peered at the animal closely. The mouth hung open exposing rows of huge, razor-sharp teeth, two deep, lining the jaws, and six legs, which accounted for its speed. "Didn't you want to kill it?"

"No. It is true they are single minded, and they attack for no reason but to kill. However, their benefit is they keep the rodents who consume the feed grains for our horses, in check. Baklai does not possess an abundance of feed, so too many losses could prove catastrophic."

"Are we likely to run into more of them?"

Makinti grinned at Kat. "No, but to run into one so close to the river is odd. I must pass this news to the rest of my men, and to the Baklai. We will all need to check to discover what is forcing them to move further east."

He stepped down from his mount. "We must bury this creature. We do not want the odor of a dead hissar to attract others to this area."

Mouse joined him. "I will help." He glanced up at Kat. "Stay in your saddle, we will not be long."

Disemboweling? Ripped tendons? Damn right I'll stay in my saddle.

Mouse was correct, they were not long in disposing of the body. On their way again, Makinti began to sing the familiar warrior ballad.

While unable to remember the words, Kat hummed along with him, happy now that her stone was once again warm against her skin.

She glanced back at Mouse. "Don't you ever sing?"

"I do, but I am not a warrior, and this is a ballad for warriors."

Kat grimaced. "Oh no. I had no idea it was only for warriors."

Makinti leaned back toward her. "Kat your voice is a welcome addition. Besides, you resemble a Rifellan warrior.

Please."

She did, but without the same enthusiasm as before. Finally, her voice petered out, and she rode the rest of the way in silent contemplation.

The Pridden star dipped slowly below the horizon by the time they rode up to the resting hut. The building was large and jutted out in all directions and, to Kat's eyes, exceedingly ugly. The entire building consisted of planks of untreated wood, not charming, but slapped together without any type of intended design. The sloped roof was covered with rough-hewn shingles, placed haphazardly. Kat could clearly distinguish gaps between the shingles, which she eyed with misgiving. *They don't look as if they'll keep out rain—or creepy crawlies.*

They waited before entering the hut to move the horses to a shelter to ensure their animals were well bedded for the night. After feeding and watering her horse, Kat hung her bridle from a large hook, hefted her saddle on her shoulder, carried her luggage, and walked to the hut.

The inside was equally lacking in any sort of order. The walls of the huge communal area, consisted of bare planks with irregular edges. Around the main room were a number of doors and some curtained entrances, leading to what she assumed were the sleeping areas. This hut appeared to be the result of additions added when needed, without thought to any plan. When she glanced upwards, pinpoints of light confirmed the gaps in the shingles. *Smells airy and clean at least.*

A small but functional kitchen occupied one corner, where two Baklai men stood preparing their food, and they nodded at the newcomers. Roughly constructed tables and chairs occupied the rest of the room. Luckily, the floors were smooth, which Kat suspected had been planed to eliminate the danger of splinters.

Kat and her companions each claimed a room, placing their saddles on wooden stands, and dropping their luggage on plain cots with thin mattresses.

Mouse and Makinti, after conferring with the two Baklai, suggested Kat make use of the single personal first. She hurried through her shower, holding back a yell when ice cold water hit her body. Dressed in her rust brown robe, she made her way back to the common room.

Makinti and Mouse appeared from their rooms soon after, and Kat, still shivering, grinned at them. "I guess a cold shower is needed after escaping a hissar."

They both rolled their eyes at her.

The two Baklai sat at a separate table, and were reluctant to answer any of Kat's questions. "Do both of you work with horses?"

Silence. A grunt from the first Baklai.

"Do either of you work at one of the farms?"

"No."

"I guess your jobs don't involve much talking."

Neither replied.

They ate the same type of rations that Makinti had packed for Kat, a form of journeyklim, dried for lengthy travel. This appeared to be the common food for those on journeys through Baklai.

Kat gave up on the Baklai males and probed Makinti for more information about hissars. "Are they good to eat?"

He laughed. "No, the meat is foul. Just as well, because, as I mentioned before, Baklai needs them. If hissar flesh was pleasant, they might be hunted from existence. Instead, Baklai makes use of blicks for their meat supply." He licked his lips. “Blicks can be delicious.” He snapped his fingers. “I forgot to inform you that the huts contain no sleeping linens. You will have to cover yourself with your robe.”

“Thanks for the warning. Aren’t these huts serviced?”

“Only on a limited basis. Almost all Baklai are involved in horses, the cultivation of grain, and the Rifellans, of course, are only concerned with protection of the land. They do not have the time for items like laundry, which the males consider female’s work. Three times a path, the huts are checked for any repairs required or replacement of broken or worn-out furnishings. All travelers are expected to clean up after themselves. It does work well.”

Mouse chimed in. “Her question may seem out of place, but Kat and I have been treated to many luxuries in the rest of the lands, and she is not used to traveling like a non-royal person.”

“Ah, I understand. When we reach the Border Keep, Kat, we Rifellans will treat you to more luxury.”

Kat smiled. “Thank you, Makinti.”

She finished her meal, washed her mug, wiped down the table, and headed to her room. She donned her night clothes and wrapped herself in her robe. Settling herself on her cot, she drifted off to sleep soothed by the low rumble of the men’s conversations.

Those Baklai hardly spoke. I wonder who they are.

CHAPTER 11

Kat woke to the sound of birds squabbling and bushes rustling. She yawned, stretched and reluctantly rose from her bed. The fresh cool air in the hut tempted her to stay in her cot a while longer.

A chirp from Wink's cage persuaded her to remain upright and feed the little pyrock. She stretched a few more times and, more alert, quickly dressed, packed her robe in her bag, and ambled out to the communal area.

Makinti and Mouse sat consuming their journeyklim and glanced up at her. Makinti eyed her beneath a lowered brow. "By Caleesh, the woman is finally awake."

She frowned at him. "Running from hissars is not energizing, and I found the cot more comfortable than I anticipated." She retrieved some journeyklim from the communal pack Makinti brought with them. After heating water on the wood stove and withdrawing some karri-san from her dwindling store, she made herself some tea. She assumed quite a few Rifellan men would be stationed at the guards' Border Keep, and it was better to be prepared.

She glanced around the hut. "Did the Baklai leave already?"

Mouse raised his eyes to hers. "Yes. They mentioned they are heading to the eastern section of Baklai to perform a count of the free-roaming horses. They will eventually end up at the foaling station."

"Are there areas where their horses roam free? Aren't they worried that those animals would be easy to steal?"

"No. All the free-roaming horses are geldings and barren mares. Therefore, no thief would be able to breed horses for sale. From what Makinti, and the Baklai we met last eve, told us, their stallions and brood mares are carefully protected and stabled near the mating house at the tip of Eastern Baklai."

Kat frowned. "I'm beginning to see now how stringent the Baklai are in maintaining control of their horses. They consider their horses more valuable than jewels."

Makinti rose, carried his dish to the sink, and proceeded to clean and store the bowl back in the cupboard. "We should set out for the guards' Border Keep, if we wish to take part in the evening meal." He grimaced. "I have eaten more than sufficient journeyklim for one turn. Please clean up after yourselves, and we can prepare our mounts for the journey."

Mouse jumped up and took his dish to the sink, followed by Kat. She found a broom to do a quick sweep of the floors. *Men never notice dusty floors.* After stowing the broom, she grabbed her packed bag from her room.

She gave a quick once-over of the hut and, satisfied, closed the door and headed after Makinti and Mouse. She was relieved the two men did not expect her to clean up after them.

At the lean-to stable, Makinti and Mouse stood saddling their horses, so Kat grabbed her saddle and heaved the heavy leather load over the back of her animal. Fortunately, the baggage horse did not stand as tall as her original mount.

Mouse strode over to help her adjust the fit of the saddle and handed her the girth strap. "You can ask for help, Kat."

"Thanks. Horses in Pridden are bigger than I'm used to, and I often forget they're not as easy to saddle."

Mouse smiled at her, and returned to his horse to complete the saddling and bridling process.

Kat cinched the girth and, to make sure it would fit well, punched the horse in the belly. When the animal exhaled, she made sure all was as tight as possible. "Hmph. This horse doesn't play games like my other one did."

Makinti laughed. "This is a baggage animal, Kat. The creature is not used to riders, and has no requirement for tricks."

She shrugged, patted the animal on its nose, and reached for the rest of the gear.

Horses prepared, the three secured their bags to the rear of their saddles, mounted their animals, and, gathering reins, set off in the direction of the Border Keep. Wider in this section, the path enabled them to travel three abreast.

Kat wriggled her butt into a more comfortable position, grateful to be on her way again.

The heat of the star beat down on them, and beads of sweat formed on Kat's upper lip. A trickle of moisture rolled from her scalp, which she wiped off with the sleeve of her shirt. *Just as well I didn't wear the robe. I'm boiling.*

They rode for some time in the heat, when a tree appeared near the road ahead. "Makinti, can we stop in the shade of that tree. I'm melting."

"I already intended we should stop in the shade for our noon-turn meal. Go ahead, but first take your horse beyond the tree to the river, and allow him to drink his fill. We can fill our canteens after our meal."

Kat slipped from her saddle, and led her horse to the river. Once he drank, she walked him to a small patch of grass under the enormous tree, and tied the reins to a nearby bush. The animal dipped his head and began to munch the short green grass with apparent gusto. Kat took journeyklim from her saddle bag and, seating herself on a lengthy log under the tree, ate her meal. A faint breeze stirred among the leaves of the sturdy tree protecting her from the searing star and fluttered through her curls.

Mouse and Makinti joined her on the log.

Mouse eyed her. “I know this might appear odd, Kat. If you wore your robe, you would find it considerably cooler than your leathers. Plus, the hood would protect you from the heat on your head.”

She stared at him. “Is that true? The robe is cooler than my leathers? But my leathers have no sleeves.”

“I did tell you the unusual weave allows air to circulate around the body.”

“Then I need to put it on now. I’m almost ill from the heat. Would the two of you turn your backs? I need to change.”

“Of course, Kat.” Makinti stood and abruptly turned his back to her.

Kat grabbed her bag from the rear of her saddle. She glanced over her shoulder to make sure Mouse had also turned his back on her, and hastily undid the buckles on the side of her leather uppers. She dropped them on the log and slipped the rust brown robe over her head. Immediately, cooler air surrounded her body. She folded the leathers, stowed them in her bag, and retied it to her saddle.

She turned back toward her companions. “Thank you so much. I’m much better now.”

They both faced her, and Mouse nodded. “You appear less stressed.”

“I am. I didn’t fully understand, when you spoke about it, how extraordinary the material of your robe is. Thank you so much for suggesting I order one.”

Mouse nodded again.

Makinti stowed the rest of the journeyklim in his bags, and picked up his canteen. "We should continue on if we wish to reach the Border Keep before dusk, so fill your canteens, and let us be on our way."

With canteens filled, they proceeded to mount their horses.

"Um, Mouse, I do need some help getting into my saddle. I'm not used to doing this with a robe on."

Mouse rushed to her, and placed his hands together as a step for her to pull herself upward to her saddle. Once seated, she adjusted her backpack and the robe to allow air flow and still be comfortable.

Kat found the balance of the journey far more pleasant, and they reached the Border Keep bridge sooner than she expected. The horses clopped across the wide wooden planks and trotted along the path through shorter grasses. The Keep itself was close to the bridge, and the three stopped before fortress-like walls that faced them.

Makinti drew up to the massive double wooden gates, reinforced with iron bands, and a guard on the parapet walk yelled for the gates to be opened. He turned to face his companions before proceeding. "Welcome to our Rifellan stronghold."

Kat gazed with awe at the fitted stone walls surrounding the Border Keep, curious as to the source of the stones. The gates groaned and ground their way open to allow the travelers access to the inner courtyard of the Keep. As she followed Makinti on horseback, Kat realized why the portals opened so unhurriedly. The barriers, over a foot thick, consisted of bulky wooden planks bound together by huge metal bands. Resembling an indestructible stronghold, this was the most ruggedly built Keep that Kat had encountered in her journey.

Makinti rode to a smaller building, redolent with a sweet pungent smell of manure and straw that suggested a stable. He dismounted. "Come along you two. We will take time for a tour later. Your horses need to be taken care of first. Our stable hands will settle your mounts, but collect your own belongings. I must leave you, as I need to send an urgent message to the Baklai Horse Master regarding the hissar we encountered." He smiled at them. "I shall request that Ildiren, who is the apprentice healer assigned to this Keep, show you to your rooms. She will collect you later to join us for an evening meal."

Kat sighed with happiness. Everywhere she looked, Rifellan warriors stood watch or moved around the Keep, intent on duties unknown to her. She felt so much at home among them. *I adore Rifellans. Mouse and I are safe here.*

CHAPTER 12

Ssestin crossed the bridge of the Farralawn River, from the western section of Baklai, and he rode through the eastern grasslands as surreptitiously as possible. When he reached the left branch of the Farralawn, he slipped across the shallowest part, positioned between the two Border Keeps of the Rifellan guards. Unfortunately, in this "shallow" section, the waters still came to his horse's chest, and he spurred the beast to swim for the opposite bank. The poor animal rolled her eyes in fear, but Ssestin maintained firm control, urged her on, and she scrambled up the bank. She stood on the firm bank in Morden, trembling slightly.

Two turns had passed since Ssestin had left the boat from Glowen at the dock in the Teeki Dow fjord, and he had ridden hard to arrive in his home land. Weariness fell like a mantle over him, and Pridden's star gradually descended, and painted the sky with the red and oranges of dusk, finally leaving the deep violet of night ready to overtake the landscape.

He paused, allowing his mount to rest, while he consulted a map. The Merga Doo, close by, would provide an excellent haven for the night. The Mordens called all their forests Doos. He shook the reins for his tired horse to continue, walked toward the tree line, and entered via one of the many animal trails.

He stopped and dismounted the beast in a clearing, affixed the reins to a tree, and removed the saddle, which he set down to act as his pillow. Retrieving his hidden dagger from his belt, he cut a number of branches, and laid them across the ground as bedding. His black Assassin's cloak he took from a saddle bag and dropped the robe over the leafy branches.

He returned to his horse, and led her to a pool of water. She drank her fill, and he then led her to a patch of grass and hobbled her, which gave her leave to graze for the night. Off to the side, well away from the horse, he set a small trap.

He returned to his makeshift bed, drank from his canteen, and lay down among the soft leaves, wrapped in the cloak. Within minutes, his eyes closed, and sleep overtook him.

❋❋❋

Birds woke him, and the first rays of dawn lightened the sky. He rose, checked his trap, and discovered a tree rodent. *Excellent, a morning meal.*

He made his way to the pool removed the Rifellan scribe's clothing he had worn during his trip through Baklai, and indulged in a brief wash in the cold water. After he dried himself with the remains of his disguise, he created a hole to bury the clothes, and covered the fresh dirt with broken branches and dead leaves. He donned his Assassin's clothing and black robe.

His stomach rumbled, so he located some rocks, and arranged them in a circle. He added kindling and small dry branches, and then he pulled a flint from his pockets, and worked it until a flame sparked.

He blew gently, and soon a healthy little fire provided him with the necessary heat to cook the rodent, already skinned and prepared with the aid of the knife he always kept concealed about his person.

While his catch cooked, he saddled his horse, removed her hobbles, and tied her again to the tree near his campsite.

Once he ate his meal, he wrapped the uneaten portion of

the rodent in leaves from the branches of his bed. He placed the leaf package in a saddle bag, buried the carcass, and extinguished all flames. He covered the remains of his fire with earth. He used the heavy branches to sweep the area of all footprints, and gazed with satisfaction at the now pristine area. He planned to drop the remaining branches, one by one on his ride through the Merga Doo, to conceal his passage.

He swung up to his saddle and set off through the forest toward the Assassins' Guild.

Alternating between walking his horse and performing an easy canter, Ssestin allowed his horse periods of rest, despite the fact he anxiously wished to speak with Ssarff. But if he pushed his horse, it would not reach the Keep alive.

He waited to consume his noon-turn meal until he reached the Heer. This river bisected Morden as it flowed from the foothills of Clog Blue to the Hyal Sea. Ssestin stopped close to the bridge just before the river plunged into a massive chasm where the water boiled through narrowed rock cliffs. Upstream from the bridge, the river expanded into a number of pools of swirling water. He allowed his mount to drink, and looped the reins over a small bush.

He seated himself on a rock, drank from his canteen, and unwrapped the last of his cooked rodent meal. Once he ate, he buried the leaves covered in the fat of the rodent, and walked back to the pools to fill his canteen.

Ssestin stretched his body to iron out the kinks from a long turn of travel. He placed his foot in the stirrup on the horse's left side and swung himself up into the saddle.

Pulling the animal's head around, he headed for the bridge and thudded across the broad wooden span. Once across. he breathed a sigh of relief. With his home so close, tempted though he was to gallop for the Keep, his horse appeared to tire too swiftly to chance it. He would still be back in time for the evening meal with his brother members.

Finally, less than a short canter away, Ssestin gave in to his desire to enter the Keep as quickly as possible. He urged his horse to gallop.

The tall gate rumbled open, and Ssestin rode in toward the stable. When he reached an assistant, he slid off the back of his animal and handed the reins to the man. "Take excellent care of her. She's ridden hard."

The assistant nodded and led the horse away.

Ssarff appeared at the doorway of the inner keep. "You bring news? The guards saw you gallop up."

Ssestin approached him. "I need to discuss much with you, Master. May we consume our meal in your quarters?"

They turned and headed swiftly toward Ssarff's rooms, and when they arrived at his door, Ssarff ordered meals for them from the guard standing at attention at the door.

They entered, sat at Ssarff's table, and Ssestin blurted out. "Has Galdin given you another assignment?"

"I received a messenger moth from him early this turn, which requested our Guild to capture the woman and bring her to him. His terms are less generous this time. I suspect he is of the mind that we would not need to travel far to snatch her from Baklai." He frowned. "Why do you ask?"

A knock at the door indicated the arrival of their meals, and Ssestin held his tongue until the apprentice left the room.

"Master, I think you should not accept the task."

"Why?"

"I met the woman on the voyage from Glowen. I do not fully understand why Galdin feels need of her, but I am positive the reason will not be in her best interest."

"I never imagined it would."

"Master. I admire her. Her name is Kat, and she is different. I cannot read her mind, yet I sense a strength of energy about her."

"Do you suspect she is a Wielder?"

"No." He hesitated. "I believe if Galdin is prevented from the destruction of this woman, she might be the cause of his downfall. Perhaps if we help her, you might replace Galdin as Thane." *I cannot tell Ssarff what I have done.*

"Ssestin, never speak those words outside this room. Galdin would convict you of treason. If you are correct, and we do come to her aid, this Kat might be our new Thane."

"Perhaps, but all I wish is that the man is not allowed to capture her. She is too valuable. Of that I am certain."

Ssarff rose and paced the room. "You have been my second-in-command for many paths, and you have always proven trustworthy. I must send a reply to the Thane. Bring me a messenger moth from the cabinet."

Ssestin rose and walked over to a tall cabinet, with many drawers. He opened one half way down, and extracted a moth, which he brought to the Guild Master.

Ssarff brought the creature to his lips. "Thane Galdin, I received your request for the Guild to accept an assignment to bring the female to you from Baklai. Although Baklai is close, there is much hue and cry over the death of a horse in her possession, and she is under scrutiny more closely than ever. In addition, Baklai recently acquired another half legion of Rifellan warriors from Lord Murwenna, and extracting the woman could prove almost impossible. Might I suggest we all wait until she enters Morden, which is most likely her next stop. At that point, your own soldiers should be more than sufficient to bring her to you. Your faithful ally, Ssarff, Assassins' Guild Master."

He glanced over at Ssestin, and raised his eyebrows as if in enquiry.

Ssestin nodded.

The Guild Master opened the window and tossed the moth to the wind. He followed its path as it fluttered off, and latched the window when the moth was out of sight. "I have done as you suggested."

Ssestin breathed deeply. *I hope the Thane will accept this.*

CHAPTER 13

Kat hefted her baggage, and, as she and Mouse reached the doors to the inner Keep, a young woman in a long blue robe approached them.

"Lady Kat, I am Ildiren. Makinti requested I show you and Sire Mouse to your rooms."

"My thanks, Ildiren, but please, I am not a formal person. Call me Kat."

"But you appear to be Rifellan royalty, and I would be at fault to be so informal with you."

"I'm not Rifellan, nor am I royalty, so you may relax."

Mouse stepped forward. "We wish to gain our rooms. The last two turns were tiring. The hissar we encountered added an unexpected challenge."

Ildiren's eyes opened wide. "A hissar? This close to the Farralawn?"

"Indeed. Makinti mentioned he found that unusual."

"It might be catastrophic. The people will need to find a way to keep the hissars contained in the west. Most of the horses roam free in this part of the land, and we do not possess sufficient grieve pieces to protect them all. It is imperative the males of Baklai prevent the hissars from crossing the bridges to the eastern part of the land."

Kat stared at Ildiren in horror. "Makinti did mention he needed to send an urgent message to the Horse Master about the hissar."

Ildiren shook her head. "Forgive me for the delay. I will show you to your rooms, and will return after you are settled to escort you to the dining hall."

She led them through the corridors and showed them their assigned rooms. As they entered, she again advised them she would return later, giving them enough time to prepare for the evening meal. She left them and returned to her previous duties.

As Kat entered her room, she peered over her shoulder at her guide. "Mouse, although my robe is most comfortable, I believe I should don my leathers to meet with the Rifellans. Do you agree?"

"I suspect this would be wise to do so. Keeping alive the resemblance to Rifellan royalty will always serve you best when you are among their warriors."

"My only concern is I'm running low on karri-san tea, and Makinti's pheromones began to have a strong effect on me. It is embarrassing to lose control of one's libido. I wonder if the Border Keep has any tea on hand?"

"I suspect they do. Remember the Kaylins are also affected by the Rifellans, and Kaylin traders do travel to Baklai to obtain horses. I suggest you request this of Ildiren."

"Good idea." Kat turned around, unlocked her door and entered her quarters. Once inside, she deposited her luggage, removed Wink's cage from her backpack, and placed it on the dresser. A squeak from the small creature signaled her desire for food.

"Wink, you're going to grow as fat as a little pig, if you continue to eat so much." Kat fed her from the container of pyrock food. Wink squeaked once more, but only long enough to burrow inside her bedding and fall asleep.

Kat removed her robe and rinsed herself in the shower, to remove the salty sweat from earlier in the turn. From her bags, she donned her leathers, and gave her hair a quick brush. She sat to complete a brief record in her journal of the encounter with the hissar and the dangers that threatened the Baklai horses. Her stone lay cool on her chest when she recalled the vicious teeth and the potential for being disemboweled. She shivered.

A tap reminded her that Ildiren would call them to a meal. When she opened the door, the healer stood in the passage way with Mouse.

❋❋❋

As Ildiren guided them through the open doors of the dining hall, Kat asked her about obtaining more karri-san.

Ildiren smiled. "I will have a supply delivered to your rooms."

Kat thanked her as they entered the hall.

Makinti waved at them from a table for ten. Three empty chairs stood waiting for them, and they were soon seated.

Kat stared all around the hall at the room filled with gorgeous Rifellan male and female warriors. She tapped Makinti on the arm. "Would you please order some karri-san tea for me? I feel in need of it."

He chuckled. "I keep forgetting you are not Rifellan. I will." He beckoned a wait person to the table, and ordered the tea, plus blick stew for the entire table. "We receive many visitors, and some of those do require the tea to help alleviate our natural appeal." He chuckled again. "I do understand what some non-Rifellans encounter in our company. Dayleeya in Glowen sent Eestred a sample of the scented ritual lip balm. We both found it quite stimulating." He grinned as if in remembrance. "We suspect this may be what some non-Rifellans experience." He smiled down at her. "I will request an apprentice bring a supply of the tea to your room."

"Thank you. I have already requested the tea from Ildiren.

While they waited for their meals, he introduced the two females and the four males to Kat, one of which was Alderon, Makinti's second-in-command, and the head of the Border Keep.

Affected to a small degree by strong Rifellan pheromones in the hall, she forgot their names almost as soon as she heard them.

The apprentice delivered a mug and a huge pot of karri-san tea to her, and she gratefully filled the cup and drained it. She poured another and sat back to enjoy the banter among the warriors.

Alderon, the tall warrior opposite her, related the story of his last encounter with a hissar. "My horse obviously decided she was a dancer, and pranced and kicked out at the vicious creature. She connected a healthy blow under the hissar's chin, and the creature flew quite a distance. When we found the animal, it was stone dead. I believe we should train all our horses to deal with hissars in this manner."

The others at the table laughed aloud and raised their mugs of Orenberry wine in a toast to the horse.

Kat unsuccessfully attempted to hide a yawn.

Makinti glanced her way. "I suspect, Kat, you are weary after our journey here. You are more than welcome to retire, and we will meet on the morrow to send you both through the rest of western Baklai."

"My thanks, Makinti. I will see you on the morrow." She rose, bid a fine night to the rest of the table, yawned, and headed back to her room. *I assume Mouse knows to meet me on the morrow as well.*

❋❋❋

Something furry and chirping woke Kat from a restful sleep. She opened one eye. "Wink. You naughty pyrock. You escaped from your cage again. How do you do this?"

Wink refused to answer, which forced Kat to depart her bed and find food for the small creature. Wink gobbled down three pieces of food, burped, and allowed Kat to return her to her cage.

She completed her packing and her morning toilette, dressed in her robe, and, carrying her bags, knocked at Mouse's room.

He opened his door. "Ah, you are ready for us to leave directly after our morning meal."

"I couldn't guess how long it would take to arrive at our first overnight shelter. I thought it best to begin our journey early."

He grabbed his own bags, closed his door, and they headed for the dining hall. As they stopped at the entrance, Makinti stood and beckoned them over to his table.

They ordered their meals and Makinti unrolled two maps for the western part of Baklai. "These maps will help you until you return to Thane Cathked's Keep. You will discover you have the option to rest overnight at four different farms, and you, Kat, also are able to stay at Dinerth Caleesh. Hissars will be a challenge until you reach the farms overlooking the Mora Waters. By the time you reach that area, the hissars are no longer present."

Kats rolled her eyes. "Hissars. Ugh. What can we do to protect ourselves?"

Their meals arrived, and they began to eat. Mouse glanced at Makinti. "I assume we will need grieve pieces for our shins, and protection for the legs of our horses."

"You are correct. We will loan you the pieces for you and Kat, and for your horses we will provide you with wrappings of both leather and brynosh fibers. Hissars will not be able to reach the tendons of the horses through that protection. You may leave the grieves and the wrappings with the farmers near the Mora Waters."

"Our thanks. We appreciate the protection."

Makinti rose. "I will take you to the stable and, once you are ready, show you the trail to the Border Keep bridge. Once you cross the bridge, refer to the maps I gave you." He and Mouse performed their Rifellan handshake and smiled at each other. "I wish you both a safe journey."

Kat gathered her bags, and she and Mouse followed Makinti from the hall, through the entrance from the outer keep to the stable.

Once there, Makinti demonstrated the way to don the grieve pieces, and how to wrap the lower legs of their horses.

Mouse tied the leg wrappings in a roll and fixed the bundle to the back of his saddle, along with his bag.

They both mounted their animals, Kat with a little help from Makinti, and gathered their reins. They waved at their Rifellan friend and set off for the bridge.

The sun warmed her face, and her robe kept her comfortable. Kat sighed in pleasure at the recall of the delightful time spent with the warriors. *Rifellans are my favorite people, but perhaps that's because of Liandock.*

CHAPTER 14

Mouse rode in front along the path. He suggested they ride single file until they reached the first farm. "Makinti informed me we are unlikely to run into any hissars until we are closer to the second farm. The grains are removed at the second settlement, and are stored at that location. Naturally, the rodents congregate at that area, attracting hissars who prefer to live where they are able to locate the majority of rodents."

"Don't they store anything at the first farm?"

"Makinti told me they only store straw in their sheds, which is why they call it the Straw Farm."

"That makes sense." Kat rocked in her saddle as the baggage animal plodded along the path. No trees disturbed the endless fields, and Kat lost all sense of time and yawned. *Miles of grasses. Boring.*

Kat's stomach grumbled. "Mouse. Are we going to eat soon?"

He stopped his horses and turned in the saddle to stare at the scenery behind him. "I can no longer catch sight of the bridge." He pulled a map from his case and studied the route Makinti suggested. "I do believe since we are quite close to the western branch of the Farralawn. The river creates many eddies close to the bank where we may water our horses." He stowed the map back in his saddle bag, and steered his horse to the right.

They rode past the edge of the grain fields, and through grasslands, until they came upon the bank of the river. The water gargled in its throat as it rushed over rocks on its way downstream.

Mouse dismounted, led his horse to the water, and allowed the animal to drink his fill.

Kat slid off her saddle, landed awkwardly on the rocks that covered the bank, and barely escaped a tumble in the river when her horse shoved past her to slake its own thirst. "Whoa, you overgrown lug. Keep pushing me and I won't be friendly to you."

Mouse grinned and shook his head. "I never encountered any other being who carries on such lengthy conversations with animals. You do not believe they speak back to you?"

Kat frowned. "No, I know they don't, except of course for the boradai in Shendea. But I'm convinced they understand me."

He shrugged. "Possibly I suspect it's your tone of voice they understand. And the boradai, by the way, are not animals, they are sentient beings."

"I guess."

"Lead your animal to the grassland and drop the reins over its head. He will be able to eat, and will not wander far."

Before she did so, Kat extracted from her saddle bag the meal the Border Keep had prepared for them. She passed half the package to Mouse, and found a smallish rock on which to sit and consume her own. The water of the river gurgled and plopped and bubbled its song over rocks and pebbles, as if directed by some unseen conductor.

Her meal completed Kat buried the leaves in which the meal packages were wrapped. She filled her canteen, and finished off by washing her hands and shaking them dry.

When they prepared to leave, none of the rocks were tall enough to allow Kat to remount. "Mouse? Can you help?"

He bent down and cupped his hands. When she placed her foot in his hands, he lifted her high enough for her to obtain her seat. *Every time he does that, I get that he's a lot stronger than he looks.*

With Mouse again in the lead, they followed the map directions to the Straw Farm.

Kat gazed across the fields. The Baklai farm hands swung their scythes, and chanted in a rhythm similar to the Rifellan warrior's song. Three passes of the scythe, and the worker gathered the stalks in a bundle and tied them together with brynosh line.

Each worked their way down the field: cut, cut, cut, stop and bundle, cut, cut, cut, stop and bundle. Drawn by a small horse, an open cart trundled down the cut paths as the workers gathered the bundles and stacked them in the wagon. Each vehicle, when filled with the bundles of grain, progressed heavily along the path toward the Grain Farm.

Carts returning from what she assumed was the Grain Farm, now piled with bundles of stalks only, headed for the sheds which Kat saw were located on the Straw Farm. The star was still shining brightly when they arrived, and a muscular and deeply tanned young Baklai ran toward them. "Welcome, Sire Mouse. Welcome, Lady Kat. We have been expecting you. I am Bryn. Please dismount and bring your horses to our stable to rest for this night."

They did as he asked, and when they arrived at the stables, they removed their saddles and placed them on trestles. They hung their bridles from hooks mounted on the walls. Finally, they brushed the worst of the dust from the coats of their animals. Bryn helped Mouse bring water to the stalls, while Kat filled both hay nets.

They exited the stables, and Kat gazed around her. The

buildings were covered in a type of varnish so that the outsides shone with burnished wood. Three of the smallest buildings were thatched with golden straw. The large sheds, which Kat assumed were for storage of the straw, had roofs covered with wooden shingles. These sheds ringed a series of even smaller buildings. The latter, Kat discovered, were houses for the farm workers.

"Sire? Lady? Collect your bags, and I will guide you to rooms for this night." He ushered them toward one of the large buildings. "In here, we have a series of rooms for visitors, plus our communal dining hall." He showed them down a long passage, with doors on either side, indicating visitor's rooms.

The interior, Kat saw, consisted of varnished wood, and wall paintings that depicted life on the farm.

Bryn led them to their doors. "If you will deposit your baggage, I will take you on a brief tour of the farm. There will still be time enough to change for the evening meal. The communal dining hall is close to the entrance of this building."

They entered their respective rooms and dropped their luggage. Kat set Wink's cage on a dresser before she left to follow Bryn for the tour.

At the first shed, a number of men cut the brynosh that held the bundles of stalks together and spread the straw to air dry. Bryn pointed to the far end of the shed. At the rear end, the men collected the dried straw which they stuffed into sack-like pallets. The pallets appeared to be mattresses.

Kat smiled at the young children jumping on the stuffed sacking. Bryn explained that the young helped break down the straw to soften the material and create a more comfortable sleeping surface. The children obviously enjoyed their jobs, as they jumped and leaped and tussled on the sacking, shrieking with laughter.

Mouse chuckled at their zeal. "Is this always a chore you assign to your young?"

"Yes. We realized that often our progeny became bored and found it difficult to act with propriety. Our females were responsible for softening the straw for sleeping mats, and the task often took them away from other duties. I decided to assign this task to our young, and we discovered they not only enjoyed themselves, but it also allowed them to expend their surplus of energy, without disturbing the rest of the farm." Bryn beamed and tapped his chest with apparent pride. "Our farm supplies pallet-like mattresses for all the homes in Baklai, and I believe the females are relieved to be rid of this task." He glanced around. "This concludes our tour, and we will all don cleaner clothes for our evening meal. Can you both locate your rooms without my help?"

Mouse nodded. "We can."

"Excellent. When the bell rings, you may then attend the dining hall, which is a short walk along the hall, to the left of your rooms."

Kat thanked him, and she and Mouse made their way back to their quarters.

❋❋❋

Kat fed Wink, and then retrieved her leathers from her bag, along with the one pair of loose pants she packed at Cathked's Keep. She hung her robe in the shower stall after she shook the dust from the folds and completed a quick wash at the sink.

Ready for her meal, she responded to the bell and exited her room. When Mouse appeared, they headed left down the hallway.

"From the noise, I suspect we do not need directions to the hall." Mouse grinned.

They entered the hall, and Bryn motioned them over to one of the biggest tables, with two empty seats. "We do not usually enjoy many visitors, so I made sure to reserve seats for you. The apprentices will bring food to the table in serving dishes, so you will be able to help yourselves. Our progeny are trained to wait until their parents, and other adults' plates are filled before they may serve themselves."

The apprentices appeared, bearing huge platters of food. Kat took the opportunity to examine the people in the hall. The dining area itself was plain and utilitarian. The tables and chairs, covered in a thick varnish, appeared to be able to resist heat and water rings with ease. The tables seated ten, and at least four children sat at each table. The cacophony of children's chatter, the clatter of eating utensils, and conversations between the adults fascinated her.

Various women approached Kat. "Welcome to our farm. Is your mate a Rifellan warrior? Do you have progeny of your own?"

"I am not Rifellan, and I am not yet bonded." Kat saw them examining her with curiosity in their eyes. "Sire Mouse, the male who accompanies me is my guide. He was assigned to me by Lord Eduardo of Kaylin."

The woman raised eyebrows. "You travel alone with a male who is not your bond mate? In Baklai, even Rifellan warrior females would travel in the company of other females."

Kat changed the subject. "Please tell me what duties the males and females are assigned to on your farm."

Kat relaxed as the women chatted about their duties on the farm, laughing and teasing each other.

By the time the meal was over, Kat left the hall and headed to her room, smiling to herself. *They all seem so happy.*

CHAPTER 15

The babble of children's voices woke Kat the following morning. While not as sweet as the sounds of birds welcoming a new day, nevertheless, the sounds of Straw Farm's progeny conveyed joy. Kat left her bed, stretched, yawned and headed for the shower.

❋❋❋

After the morning meal, she and Mouse would head for the Grain Farm. They might encounter hissars and would need to attach grieve pieces to their shins and wrap their horse's legs before they departed.

For safety over comfort, she donned her leathers and packed her robe. *I hope I won't be too hot.* She fed Wink, attached the cage to her backpack, and set out for the dining hall.

When she entered, Mouse waved her over to a table. "Most of the Baklai are already at their work. I ordered a substantial meal for you, because we will not wish to stop for the mid-turn. I do not fancy being a sitting snack for a hissar."

"You'll receive no disagreement from me."

"Bryn lent us additional canteens so we do not need to dismount to drink from the Farralawn. He suggested an area, which he marked on the map, where we may water our horses without the need to get down from them. In addition, we were given a hand-carried snack for mid-turn refreshment. You may consume this as we ride."

"With leg protection, would we be able to outrun hissars?"

Mouse smiled. "We will not need to. Bryn gave me two

containers of reeker fetor to throw at them should they attack us."

Kat blinked. "Reeker fetor?" She shook her head. "What the hell is reeker fetor?"

"This is the odor reekers expel if they are in danger. Before you ask, a reeker is a small furred rodent that consumes fruit. The problems they cause are serious, because the fruit supplies are an important part of food the Baklai require to survive."

"Can't the hissars keep these reekers in check, like they do the grain rodents?"

"Before a hissar can arrive close enough to kill a reeker, the animal expels an odor so foul, so choking, that any unfortunate creature caught in their spray becomes unhinged in their attempts to rid themselves of the disgusting scent. The noxious smell can last almost five turns before dissipating. During the time any animal that is covered with reeker fetor, cannot hunt because the odor warns all of their approach."

Kat eyed him with trepidation. "Is it safe for us to carry these containers?"

"Bryn assures me they will not break unless thrown on the ground. He is proud of the fact that he helped in the design of the containers."

"Baklai is not a friendly land." Kat shuddered. "Don't they possess anything to reduce the smell on someone?"

"They douse the affected person or animal with plenty of water and bury the poor creature in sand for half a turn, except for their mouths and noses. This apparently speeds up the process of eliminating the stench."

After finished his meal, Mouse rose from his chair. "We should leave for the Grain Farm. We do not want to arrive after dusk, and we must travel with care."

Kat stared up at him. "Oh no, not another nasty creature?"

He grinned as she stood. "No. However this is blick country, and the Baklai do attempt to keep the pathways clear of their holes. By traveling slowly, we allow the horses to pick their way around any blick holes that may appear, and avoid leg injuries."

"I thought blicks were from Rifella, and I've never seen one."

"They are. Blicks are about the size of your boradai, but with much more fur on them. They only eat grasses, and are benign little creatures. The Baklai discovered blicks thrive in their land. They purchased a number of breeding pairs from Rifella, and have established a flourishing colony."

Kat twisted her mouth. "Interesting." She picked up her bags and followed Mouse from the hall, deep in thought. *Hissars and now blick burrows. I don't want to live here.*

Bryn waited for them at the stables. "Since you are probably not familiar with protection from the hissars, I am to show you how to properly install the leg pieces for both you and your horses."

Kat nodded. "Great. We were shown briefly how they work. But I certainly would appreciate a step-by-step lesson."

Bryn laid out the grieve pieces for the two of them and the bindings and protective covers for their horses' shins. "Lady Kat, would you step forward." He took a grieve piece, created by the armorers in Rifella, attached it to the front of her lower leg, and buckled the straps at the rear. "Please note the front of your leg is protected, but you still possess open areas at the back. However, the primary concern is to protect the bones and tendons, and the Achilles tendon is protected by the wide leather strap holding the grieve pieces in place."

Kat stared down at her leg. "I do not intend to be on ground level with a hissar, so my legs are bulky enough."

Bryn grinned at her. "Now we will protect your horse." He tied the reins tight to a bar outside the stall. He placed the odd shaped armor on the back of the horse's lower leg and held it in place with one hand. With the other he began to wrap the brynosh enforced material around the leg, keeping the armor in place as he did so.

Kat peered at the result. "My horse actually seems comfortable, and he moves with ease."

"We needed to spend much time making sure our horses in the west are well protected. The armor is in two pieces, held together by thin straps on each side. This means the tendons both below and above the bone are armored."

"Thank you, Bryn. I feel so much safer now."

"We do still suggest the best method is escape when dealing with hissars."

"I do not disagree with you."

Bryn continued to help both her and Mouse don their armor, and helped saddle and bridle their horses, before they mounted.

She waved farewell, and she and Mouse set off for the Grain Farm.

❋❋❋

The passage was slow, because Mouse, in the lead, kept an eye out for any blick holes. Only twice during the journey did he need to warn her, and luckily, they did not encounter any hissars.

Kat again, found the rocking motion sleep inducing, and she struggled to stay awake. She knew she could not afford to lose her concentration with the possibility of hissars in the area. She grabbed her canteen a few times to drink cool water, and when a hunger pang struck, reached around for her saddle bag and extracted some food.

"Mouse?"

He swung around in his saddle to face her, a frown on his face. "What?"

"How far is it to the farm?"

He breathed a sigh. "I thought you caught sight of something. We are close. The road ahead appears to make a sharp turn to the left. The farm is only a few lengths beyond that."

"About time. This part of our trip is so boring and slow, I'm surprised I didn't fall off my horse."

"I hope you are making a joke. You must be alert in hissar country."

Damn. Sometimes he takes things so literally.

They continued to plod along the path, and as the road swung to the left, a series of buildings popped into view. The buildings were plain in their design, built of wood, and whitewashed. They were scattered over a substantial area, with plenty of cleared land around them. The section around the houses, kept free of growing grain, made it easier to see if hissars approached.

Kat suspected they lacked any adornment, because the inhabitants needed to devote their time on ensuring protection from hissars, rather than indulging in home decoration.

When they arrived, an apprentice came out to greet them and guide them to the stables. "When you have settled your mounts, collect your baggage, and I will show you to your rooms. Didahanus, the leader of our farm, will give a brief tour of our facilities, and will later, also meet you in the dining hall for the evening meal."

❁❁❁

Kat settled her luggage in her room and removed the

grieve pieces from her legs. *Ouch, cramps.* She had been so aware of the possible danger of hissars, she had held her legs tightly against her horse's sides. A walking tour she knew would help relax her muscles.

She and Mouse met Didahanus at the huge threshing shed to watch how the Baklai separated the grains from the stalks. Surprised at how simply they accomplished the separation, Kat was delighted that the Baklai once again involved the children. The males inserted each bundle of grains into a sack, and a child would jump on the sack and beat it until the grains and stalks were separated. The stalks, still tied together, they stored upright in the back of a cart, which would be returned to the Straw Farm. They dumped the grains into larger containers.

The grains from the large containers were poured into a bigger one--this time from a height of about five feet, which allowed the chaff to blow away in the constant breezes.

Didahanus asked Kat what she thought of their system.

"What you've accomplished here is astonishing. I enjoyed seeing you bring your progeny into the whole process, and that they find the situation so much fun and so satisfying. It is similar to how the young help at the Straw Farm."

"We dedicated many paths to discovering a system which would work for our land. We raise our progeny to be useful members of our society. Each one serves a different purpose each turn." He chuckled. "This way they never become bored, and we do hand out incentives occasionally."

At that moment, Kat heard the growls of a hissar. She whirled around and stared in horror as the animal headed full tilt toward one of the children. The nasty piece of work had something pink attached to it. Horrified, she drew her dagger and threw herself toward the hissar.

Cries of "Stop! He is mine," interrupted her charge. A young child ran and clutched at the hissar, effectively barring Kat's intent to kill the creature. Sliding in the dirt, Kat raised a considerable amount of dust and came to rest inches from the young Baklai. She stared with an open mouth at the pair.

The child hugged the hissar tightly, and the animal licked the face of its benefactor. The hissar did not possess the normal two huge fangs, and the claws were all blunted. In addition, it sported an enormous pink bow around its neck.

The small girl smiled at Kat. "This is Meena. You must not hurt her. She loves me."

Didahanus hurried over to Kat and helped her regain her feet. "I do apologize, Lady Kat. I neglected to inform you about my progeny's pet. A full-grown hissar attacked one of our people, and he was forced to kill it. If only he knew, he could have easily escaped, because the hissar was a female who had given birth moments before to four small kits. Joona here" -- he pointed at his daughter-- "attempted to save them, but only this one survived."

"Weren't you worried about the danger to the child?"

"Child? Ah, you used Rifellan words. No, the animal bonded with Joona, and when Meena became older, we removed the dangerous fangs and blunted the claws. We would never have been able to raise her and return her to the wild."

"How extraordinary. I never anticipated meeting a tame hissar."

Mouse stood close to her, sheathing his own dagger. He shrugged. "I, too, thought we were faced with danger, but you were closer to Joona."

How odd, my stone remained warm. She often wondered how it knew when danger did or did not exist. "Didahanus, I would appreciate the opportunity to change my clothing before we meet for the evening meal."

"We do understand. Your attempted rescue raised a great deal of dust. When the bell rings, we would invite you to join us at the hall."

She thanked him and favoring her left arm, walked with Mouse to the main building. "Did I make an idiot of myself?"

"No, you did not. If I were closer, I would have done the same thing. Didahanus is most likely grateful you thought you needed to save his progeny from danger."

At her door, she glanced at Mouse. "I'll meet you here when the bell rings, but I need a decent shower. I've got dust and sand in every crook and crevice."

Mouse's face turned pink at her words. "Fine."

Kat noticed his discomfort and was curious as to what he had envisioned.

Once in her room, she fed a grumpy, neglected pyrock.

In the personal, she took off her Rifellan leathers and shook the top in the shower stall to shed the sand and dust. *If I hadn't had on my leathers, I might have left a lot of skin behind.* She placed them on a stool outside the stall and returned to the shower.

Clean, she pulled her robe from her bags and slipped it over her head. As she fluffed her still damp hair, the bell rang, and she exited her room to meet Mouse in the hallway.

❋❋❋

Once again, the din was extraordinary. Children laughed and yelled at each other, and adults' voices rose when they tried to carry on a conversation amid the uproar. All added to the mayhem. Seated with Didahanus and his family, Kat dug into the delicious blick stew. The spicing, slightly different from that of the Straw Farm, tempted her to indulge in a second helping.

Joona piped up. “You will not have room to eat dessert now.”

Kat smiled down at her. “I need more stew. I expanded much energy fighting off your tame Meena.”

Joona giggled. “Meena would not fight you. I think she likes you, although you did scare her a bit.”

Didahanus frowned at her. “Joona, I suggest you and your friends collect your desserts and go to the play room.”

The girl squirmed from her seat and rushed to the dessert table, apparently searching for the biggest serving.

Didahanus grinned, shook his head, and rolled his eyes at his youngster. He turned back to Mouse. “We understand you will be lodging with us a second and third night. Am I correct?”

Mouse nodded.

“And, Lady Kat, you will depart on the morrow for Dinerth Caleesh?”

“I will, and since I will be leaving early, if you will all excuse me, my bed calls me. Today was tiring.”

“By all means, do. We will no doubt meet with you at the morning meal, and I will arrange for our apprentice to help you with the rebinding of your horse’s legs.”

“Thank you.” She rose and left the dining hall, dragging her weary feet to her room.

A tame hissar. How many other surprises am I in for?

CHAPTER 16

The horizon had just barely blushed with the first appearance of Pridden's star when Kat opened her eyes. She blinked a few times and stretched until her spine cracked. She sat up and tiptoed out of bed but too late, a mournful chirp came from Wink's cage.

"Come on Wink. I've not starved you. Come to think of it, the last time you took any messages we were in Glowen." She walked to the cage, carrying a container of pyrock food. She withdrew Wink from her cage and popped two treats in her mouth before the creature could complain any further. "I think you're just feeling neglected." She stroked the small pyrock and gently laid her back in her cage among her cozy blankets.

She opened the window, and breathed in a huge lungful of crisp air, grateful that the air nights were always cooler.

She prepared for her day, dressed in her Rifellan leathers, packed her robe, and placed her luggage in a pile on the bed.

She left her luggage in her room to be picked up later, and walked to Mouse's room. When she knocked, the door opened almost immediately, and he peered out.

"You are up early."

"I had a terrific sleep last night. I wonder if you are ready to join me for the morning meal."

"I am. We can discuss your visit to Dinerth Caleesh." He closed his door behind him and followed her toward the hall.

At the entrance they found only a few people milling about. Mouse led them to a small table for four, and they sat and ordered meals from the apprentice.

"So, Mouse, what do you think I'll encounter at Dinerth Caleesh?"

He dropped his gaze and shifted in apparent discomfort. "Well…being truthful, Kat, I have absolutely no idea what you should expect."

"I guess that was unfair of me, since you did tell me you've never been to Baklai before. I'm surprised Makinti didn't give you some idea."

"Makinti has no idea either. Eestred has not revealed anything to him. Apparently, the females wish to keep their ceremonies familiar only to other females."

"Odd. You said we should discuss my visit though."

"I meant the travel to Dinerth, and where you and I will meet in two turns."

Kat smiled. "That makes sense." A movement at the doorway and a familiar face caught her eye. She rose and waved at a woman. "Eestred. I didn't expect to see you."

The Rifellan woman approached their table, a cheerful grin on her face. "I decided to accompany you to Dinerth Caleesh."

Kat hugged her. "I'm so glad. Please sit. Will you join us for a morning meal?"

The woman seated herself. "I would be delighted. I departed the Dinerth pre-dawn and pre-meal and rode to arrive here before light. Hissars do not hunt in the dark, as their eyesight is not sharp. This way you and I can accompany each other during the light and, thus, guard each other."

Mouse who had risen to welcome Eestred, sat down. "I am most pleased you will accompany Kat. I intended to arrange for a female from the farm to guide her." He smiled. "However, a Rifellan warrior is a much better escort."

Eestred laughed. "Not a definitive truth, Mouse. Farm women are most capable in the way they handle hissars. They live with the creatures every path."

"I suspect you are correct. I must admit I hold a prejudice when I consider Rifellan warriors. Perhaps I tend to endow them with all-encompassing powers."

Eestred grinned at Kat. "It appears your Mouse is most adept at flattery."

Kat glanced at her guide, his eyes wide, as a blush crept up his face. *Poor Mouse, he embarrasses so easily.* She wondered if Eestred was aware he wasn't flirting with her.

An apprentice approached their table to take their orders.

They waited for their meals, and the two women chatted. Eestred asked about their journey from the Border Keep. "I meant to ask you, Kat. Did you obtain extra karri-san?"

"Yes. Makinti and his guards were most generous." Kat screwed up her face. "My most dangerous encounter was when I met Meena."

Eestred wrinkled her brow. "Meena?"

"A tame hissar."

"Ah yes. I recall one of the guards mentioned a young one possessed a pet hissar. Is the creature truly tame?"

"Yes. The parents had the large fangs removed, and maintained cut claws. He told us the young hissar would never be able to be returned to the wild, so they had no choice but to adopt it."

Eestred shrugged. "Nevertheless, I would be reluctant to keep such a creature around, tame or not."

"I agree with you, but the Baklai seem to have their own way of doing things."

"They do indeed. Which brings me to the Dinerth. We will stay this night and that of the morrow. Mouse, we will meet you the morning of the third turn at the small protected hut outside the Dinerth. I suggest you travel before first light. We will bring morning meals for us."

Mouse nodded. "I will be at the hut before dawn."

Their meals arrived, and conversation ceased.

***

Once the meals were completed, Eestred and Kat said farewell to Mouse, and Kat returned to her room to pick up her luggage.

Later, Kat, with bags in hand, headed to the stable with Eestred. Grieve pieces in place, and their horses' legs wrapped, the women set off for Dinerth Caleesh.

They both kept a close scrutiny for hissars and, as they passed a wooden hut, painted a deep brown, Eestred pointed out that was where Kat would later meet Mouse. They rode on, and a number of narrower paths branched off the main thoroughfare. Kat had no idea where any of them led. The Rifellan female guided them down the fourth one to their left, which meandered through grasses and small trees.

They rounded a bend in the path, and the Dinerth burst into view. The building was most unusual. The construction of the entire lower section was of stone, similar to that of the Master Builder's village in Kaylin. Each block, streaked with crystals in a myriad of colors, reminded Kat of Liandock's village of Lanfair, and the memory warmed the deep green stone in her pendant that nestled between her breasts.

The upper part of the structure consisted of wood, light in color and burnished to a brilliant sheen. The building's stunning construction sang of praise to a deity of supreme importance.

Kat's breath caught in her throat. Something of this beauty was unexpected in Baklai. It appeared so out of place in this land, a place of horses and tough men, dark of skin, and in the Thane's case darker of mind. *This is one huge difference between men and women in Baklai?*

Eestred led them to a building attached to the outer edge, also constructed of wood, which proved to be stables. Two male apprentices approached and helped them from their mounts, removed the saddles, bridles, and leg wrappings, and proceeded to groom the horses for them. Since men were not allowed within the walls of the Dinerth, Kat was curious as to where these men lived.

Eestred explained they resided in a small village down one of the narrow paths that led from the main thoroughfare. "Men, Kat, are always used in the care of horses."

Kat and Eestred took their own bags through the huge iron gates of the Dinerth, where, clad in a blue robe and her face alight with a welcoming smile, Layleene greeted them.

"Welcome. I am considered the healer for the women of Baklai. Let me show you to your room, Kat."

"Layleene, I'm so delighted to meet you again. I didn't expect you to welcome us to Dinerth."

"You will find almost all the women of Baklai at the Dinerth at this time. Only a few remain at the farms to ensure they continue to operate smoothly. We have celebrations four times per path, and those who cannot attend this one will be at the next. Every woman in Baklai attends at least two, and preferably three, celebrations per path."

Eestred touched Kat on the arm. "I will give you time to settle yourself in your room, and I will take a nap in mine. I will come for you to attend a noon-time meal."

"I will enjoy that, Eestred." She glanced at Layleene. "I would appreciate being shown to my room. I too need a nap."

The healer led her down the hallways of the inner Dinerth and up a series of stairs to the second floor, past wooden walls painted with breathtaking murals of Baklai. Life in the land, represented by young horses galloping through lush green meadows, golden grains waving in the winds, young Baklai skipping between the farm buildings, and fruits and vegetables piled on carts, drew her eyes in every direction.

At Kat's door, Eestred handed her an ornate gold colored key. "This is for your door only. The tassel in your room will call someone to help you should you need it. Every woman in Baklai acts in a service capacity at least once per path. The only women who are exempt are those who serve on the Council of Seven. They serve all the women of this land throughout the entire path."

"Thank you Eestred." Kat entered her room and dropped her bags on the floor. She removed Wink's cage from her backpack and placed it on the dresser.

Built of the same type of wood found in the halls, the furnishings, covered in a shimmering varnish, gleamed under the light of the globes in the room.

She yawned, moved to the bed and, sank gratefully on it.

❁❁❁

Kat woke to the sound of women singing. She rose from her bed, stretched, and followed the voices down the hall. She peered in at a roomful of mostly Baklai women, with a healthy smattering of Rifellans among them.

The woman closest to her turned and smiled. She was stunning, with skin like smooth dark chocolate, and brilliant blue eyes. "You must be Kat."

"I am. I must apologize. I am sure I should remember your name, but I have met so many new faces recently, I'm drawing a blank."

The woman laughed. "What an odd expression, but it

does convey what you mean. We were not introduced, but did see each other at Thane Cathked's dinner. I am Grayseen, and am bond mate to Hunter Master Galakis."

"I remember you now. I thought at the time what extraordinary eyes you possess. All the other Baklai I've met have brown eyes." Kat tilted her head and gazed at the woman. "Are you full Baklai born?"

"I am. Our family all were birthed with brown eyes, so we suspect somewhere one of my ancestors may have been from Rifella, and passed on their gift to me."

"A gift indeed, Grayseen. You are a striking woman."

The woman smiled and bowed her head in a gesture of thanks. She cocked her head at Kat. "You are not wearing a robe. Did no one give you one when you arrived?"

"Eestred brought me here, and we were both so tired we retired to our rooms for naps. I believe I am to meet her for the mid-turn meal, but she never mentioned a robe to me."

"Let me help you. First let us check your room."

Kat led the way, and shortly they entered her quarters. Grayseen opened the closet door, and pulled out a snowy white robe. "Here we are. I am pleased someone did remember to make sure you would be properly outfitted."

"Why a robe, Grayseen?"

"The Dinerth is a place for women to relax yet perform the duties for which we are well suited. We do much work here, but we make sure our surroundings are beautiful and restful. We achieve much that is needed in Baklai because we cater to our well-being. I will return to the hall to sing some more, but I suggest that to help you relax fully, you shower the dust from your travels, put on the robe, and join me when you are able. The hall is also used for dining, and we will share a mid-turn meal."

Kat thanked her, and Grayseen left the room.

Kat laid the robe on her bed, and hung her leathers in the closet. She entered the shower, which was one of the most luxurious she had encountered, filled with containers of sweet-smelling soaps and lotions. When she was dry and powdered and relaxed, she donned the robe. The material, soft and silky on her skin, enhanced the sensation of royalty. *This is so luxurious. I am spoiled.*

Kat exited her room and headed back to the massive hall. She located Grayseen at a table for eight.

Kat slipped into a seat, and within minutes, Eestred, Layleene, and four Baklai women joined them. Kat recognized one of the women from the Straw Farm.

She gazed around the enormous hall, her eyes darting everywhere. Hundreds of women either sat at tables, moved around the area, filled meal orders, or worked in the enormous kitchen she glimpsed whenever the door swung open. "This is extraordinary. You do this four times a path?"

Layleene smiled at her. "We do. During the time Caleth and I are assigned to Baklai, I am always able to attend, particularly in my role as a healer. Healers are assigned to a land for five paths, or for life, if they and the Thane or Lord of the land desire they stay."

"How many paths have you served here?"

"We have been in Baklai for three paths. My duties are a little different than many of the females. As a healer, I must always be available, so I am not permitted to be in a service capacity. However, although I am not part of the Council of Seven, I am called upon from time to time for my expertise in the health of those in this land."

"Who and what are the Council of Seven?"

"They are responsible for the governing of Baklai. They

determine the policy of interaction and commerce with the other lands. They oversee the laws of the land, and determine the responsibilities of the males in Baklai. There is no corner of Baklai life in which the Council are not involved."

Kat opened her mouth and breathed out a "Wow. The females of Baklai are the ones who run the land."

"Generally, we do, because we are best-suited to these tasks." Grayseen raised her eyebrows and laughed quietly.

"So, the males are little more than figureheads."

Grayseen frowned. "Not at all. Our biggest commercial assets are our horses. The males are totally responsible for everything to do with these creatures. They determine when to breed, who to breed with, which horses are for sale, their food, health, and areas in which to graze. Our males are ideally suited to deal with these valuable animals. Because of their expertise, Baklai enjoys a unique position in Pridden. Our horses are worth more than jewels, or wine or goods from any other land. Our males are not figureheads, but important members of Baklai."

A woman, whom Kat was sure she had seen before, delivered meals for all at the table.

As they began to eat, Kat turned to Grayseen again. "You still haven't told me who serves on the Council of Seven."

"My apologies. Each member serves for three paths, with the exception of the head of the Council, who is always the bonded mate of the Thane. In our current situation, that is Kerdinon, who is bonded to Thane Cathked. There is always one Rifellan, and Eestred, as bond mate to the praetor, Makinti, was invited to serve but has requested that Eeloria, bond mate to Alderon, leader of the Border Keep, serve in her stead." Grayseen held up her hand and ticked off her fingers. "Nellabon, mate of our Horse Master, Bannigus; Kitterin, mate of Didahanus, who is head of Grain Farm; Gayzella who is the Thane's Head of House at the Keep; Larryna, mate to the head of the Fruit Farm, and myself, as mate to the Hunter Master."

Kat pinched the bridge of her nose. "My head is spinning."

Grayseen smiled at her. "There is much to learn about Baklai." She held up a hand. "Do please remember, Kat, this information is not ever spoken of outside these walls."

"I can keep confidences." *The Sha-hee were never this complicated.*

"I was sure you could be trusted with our secrets. Now, let us complete our meal and you may spend the rest of this day however you choose. Please explore anywhere within our walls. You may return here for the evening meal or request food be delivered to your room. On the morrow, we all meet in this hall for the morning meal and the beginning of our celebration. We will see you when you hear the bells calling for the commencement of our day."

❋❋❋

Kat excused herself and headed to her room but remained there only long enough to check on Wink. She spent the afternoon wandering through the magnificent Dinerth building, in deep thought about the relationship between the males and females in Baklai. She eventually returned to her room to order a light evening meal and extracted her journal to write up the experiences of the day.

Stiff from being seated most of the evening, meal and journal both completed, she stretched and yawned. Bed called her. She fed Wink, hung her robe in the closet, and stumbled onto the thick mattress, which enveloped her in its downy folds. *Wow The women of Baklai may not be fighting warriors, but their strength of mind and purpose is unparalleled.*

CHAPTER 17

Kat woke to the music of some incredibly talented bird. *Birds?* She gazed around the room. *A window?* She had seen no windows when she first rode up to the Dinerth. She left her bed and walked toward the unexpected window. Puzzled, she opened it and leaned out. What she saw initially was an outer rim of walls surrounding the courtyard below her. There were no discernable openings in the outer wall.

As she continued to glance around, the view suggested how the builders constructed the Dinerth. She leaned further out. The inner building, which housed everything and everyone, possessed the same crystal-imbedded stone on the first level, and an upper level of wood. A covered walkway led from the entrance gate, and what she had assumed to be an inner passageway now appeared to be the only link between the outer fortress and the primary building of the Dinerth. The walkway contained two doors, which opened to the courtyard.

Curious. I saw no openings in the outer fortress. This is a settlement of secrets.

The courtyard contained a combination of gardens and a few stalls that displayed items of clothing, jewelry, and shoes. Tranquil, except for the birds, this inner area gave the impression of peace. Women in white robes glided through the yard with grace. Spaced regularly within the area, slender trees reached toward the heavens, but never stretched above the outer walls. Song birds lived hidden among the leaves. Kat did not remember seeing the tops of trees when she first approached the walls of the Dinerth. *No wonder bird sounds are unexpected.*

A chirp from Wink indicated the pyrock wished food. Kat fed her. "Don't go back to sleep. I need you to take a message to Mouse." She extracted a piece of parchment and her cathnog tooth pen, which she dipped into the Kaylin ink. "Mouse. I will meet you on the morrow just before dawn at the hut that is painted a deep brown. Do not proceed any further, because you would not be aware which road I will come from. Kat." Because the note was meant for Mouse, she was able to write it entirely in her own writing, rather than Priddanese script. She placed the note in a tube and attached it to Wink's foreleg. "Go to Mouse, Wink." The little creature flapped her wings, lifted from the desk, and disappeared.

Kat stowed her writing materials in the diplo bag and prepared for her day. She once again donned the white robe and straightened her bed covers. Eestred mentioned functions in the Dinerth were handled by the women themselves,

A series of gentle bells began the call for all to attend the morning meal, and Kat locked her door and hurried down the passageway to the huge hall.

At the entrance, she paused to gaze around the room. Seated at a table for ten, Eestred waved at Kat to join them.

"Thank you for directing me. I wasn't sure with whom I should sit. Layleene originally invited me, you guided me here, and Grayseen explained the ways in which the Dinerth worked."

"You will enjoy even more contact with other females here. However, Grayseen is a member of the Council of Seven and must sit with her fellow Council members. Layleene is the current healer for the women of Baklai, and, although not a Council member, during the ceremonies she is required to sit beside them." She grinned at Kat. "I alone of the three you mentioned am free to sit with whomever I please. The Council requested I serve with them, but I asked that Eeloria, who is the bond mate of Alderon, report on behalf of the Rifellans instead."

"Grayseen mentioned this to me. Why didn't you want to be on the council?"

"Because Makinti is the Praetor. He travels throughout Baklai often, and I usually travel with him. If I did not, we would rarely see each other. As such, I am not as available to serve on council matters as the others."

"I can understand why you would not wish to be separated from Makinti that often."

Eestred smiled and nodded.

The women who acted as servers for the entire celebration emerged from the kitchen area, laden with trays of food and drink, which they deposited at the tables of attendees.

As they ate, Eestred introduced the other eight women to Kat. They came from all over the land of Baklai, two from farms, one from the Keep, and five were mates of the men who handled horses in the eastern part of the land.

Kat, awed by the sight of hundreds of females in the room, sat in silence. The babble of various conversations overwhelmed her as she tried to follow only those at her table. The women discussed a number of topics about family life, offspring, and the challenges of how to maintain the function of a household with often limited finances.

Eestred, who had been discussing how the women from other lands managed their lives when they lived away from their own lands, turned to Kat. "You are in a unique situation, Kat. You move to a new land every number of turns. We are all aware your challenge is that you have no idea when you will return to your home." She patted Kat's arm.

She waved her hand over the room of women. "Healers serve in a land for five paths, but may stay longer if they wish. Rifellan warriors serve only five paths, but Praetors serve the Lords or Thanes for a minimum of ten paths. All those from other lands are allowed to visit their homes at least once per path."

The servers returned and cleared the tables of all dishes, and then returned with mugs and large pitchers of tea. The din of conversation slowly receded.

The servers brought out a long table with eight chairs, which faced the room. The Council of Seven took their places at the table, joined by Layleene in the eighth seat. Silence reigned.

The woman whom Kat recognized as Kerdinon, rose. "As the chair for the Council, I welcome you all to our third celebration for this path. We are fortunate. The past number of turns have been most successful, so our business discussions will not be as lengthy as expected. Before the Council deliver their reports for the past quarter of this path, we would ask you to welcome Kat, who is here on behest of Lord Eduardo of Kaylin." Kerdinon raised her arm and beckoned for Kat to rise.

She rose, and the entire hall called out, "Welcome, Kat."

Odd. Kerdinon didn't join in the verbal welcome. She's also taller than most Baklai women. Interesting.

Kat lowered herself to sit, when Kerdinon again raised her arm, her face without warmth. "Pray tell us, Kat, why did Lord Eduardo send you here?"

Kat stood straight again. "You all made me feel so welcome in Baklai that I am sure Lord Eduardo wished me to experience the warmth among all the lands in Pridden."

Kerdinon kept her arm in the air. "I believe you experienced the loss of a horse on the way here from Glowen. Am I right?"

The woman's face, frozen like a block of ice, displayed no welcome in her eyes.

Why is she angry? The stone on her pendant cooled. Kat, nonplussed, lowered her eyes and gazed at her table mates.

Eestred's eyes narrowed and her brow furrowed.

I can't ignore Kerdinon. I must answer. "You are correct. My horse was unaccountably murdered on board the Glowen vessel. My guide has applied to Thane Cathked for a replacement, which Lord Eduardo will pay for on my behalf."

Kerdinon lowered her hand, and allowed Kat to seat herself.

The chairwoman remained standing. "I do hope, Kat, that should my Thane allow this, you will take better care of the new animal. Horses are precious in our land."

Bitch. Kat bit her tongue to hold back expressing herself out loud. She had ridden the horse through four lands without any problems. How could Kerdinon assume it was Kat's neglect that killed the unfortunate animal? *Double bitch.* She caught an expression of disapproval on the face of Grayseen, and shock in the expressions of the rest of the women at her table.

Eestred leaned toward her and whispered in her ear, "That was undeserved. Why does Kerdinon dislike you so much?"

Kat glanced at her and shrugged. Her facial muscles tightened.

Kerdinon, now seated, read out the minutes of the report from the previous quarter and asked the women to accept or change it. The women all voted to accept the document. The chairwoman, called on the each of the other Council members for their reports.

Nellabon was first to stand, since she was mate to the Horse Master and in the best situation to advise about the sales of horses and the accounts of the herds and their requirements. "The hissars have kept the number of rodents to a manageable level. However, we received notification of a hissar sighting close to the middle branch of the Farralawn River. Horse Master Penabon, when advised of this, arranged for his men to ensure the hissars are not able to cross any bridges to the east part of Baklai."

With the next report, the all-important one about food and other amenities for the horses, Kitterin, mate to Didahanus, assured them that these items were in excellent supply. "We are most fortunate to have increased our stock of grain with which to feed the animals. Both for the past quarter and based on our current supplies, grains will remain in a positive position for the last quarter of this path."

Larryna advised them the fruit and vegetable supplies for the population surpassed their estimates, and Gayzella happily mentioned that life at Thane Cathked's Keep was proceeding as expected.

"Security is always a concern for those of us in Baklai, particularly because we share a lengthy border with Morden." Eeloria assured the room that no infiltrations from Galdin's men had occurred in the current path, nor had they picked up any rumors of intended challenges.

Layleene's report, brief and simple, revealed only the number of new offspring who birthed in the past quarter.

Kat sighed silently in relief at the brevity of the reports. It was a great deal to take in.

Kerdinon again addressed the females in the hall. "If any female here has new business to be discussed, please do so now."

The groups of women stared about, curious if anyone would speak. Not one woman did.

Finally, Grayseen stood. She put her arms out, palms up, as if she held up the heavens. "Caleesh. We stand and invite you to bless our land and our people." Kat and the rest of the women in the hall rose and assumed the same position as Grayseen. They repeated her words. She continued to speak, one phrase at a time, and waited after each line for the rest of the hall to repeat her words.

"May our bodies be well-nourished.

"May our spirits be cleansed by love.

"May our souls be filled with joy.

"May our precious elderly transition with ease,
And always reside in our hearts."

The women in the hall placed their hands together as if in prayer, bowed from the waist, and said in unison, "Caleesh, may you grant us unconditional love."

Bet that bitch Kerdinon isn't thinking love.

Grayseen addressed them again. "The business for this turn is concluded, and we may now take part in a celebratory mid-turn meal."

Before any of the servers could begin to bring the meals, a growl of thunder from outside the Dinerth rumbled throughout the hall. Grayseen asked for their attention. "We are about to receive a serious storm, and we are fortunate to be in a strong shelter. However, I believe three stalls of goods are still left open in the courtyard, and the songbird houses need to be unlatched to allow them to seek shelter. We ask for volunteers to help with these items."

Kat began to move toward the hallway to the outer gate, but Eestred caught her by the arm. "No Kat. We appreciate your intention to help, but there are females in the hall, who are experienced in these preparations. Let them handle it."

"I was about to check that the window is closed in my room."

Within minutes a number of women headed for the courtyard and returned quickly with goods from the stalls, and the basic frames and fabric of the stalls themselves. Kat blinked as a brilliant flash of light appeared from the upper windows in the hall.

Eestred called out to Kat, "Go check your window."

Kat ran to her room and shut the window. As she turned to leave, Wink appeared, squeaking in fright. Kat took the tube from her foreleg, unrolled the piece of parchment, and read the message, "Okay" from Mouse. She chuckled at his use of her expression. Rewarding the shivering pyrock with a treat, she swaddled Wink in her bedding and placed her back in her cage. The small creature's eyes closed, and she dropped off to sleep.

The rain pelted down with a vengeance, drumming on the outer walls of the Dinerth. The rhythm increased in volume, and Kat, as she hurried back to the hall, was certain she heard hail strike the wood of the upper layer.

Laughing and chatting to each other, the women had returned to their seats, and the servers now carried food and drink to the tables.

Kat rejoined her table mates, with Eestred again beside her. The Rifellan laughed at joke from a woman on her other side. She leaned back to Kat. "This is not usually part of our celebration, but it is most appropriate. Thunder storms bring precious moisture to our land. Caleesh has blessed us."

New dishes continued to emerge from the kitchen, females toasted each other with Orenberry wine, and the hall echoed with laughter and song and joyous celebration. Some women rose and performed the dances of their villages. The feast and celebrations of the mid-turn meal morphed into early evening.

By the time the storm ended, so had Kat's energy. "Eestred, I am to meet with Mouse before dawn at the hut. Is it possible for someone to wake me early and supply me with a meal for both Mouse and myself to consume at the hut?"

"Of course. I will arrange it for you. Attend your bed."

Head spinning from too much wine, Kat staggered off to her room, threw her robe on a chair, and stumbled into bed. The moment her head hit the pillow, she had time for only one last thought.

I like the women of Baklai. They are the ones who run this land.

CHAPTER 18

A loud cheeping beside her head, woke Kat. A pyrock stood on her pillow, but the creature was not Wink, who also cheeped frantically from her cage.

Kat peered at the newcomer. "Who are you, and where do you come from?"

The creature held out a foreleg with a tube attached. Careful not to touch the animal, she removed the tube, and extracted the note. Unfortunately, Kat wasn't able to read the lengthy missive written in Priddanese, but she recognized Liandock' signature. Her heart skipped a beat.

She rose from the bed, and withdrew a blank piece of parchment, her writing materials, and the list of Pridden words Mouse had helped her record.

As swiftly as possible, she penned a reply from her list of Priddanese words. "I will reply later. Kat", and inserted her note in the tube. She reattached the tube to the foreleg of the strange pyrock, and ordered it to return to Liandock. Seconds later, with wings flapping, it lifted off the desk and disappeared from the room.

Although not yet dawn, she hoped to find Layleene to help her interpret the parchment from Liandock. She took a cold shower to properly waken herself, dressed in her leathers, and packed everything else in preparation for her departure for the hut. She gathered her bags in a small pile, together with her long bow, when a light knock sounded at the door.

Layleene stood in the passageway, a package of food in

her hand.

"Layleene, I didn't expect you to be here. I'm sorry you had to leave your bed so early."

"It is not a problem, Kat. A number of us will be heading directly for the Thane's Keep after our morning meal. We must leave early to arrive at the Thane's home before dark, because we will not be able to find any shelters prior to the Keep." She tapped her on the arm. "Come, we should leave for the stable now."

"When we arrive at the stable, and while I prepare my horse for departure, would you read me a note I received via pyrock?"

"I will."

They hurried down the passageway, and as they departed the huge entrance gate of the Dinerth, they headed left to the stable which stood close the entrance gate.

Once inside, Kat handed Liandock's note to Layleene, and began the task of preparation for her trip to the hut. She saddled and bridled the horse as the healer read the letter aloud.

"The letter says, 'Kat, Irina contacted me and advised me someone killed your horse on board the vessel from Glowen and you may encounter a challenge to replace her. I am friends with Galakis, the Hunter Master in Baklai, and he possesses much influence with the Thane. I will request his help on this matter. He, in turn, enjoys a similar friendship with Penabon, the Thane's Horse Master. We will obtain a horse for you.' " Layleene smiled at Kat. "This male must be a fine friend to help you in this way."

Kat sighed, relieved there were no problems for him in Kaylin. "Is that all he wrote?"

"No, he wrote more. He continues to say, "I was much

amused when Irina informed me about Eestred, Makinti's bond mate, who suggested you and I should be introduced. She believes we would be an excellent couple. Irina is aware of our relationship, and she laughed as she told me of Eestred's plan. Please be safe and remember, if you need me, I will come. Penrow has requested I send you greetings, and he too has pledged his help should you need it." He signed the missive as Liandock."

"Thank you so much, Layleene. I would appreciate if you would keep this knowledge to yourself. I believe Mouse does not wish me to enjoy time with Liandock, so I would prefer he is not informed of this note."

"Naturally I will say nothing." She smiled. "You do not need to don grieve pieces for the short ride to the hut. You can wait until you and Mouse are ready to leave." She hugged Kat. "May your journey be safe. I will no doubt meet you again before you leave Baklai."

Kat pulled a small folding ladder beside the horse and easily mounted the animal. With her backpack on, her diplo bag stowed inside, and Wink's cage attached, she inserted her long bow into the holder on the side of the saddle.

Layleene handed her the food package and a canteen of hot tea, which Kat slipped into a saddle bag. She had rolled together grieve pieces and bindings for the horse's legs and tied them to the back of the saddle next to her baggage. Kat swung the horse's head around and set off for the hut. She looked back and waved at the healer.

❋❋❋

When Kat arrived at the hut, she was the sole visitor. She guided her horse into a stall but did not remove the saddle or her baggage. They would not be stopped for any length of time, and her animal was still fresh from the brief journey.

She removed the meals and the canteen from her saddle bag and entered the hut to wait for Mouse.

Soon she heard the rhythmic beat of a horse approaching, and the baggage animal Kat had placed in the stall, whinnied a welcome.

She peered out the door. Mouse led his horse into another stall, dismounted, and strode toward the hut. He held a map in his hand.

"Good morrow, Kat. Were you waiting long?"

"No. I received a meal for us." She pointed at the wrapped food on the table. "Even better, the kitchen at the Dinerth supplied me with an extra canteen filled with hot tea."

"The tea is most welcome. I tied my horse in a stall with a water trough. This should last him until we reach the Frothan Farm, which is where the fruit growers reside." He sat at the table, and Kat removed two mugs from the shelves over a small sink, poured tea from the canteen, and served one to him. Steam rose from the surface of the cup, and he drank. "Delicious."

Kat poured some for herself, drank gratefully, and passed him a wrapper of food. "Baklai is so different from some of the other lands. The heat during the turn is almost unbearable. At night, though, once the star sets, I am quite chilled. I wonder why."

Mouse frowned. "I suspect because Baklai is enclosed by the three branches of the Farralawn River, and a lengthy coast line. The winds over such a huge amount of water cool the land when it is not being scorched by Pridden's star."

"I guess." She unwrapped her food and began to eat.

Mouse did the same. He tilted his head and gazed at her. "Did the Dinerth Caleesh meet your expectations?"

"I find your question difficult to answer because all that

occurred in the building, I must keep as a secret. Sorry, Mouse. However, I will say that the place itself is beautiful. The artistry in the structure is magnificent." She sighed.

"No matter. I gathered as much from my discussions with the males at the Grain Farm." He frowned and pursed his lips. "I suspect Baklai males are wary of the females. Why, I do not understand."

Kat nodded. "The males and females of this land appear to enjoy a strange relationship. There's an element of grudging respect. Both also show no desire to perform the tasks of the other. Yet bonded pairs seem quite normal."

"I suspect if the other lands understood this about the Baklai, they might show more respect for them."

"Do you believe Eduardo is aware of this about Baklai?"

He shrugged. "I am not sure, Kat. I doubt the females here allowed him to visit the Dinerth, so it is unlikely he is privy to the depth of the situation."

Kat snorted. "The males and females need to share how they each operate. They can still perform their own tasks, but to keep each other in ignorance of how they do so, makes no sense."

Mouse grimaced." I doubt we will be able to persuade them to be forthcoming with each other."

Kat drank more tea and pointed at the papers in Mouse's hands. "Is that a map of the rest of our journey back to the Keep?"

"Yes." He placed it between them and pointed out their stops. "We should reach the Frothan Farm shortly after their noon-turn meal, and they will, I am sure, serve us some food. We will have an opportunity to tour their premises and later join them for their evening meal." He took another drink, and continued to consume his food. "On the following morrow, we will depart for the Losgayrin Farm."

Kat sighed. "I am not fascinated by the prospect of visits to farm after farm. I'd much rather see more of the horses."

"Think of this as a prelude."

"I'll do my best. All I want is a horse of my own. This baggage animal is boney, and I find his gait uncomfortable."

"A possibility exists that before he grants you another, the Thane wishes to be sure you appreciate everything about his land."

"Perhaps. We should set out now. You may leave the canteen on the counter. Layleene advised me they would retrieve it later."

They rose from their seats, left the hut, and walked to the horse stalls. They removed the animals from the stalls, where they put on their grieve pieces and wrapped their horses' legs. Finally ready, they mounted their animals, Kat with assistance from Mouse.

Side by side, they set off along the trail which led to the Frothan Farm, and the sky, now alive with the pallet of dawn, lit their path.

Another secret. The Sha-hee and now this. Although Mouse can be annoying, I hate keeping secrets from him.

Chapter 19

Ssestin worked with some of the apprentice Assassins, including Seegal, who, as usual, showed off for the women who watched from an upper gallery.

Ssestin sighed. "Seegal." He shook his head in frustration. "If you continue to battle in such a shoddy manner, you will become a fine meal for a drag. A large sized one should be easily able to swallow you completely."

Seegal grinned at his parent. "A drag would never catch me. I am too fast."

"Perhaps not a drag. However, walk too close to a kokas nest, and you will find yourself as a repast for their young. I doubt you possess the ability to outrun a kokas. Pay attention when you spar."

Seegal lowered his gaze and shuffled his feet. "Yes Sire."

Positive the boy still grinned, Ssestin grumbled to himself. A servant of the Keep ran up to Ssestin and murmured to him, "Master Ssarff wishes to meet with you in his quarters, Sire."

He nodded at the man. "Fine." He eyed the young apprentices and called over his best student. "I must attend Master Ssarff. Please take over the class, and do not allow Seegal to neglect his sparring."

The young apprentice nodded and bowed to Ssestin, who turned and left for the inner Keep, and Ssarff's quarters.

❁❁❁

Ssestin knocked on Ssarff's door, and entered when the Master called, "Come."

Ssarff sat at his desk recording the happenings of the Keep in his master journal.

Ssestin approached him. “You summoned me, Ssarff?”

The Guild Master sighed. “I did. My worst fear is here. Galdin is most unhappy at my reply and I am ordered to his Keep.”

Ssestin stared at him. His heart thumped in his chest. “I suspect you cannot refuse to go.”

“No.”

“I worry you will be in grave danger if you attend Galdin at his Keep.” Ssestin rubbed his brow. “Perhaps you might be wise to allow some of your best Assassins to accompany you, but they should remain out of sight.”

“You speak wisely, Ssestin. I cannot take you. Should something happen to me, you must head the Guild. I will take only two, and I agree I will request they travel unseen on a parallel course. I still doubt Galdin would be foolish enough to order me killed.”

“It would be illogical for him to do so.” Ssestin twisted his brows in worry. “Although Master, he has not shown much logic since he became obsessed with that woman, Kat.”

Ssarff smiled at his second. “Galdin may often wish to kill me, but despite the loyalty of his guards, he is aware they still fear our Assassins’ Guild. They fear our snakes, and they fear our magics. He is never sure if we are allies or dangerous enemies. He judges all others by his own past actions.”

“His past actions prove he is not a man to be trusted.”

Ssarff rose from his desk and laughed as he slapped Ssestin on the back. “You need not worry. I will return safely.”

“I have faith in you Master. Shall I choose the two who will accompany you?”

“Yes please. You are the best one at being aware of your

Assassins' qualities and skills."

Ssestin extracted a messenger moth, and handed the creature to Ssarff, who whispered to it. "I will be at your Keep in two turns, Thane Galdin." He threw the moth from a window.

Ssestin left to assign the men to travel with the Guild Master.

❋❋❋

Ssarff met with the two tall, dangerous Assassins who would accompany him. He pointed out his intended route on a map. "I will travel on this side of the Heer River, and you must make you way through the trees of Skinya-Doo and Merga-Doo."

The men studied the map carefully and handed the parchment back to him. His last-minute instructions were brief. "You must always remain out of sight. Do not show yourselves, unless I call out for you. The greatest danger to me will be when I am in Galdin's meeting room, but you will be outside the walls of the Keep."

Enveloped in black robes to shield them in the confines of the forests, both nodded.

Ssarff and his guardians set off toward the Heer, which they did not reach until the noon-turn. He watched his Assassins cross the rickety bridge near the start of the chasm. By the time he arrived further up the river at the Heer Falls, where the water fell hundreds of feet to the pointed and jagged rocks below, the two men were no longer visible.

Ssarff halted briefly near the edge of the Heer to water his horse, without dismounting. He consumed some journeyklim, which he had stowed in a saddle bag, and drank from his canteen.

His horse took the opportunity to crop grass while Ssarff ate. His appetite sated, he dug his heels into his animal and continued on. He rode until night swallowed the colors of evening. He had not seen his pair of Assassins cross from the Merga-Doo through a brief section of grassy plain into the Skinya-Doo.

Confident they were now within the forest he rode among the tall grasses of the upper plains of Morden. He dismounted, unsaddled his horse, and led the animal to water. The horse drank its fill, so Ssarff hobbled it in a small clearing among the tall feathery grasses. He placed his saddle on the ground, ate more journeyklim, and refilled his canteen. Wrapped in his cloak, he laid his head on his saddle and slept.

The sounds of creatures who rustled among the strands of grass woke him as dawn began to paint the sky with pinks and oranges.

Ssarff rose and stretched, and his muscles cracked as he worked out the kinks from sleeping on the ground overnight. Another meal of journeyklim, and he removed the hobbles and saddled his horse. He mounted his animal and set off again for Galdin's Keep.

He spent the rest of the turn moving through the lengthy grasses, occasionally disturbing a ground bird into flight. The light fled from the land, and Ssarff plodded along on a very tired animal to the gates of Galdin's Keep. He threw back his hood to allow Galdin's guards to recognize him.

They opened the gates, and bowed their heads as he slid off his horse. He handed the reins to one of the guards. "Please make sure he is watered and fed. We rode long to get here."

The guard nodded and led the animal to the stable.

Another guard appeared from the inner Keep. "Guild Master, Thane Galdin requested you join him to dine when you arrive."

Ssarff widened his eyes. *Dine?* "I appreciate the invite. Would you lead me to Thane Galdin?"

The guard bowed and walked ahead of Ssarff. He moved through a number of passages and ended up at a huge iron-clad door, guarded by two burly men who held heavy metal spears. One of the guards opened the door and announced the Master Assassin.

Ssarff entered, and Galdin, who stood behind his usual throne-like chair, waved the Guild Master to a seat at the end of a highly polished table, set with silver and glassware.

The Master Assassin sat and regarded Galdin curiously, although he tried to keep his expression neutral. "My thanks for the meal, Thane Galdin. I rode to arrive here with speed, and have not enjoyed a hot meal since I left my Keep."

Galdin flapped his hands. "Yes. Yes. I felt we needed to meet in person. I became most upset to receive your message about the woman. I cannot understand how your Guild would encounter challenges to capture her in Baklai."

Ssarff swallowed. "My Thane, because our appearances are so different, we are unable to blend in with the Baklai because of our height. Nor are we able to disguise ourselves as Rifellans. In other assignments you asked of us, we met with your allies in those lands. I cannot recall that you mentioned an ally in Baklai."

Galdin frowned, and his eyes narrowed. "I thought you Assassins were able to do anything."

"We do our best, my Thane."

The man's face contorted in an angry expression. "We will eat, and I will think on this problem."

Ssarff bent his head to his plate and ate in silence, but the meal tasted like ashes in his mouth. *I am glad I cannot read his mind. And doubly so that he cannot read mine.*

❋❋❋

Two black-robed figures eased over the walls of the Keep and glided stealthily over the roof-top of the inner Keep. As they slithered over the various towers, they paused near each of the inner rooms, until they rested behind a parapet, concealed by a dark crevice. They remained on the roof as guards to the Assassins' Guild Master.

***

Galdin finally pushed back his empty plate. "I believe I may possess an idea that I can supply you with an ally of mine in Baklai. I will need some time to engage with this person. I will contact you again when my arrangements are complete."

What is he up to? Ssarff shifted, discomfort sweeping over his body.

"Since the evening is late, you may stay for the night in one of the tower rooms,"

"My thanks for the offer, my Thane, but I cannot afford to neglect my duties at my own Keep. I will depart now for the Guild and will await your message about your ally." *Sleep? Under Galdin's roof? Never.*

Galdin shrugged. "As you wish."

Ssarff rose, bowed to Galdin, and backed from the room. He hastened from the inner Keep and called to a guard to fetch his horse. When the animal appeared, he mounted it and left via the enormous iron gates. He lost no time as he headed back through the long grasses, but this time toward the trees of the Skinya Doo.

As soon as he rode out of the sight of Galdin's Keep, he whistled for the pair of Assassins. He did not see where they were hidden, but they appeared quite suddenly, and bowed to him.

He raised his hand in acknowledgement of their presence. "I am safe, and we are able to return to our Guild. We will travel the route you took through the Doos."

Both nodded and led the way across the bridge toward the trees. Once concealed in the forest, they made a request. "Guild Master, our horses are still tired and we have eaten no meal since the noon-turn. We would request we stop here and set traps for food."

"I agree. My animal is also spent. We will take our mounts to drink, but return to this clearing where there is plenty of grass for them."

The two agreed, and each watered their horses, then led their animals back into the forest and tied them to small bushes within the grassy area. They unsaddled their mounts and placed the soft leather saddles on the ground as pillows.

The two guards set a couple of traps deeper among the trees for any creatures they might use as food. They then cut leafy branches to cushion the ground. One Assassin sat beside his make-shift bed. "I will take first watch."

Ssarff and the other one wrapped themselves in their robes, lay down on the leaves, and slept.

❋❋❋

Morning brought the first rays of Pridden's star. Overjoyed to find their traps filled, the guards skinned and prepared the medium sized rodents to be cooked over a smokeless fire. As they waited for the meal to complete cooking, they once again watered their horses, and resaddled them.

Once they consumed their food, they wrapped the leftovers, in leaves from the bedding. They planned to eat the wrapped bundles that evening. One guard buried the bones and skin of the animals, and swept the area clear of any signs of their overnight stay.

The three set off to return to their Keep.

❋❋❋

Two turns later, the sky black from night, the three rode through the gates of the Guild's Keep, and Ssarff headed wearily for his rooms.

Unable to keep his eyes open any longer, he sank into his bed and slept.

❋❋❋

A knock on his door roused him. "Who is it?"

"Ssestin, Master."

Ssarff rose and dragged himself to his door, and yawned so widely his jaw creaked. "Enter." He greeted his second-in-command, then walked to his personal and splashed cold water on his face. "That feels better." He faced Ssestin. "How long did I sleep?"

"Only overnight. The star rose moments ago."

"Excellent. I feared I might sleep for a full turn." He cleared his throat. "Did anything of note occur in the Keep while I was absent?"

"No, Master. What about your visit with Galdin?"

"Inconclusive. Nothing will happen while he attempts to chase down a potential ally in Baklai."

Ssestin's eyes widened. "He has an ally in Baklai?"

"Apparently so."

Ssarff strode over to his desk and opened his journal and began to describe his journey in its pages. He paused and rubbed his brow.

What is Galdin planning?

CHAPTER 20

Kat, well fed and fully awake, followed Mouse toward the Frothan farm. The light of the star blazed bright in the morning sky.

He turned in his saddle. "We are now about halfway to the farm, and will be in time to share a mid-turn meal. After that, I suspect our hosts will guide us in a tour of the farm, and we will spend the night. I suggest we depart for the next farm at dawn on the morrow, because the journey to Losgayrin is lengthy."

"I will follow your lead." She sighed. "I'm bored from touring farms so often. I think I feel about farms like you feel about shopping."

Mouse grinned. "Your comparison makes this clear to me, but I suggest you pay attention despite your feelings on the subject. You may find some part of the tour will aid you later in your journey. This is an odd land, and it is not one with which I am familiar. We will both learn much about Baklai during our time here." He turned back and continued to lead the way.

Kat moved closer to him, so she could speak without yelling. "You are probably correct. My challenge is, Mouse, I am frustrated about not being able to obtain a replacement for my horse." She screwed up her face. "I never mistreated my animal. So why are they punishing me?"

"I am positive the people of Baklai are not punishing you. They consider their horses incredibly valuable. Remember, without horses, Baklai would be severely challenged. They would not enjoy Rifella's protection from the Mordens. They would have little access to goods from other lands, and would not exist as free beings."

"I'm sure you understand them better than I do. I wish I had spent more time at Dinerth. The females of Baklai are… are…" She frowned as she searched for a word to describe them. "Strong. Brilliant. Unusual."

Mouse turned to gaze at her again. "What do you mean?"

"It seems to me the females run Baklai. Not the males."

He twisted his brows as he continued to gaze at her. "I doubt you are correct in that. I spent time with the males when you were at Dinerth, and they appear to be definitely in control in this land."

Kat sighed. She was convinced otherwise.

They continued to ride, silent once more, and the star rose higher.

Kat yawned, even more bored than before. She would almost welcome the appearance of a hissar. At least that would be exciting.

They rode on, until Mouse eyed the road ahead and pointed. "Those are the buildings of Frothan."

They reached a circle of buildings and houses, each painted in brilliant white, with colorful illustrations. As they moved closer, Kat stared at the paintings. "Those pictures. They're of different fruits. I wonder if they use those buildings as storage for the fruits in the paintings."

"Possibly."

They rode toward a building with horses painted on it, where two people waited for them.

Kat, startled, recognized one of the women. "Eestred." She stopped her mount and slid off his back. "What are you doing here?"

Eestred ran over to Kat and hugged her. "I am accompanying Gayzella on her journey to order food stuffs for the Keep."

Kat faced Gayzella. "I remember. We met at Dinerth. You are the Head of House for Thane Cathked, are you not?

"I am. I am on my quarterly visit to the food farms to arrange for deliveries to the Keep. Eestred accompanies me because no one in Baklai journeys alone. Creatures such as hissars, reekers, and often wild horses can be dangerous to a single traveler."

Mouse approached the women. "Kat, we should see to our animals. The building with the picture of a horse is the stable."

"Yes, of course."

Mouse smiled at Eestred and Gayzella. "Perhaps after we have settled our animals, we may join you both for a mid-turn meal."

Kat glanced at the two women. "If I don't attend to my animal, the Thane may never grant me another horse."

Gayzella patted her arm. "Patience, Kat. Eestred and I will meet you in the dining hall."

***

Horses watered and fed and bags delivered to their rooms, Mouse led the way to the hall, followed closely by Kat. They joined Eestred and Gayzella, who were seated with two females from Frothan.

As Mouse seated himself next to Kat, the servers delivered food to the table, along with a refreshing tea.

Kat, curious about Gayzella's position at the Keep, asked a series of questions. "What do you do when you travel to the farms?"

"Well, the grains that feed our horses are also needed at

the Keep to be ground into flour for our breads. I only need to visit the Grain Farm once per full path. Here at Frothan, I personally inspect the fruits available during each quarter and order what will be needed at the Keep. This is because we can choose from different fruits grown during different quarters of the path."

"You also visit Losgayrin?"

"Indeed. From Losgayrin, I order the vegetables and spices available during each period of a path. And Losgayrin also farms blicks. These animals are so delicious, but the natural population of blicks would not be sufficient to sustain all our people."

"Are you supplied with live blicks, or are they terminated at the farm?"

Gayzella laughed. "Terminated. Delicately put, Kat. These creatures are raised to provide food for all those in Baklai, so they are killed at the farm and prepared in sections for later cooking."

"How do you keep the sections fresh?"

"At the Keep, the storage facilities for our foodstuffs are in caverns constructed well below ground level. Far below the surface, the air is extremely cold, and the foods all stay fresh. Some of the sections, we cover with a spice which preserves it."

"I had no idea how demanding your duties are."

Gayzella smiled. "Every female on Baklai owns demanding duties, Kat. However, since we love our land, our duties seem more like privileges."

The servers began to clear the tables of the dishes, and Eestred rose. "I need to help Gayzella inspect the foods. Would you join us in this, Kat?"

Mouse grinned at the women. "I, as you know, Kat, do

not appreciate shopping. Inspecting sounds like shopping to me. I will seek out the leader of Frothan and compare notes with him about hissers and reekers.

***

Kat followed the two women through the sections of fruit bearing trees and bushes.

As they walked, she thought about Mouses' words about the situation between males and females. "When I was at the Keep, I thought men controlled this land, but after visiting Dinerth, I now believe women are in control. If that is so, can you help me obtain a replacement horse?"

Gayzella laughed. "We must seem curious to outside visitors, but you cannot be more incorrect. We are neither a patriarchy nor a matriarchy. Males and females share equally in the running of Baklai. We each possess our areas of expertise."

"How do you mean?"

Gayzella bent to examine a low-growing vine of scarlet berries. "Females are naturally excellent at organization, at items relating to progeny, and at keeping our land fed and able to survive financially. We are the ones who also deal in trade with other lands. We are the ones who can handle politics between Baklai and the rest of Pridden."

"I still believe the females are in control of Baklai."

Gayzella glanced at Kat, amusement in her face. "Our males are strong and are excellent at building, assuring their family groups survive from outside interference, and, of course, they are particularly able with horses." She continued to bend down to view yellow berries growing on small bushes. "Our animals are large and require vigorous control to provide us with a valuable resource to trade with other lands."

Gayzella puffed out her chest in apparent pride. "Our males are not as robust as Rifellans, but they and the Rifellans bond well. Our needs are different from those of our males, but we respect each other's abilities, absolutely."

"Well then, Gayzella, can you find me a new horse, or are the men too controlling in this respect?"

"Kat, you must be patient, as I said before. When one side wishes something from the other's domain, negotiations tend to move slowly." She gave an uncharacteristic giggle. "We normally win our requests. We have a passionate spirit behind us. Calanta, the Hunter, almost always bows to Caleesh's desires."

"Patience? I will attempt to be patient, but it is difficult for me."

"Kat, we will help you. Both Eestred and I feel you deserve a replacement animal. Oh my, enough bending." She stretched, and her back muscles cracked into place. "My inspection is complete. Let us head for the evening meal, and we will join you early on the morrow for the journey to Losgayrin."

"I anticipate traveling with the two of you with much pleasure." She turned to Eestred. "I would appreciate your advice about a message I must send to a Rifellan with whom you are familiar. Would you mind accompanying me to my quarters to help me prepare the note?"

"Certainly. Gayzella, I will help Kat with her missive, and we will both see you shortly in the dining hall."

Gayzella waved her assent at both of them. "Excellent. This will allow me time to complete my list of requirements from this farm."

Kat and Eestred headed to Kat's room. When they entered, Kat extracted from her bag, a piece of parchment and her writing materials, which she handed to Eestred. "I am not as adept as I would like to be at Priddanese writing. Would you mind saying the following for me: "My thanks for your message. To understand that I have your help and that of Penrow is of much comfort. I know I will also have support from many of the women in Baklai to achieve a new horse. My friend Eestred is writing this letter for me, and I will end my words now, so I do not tire her out." And sign it Kat."

Eestred bent to the task and, when she completed her writing, handed the parchment to Kat.

"My thanks, Eestred. I will leave this on my desk to allow the ink to dry. I will send it off with my pyrock after our meal this eve."

"I am delighted I could be of help."

"We should join Gayzella in the dining hall. I will advise Mouse he should be ready to leave in the morning."

Kat considered all Gayzella and Eestred had told her of the ways of men and women in the land. *Are the Baklai the perfect embodiment of yin and yang?*

CHAPTER 21

A loud series of squeaks woke Kat from a dreamless sleep. She opened one eye and peered over at Wink, who had already returned from her visit to Liandock.

"Sorry Wink. I did not hear you arrive last night." She yawned and left her bed. Picking up two treats, she fed the hungry pyrock. As she didn't require a reply from Liandock, no tube was attached to Wink's leg. She popped her in her cage, and the tired pyrock slept almost instantly. *Glad I packed everything last night.* She showered and dressed in her leathers, attached Wink's cage to her backpack, and piled her baggage on the bed.

She left her room and knocked on Mouse's door. When he answered, she reminded him they were scheduled to meet Eestred and Gayzella. "I'm not sure if they will join us for the morning meal, but are you ready to head for the dining hall?"

"I am prepared to depart after we eat because the journey to Losgayrin is lengthy. It would be best undertaken with a substantial morning repast."

Kat grinned.

"Why are you amused?"

"Sometimes, Mouse, the words you use are so old fashioned on my home world."

He smiled back at her. "And, sometimes the words you use are so odd to us." He walked beside her along the short passageway.

They entered the dining hall and stopped beside a table

for four. Eestred and Gayzella both looked up and chimed a welcome.

Eestred, the Rifellan woman waved them to seats. "We took the liberty of ordering for you."

They seated themselves as a server approached with food and drink. She pointed to Kat's beverage. "Your tea is karri-san, Lady Kat."

"Thank you." Kat turned and raised an eyebrow at Eestred.

"I thought you might need it by now. Many Rifellans reside in Baklai, and although you appear to be only mildly stressed by our pheromones, Irina in Kaylin told me of your first meeting with her and Bardu."

Heat crept up Kat's face. "She did? I was so embarrassed. But thanks to karri-san, I'm no longer subject to such strong…um…sensations."

Mouse leaned forward. "Gayzella, I am aware Losgayrin produces the majority of vegetation type foods for Baklai, but what type of creatures should we expect to encounter?"

"An excellent question, Sire Mouse. The farm is located at the part of land which leads to the high rock cliffs, overlooking the Mora Waters. Losgayrin is located in a basin which contains the most fertile soil in our land and where our foodstuffs are grown. The rocks, which extend to the edges of the escarpment are home to gondal lizards." She paused and licked her lips. "Gondals are delicious. Their meat is sweet and tender, and they breed frequently."

"I am aware of their existence, but I've never seen them available in other lands."

"They do not breed often enough to sell elsewhere. Plus, we Baklai are most partial to the flavor of braised gondal steaks. But you are in luck. You will be able to sample gondal meat at Losgayrin."

Kat pushed her empty plate aside. "I like blick meat, so I'm bound to enjoy gondal steaks. Let's head to the farm. I don't want to miss the evening meal if there's gondal on the menu." She rose from the table.

Gayzella rose as well. "We should indeed leave now." She waved at one of the servers, and the woman brought her four containers. Gayzella accepted them and handed each of the other three one of the packages. "These are your mid-turn meals, for when we take a brief stop to rest our horses."

The other two rose and left the hall. Kat waited at the entrance for Mouse to return with her to their rooms to obtain their luggage, while the other pair headed directly for the stable.

Once they arrived, they saddled their mounts. Mouse brought out the grieve pieces and shot an enquiring glance at Eestred.

"Yes, Mouse. We might still encounter hissars on the first section of our ride to Losgayrin. Once at the farm, we can dispense with them and leave them for travelers who are headed toward Frothan."

He nodded and began the process of binding the legs of his horse.

Kat led her horse outside the stall and bound its legs as well.

"Eestred, I noticed you and Gayzella left the bindings on your horse's legs overnight. Is this allowed? This won't hurt the animals, will it?"

"No, the bindings are comfortable for them, and they protect the horses in the stalls from stray bumps."

"On my world, we often bind the legs of horses when they are stiff or sore. Plus, sometimes when they exercise."

"Interesting. The sole time a horse requires sore legs to be bound is when someone has overridden them. A practice we discourage."

The three women used small stepladders to gain their saddles, but Mouse stretched his leg high enough to place his foot in his stirrup, and hauled himself up on his animal.

Kat gaped at him in awe. *He always makes mounting his horse appear so easy. Yet he's not tall.*

Mouse and Gayzella led the way to Losgayrin, with Kat and Eestred, riding side by side, following them.

They travelled for a while, and Kat turned toward Eestred. "Mouse asked about creatures, and Gayzella told us about gondal lizards. Should we be aware of any other animals?"

"As I mentioned before, by the time we stop for our mid-turn meal, there will no longer be the grain-consuming rodents in the area, and thus no hissars. If we are lucky, we may sight some hunters. The hunters are magnificent birds with a wingspan about the width of this road, and they possess extraordinary eyesight. They ride the air currents and search for small animals to feed to their young. Once they capture their prey, they carry them to their nests in the hills near Losgayrin. If we do encounter at least one, supposedly we will be blessed with excellent fortune."

"I hope we do see one."

Mouse turned back in his saddle and hailed them both. "Around the next bend, according to my maps, you will find a small pool of water fed by a spring from the Farralawn river's western branch. We should stop to water our horses and consume our meals."

"This part of our journey has flown by, because we enjoyed our conversation. But--" Kat stared upward, "--your star is overhead, and my stomach growled. I am ready for food."

They continued to follow Mouse who, after they rounded the bend, waved them over to a small pool, which bubbled and frothed from some spring below ground. They dismounted, and stretched to ease muscles cramped from being in the saddle for such a lengthy time.

Mouse led his horse to the pool to drink, followed by the other three. Once the animals drank their fill, the travelers each looped their reins over small bushes in the middle of grassy patches.

They left the horses to forage, and located stones on which to sit.

Kat sighed, sat, opened her meal package, and took a bite. "Yum, blick meat. You are correct, Gayzella. Blick is delicious. The spicy sauce seems familiar."

Mouse chimed in. "The spice is Fire Mouth, and we experienced it in Rifella. Do you remember the sea-swimmer dish we ate?"

"I do."

Gayzella sampled her meal. "Perfectly cooked and spiced. Our Fire Mouth spice is sold mostly in Rifella, but other lands do purchase it sometimes. We grow many different spices which we trade with other lands, and our red leaf tea is excellent to curb nausea." She smiled. "The Glowens purchase much of this tea."

The four sat comfortably on rocks, munched their food, and drank from their canteens.

Their brief pause over, Gayzella directed them to bury the remains of their meal and fill their canteens for the rest of the trip to Losgayrin. The group remounted their horses, and Mouse and Gayzella continued in the lead.

❋❋❋

Kat, riding on the baggage horse, stretched her spine. *This is not a comfortable horse.* As she moved in her saddle, her back muscles crackled, releasing the stiffness in her shoulders and the kinks in her neck. *That's better.* "Your star is approaching the horizon, Eestred. How far are we from the farm?"

Eestred opened her mouth to reply, but Gayzella's horse stopped abruptly, and she held up her hand. "Stop. Silence." She pointed ahead.

Kat blinked rapidly searching for some danger.

Gayzella whispered a warning. "Reeker."

Far down the road, Kat glimpsed a fat furry rodent nibbling at shiny red bulbs hanging from a small bush at the side of the road. What caught her eye, however, was a creature that resembled a spotted cat. The cat, sinewy, with a short, glossy coat crouched motionless, but as she peered at it, the animal slowly raised a paw and barely perceptibly moved forward. Kat held her breath, as she waited for the final leap that would end in the death of the reeker.

Without warning, a flash of huge wings, silent but deadly, with massive claws plunged into the back of the reeker and shook the life from its body. An enormous bird with a wingspan, that, to Kat, appeared to be over eight feet, rose with the limp body of the reeker hanging from prodigious talons.

The spotted cat yowled and spat skyward, and turned and tore into the vegetation at the side of the road, growling and spitting continuously.

Kat expelled her breath. "Wow. Is that a Hunter?"

Eestred nodded. "Yes. So magnificent." Her mouth opened and she dissolved into laughter. "A Hunter. Our journey will be filled with joyous happenings."

Kat cracked up. "I think the poor cat is pretty angry at the

Hunter."

Gayzella joined in the laughter. "That poor cat is called a mowzer, and they generally are successful when they stalk reekers. It is not often they lose their prey to a Hunter."

"I thought the reekers spray out a nasty stink?"

"They do, Kat. However, both the Hunters and the mowzers pounce and break their necks, which prevents them from releasing their spray. The reekers die instantly." Gayzella gazed at the star, which had kissed the horizon. "Around the next bend is the farm. I suggest we move before we lose the light."

The four travelers continued and, as promised, when they rounded the bend, the buildings of the farm appeared. A two-story building held center court, surrounded by dozens of smaller houses. Built of wood, these structures were the first that Kat had encountered that the Baklai allowed to age naturally. Instead of painted colors or wood varnished to a high sheen, the buildings had taken on a patina of soft gray.

Gayzella led them to the stables, where they dismounted and tended to their animals. She advised them to collect the grieve pieces, or gee-legs as some called them, and roll them together with the bindings for the horse's legs. "We can leave these here, and anyone who needs such protection will use them in the future."

As they brushed the dust from the coats of their mounts, a husky young Baklai male appeared. "Welcome to you all. Eestred and Gayzella, welcome back." He addressed Kat. "May I assume you are the Lady Kat?"

She nodded.

"And, you must be Sire Mouse."

"I am, and what are you named?"

"My apologies. I am Ivenon, the assistant apprentice for

Losgayrin. I will show you to the rooms we have assigned for you, so you may leave your luggage. I will then escort you to the great dining room, where we are now serving the evening meal." He bowed to them and led them to the largest building, up a flight of stairs, and along a passageway to their rooms.

❁❁❁

They left their luggage, and Ivenon ushered them to the dining hall. Soon the four sat together, meals and drinks on the table.

Kat took a mouthful of food. "What is this delicious meat? It's better than gornog."

Gayzella patted her arm. "We have converted you. Kat. That is gondal lizard, prepared with some of Baklai's best spices."

"No wonder you keep this meat for yourselves. My mouth is happy."

"Tomorrow, you must come with me to inspect the various sections of the farm. I always find the spice and herb gardens to be my favorite."

Mouse cleared his throat. "I wish to accompany you on the morrow, Gayzella. I am intrigued by Baklai's spices."

"We would welcome your presence, Mouse."

The four continued to chat about their journey to Losgayrin, including; the extraordinary sight of a Hunter stealing a reeker from a mowzer, the benefits of karri-san, stories of spices and gondals, and tales of the horses of Baklai.

The hall was almost empty when Mouse rose from his seat. "I must be honest with you. I admit to being outridden by you three females and beg your leave to seek my bed."

Kat laughed. "You flatter us, Mouse. But I too am weary, and would like to head to my bed as well."

They all rose, and headed to their rooms., calling good night as they reached their doors.

Kat hauled her tired body to the desk to feed Wink. She undressed, forced herself to take a brief shower, and, too weary to locate a night dress, climbed naked into bed and yawning, drifted to sleep.

I've asked for a new horse. Will I get one?

CHAPTER 22

Dressed and ready for the day, Kat strolled along the passageway and down the stairs toward the dining hall. At the entranceway, she spotted Mouse seated with Eestred and Gayzella. Eestred glanced up and waved at Kat to join them.

Kat sat next to Gayzella and smiled. "I enjoyed the best sleep. I'm refreshed and ready to spend time with you inspecting the gardens once we've enjoyed our morning meal."

"You do not need to inspect. That is my job. However, I will show you what qualities I seek in Losgayrin's gardens." She turned her gaze toward Mouse. "Is this something in which you would also be interested, Sire Mouse?"

"Yes, but my primary interest is in your herbs and spices."

"Oh, why?"

"Traveling with Kat has exposed me to many different types of food, most of which I found delightful. However, when we needed to camp or make use of traveler's huts, our food was generally only journeyklim. I would appreciate having a spice to make those meals less monotonous."

Kat stared at him. "Mouse, perhaps you should consider expanding the idea. Instead of only one spice, why not a packet of different spices to enhance the klim."

Gayzella smiled at her. "What an excellent idea. I believe I am able to create such a packet, and the Baklai would be able to market this to other lands."

"Even better. Create containers for travelers so that each one would be designed to enhance not only the journeyklim, but also any animal which travelers may trap for a meal in that particular land."

Gayzella grinned at her. "Kat, I do believe you should be an advisor to our Council of Seven. You may have come up with an excellent addition to the goods which we can market to other lands."

"Do you possess enough growing land to produce a sufficient number of packets?"

Gayzella frowned and pursed her lips. "I would need to check. Too many might place considerable strain on our abilities." She tugged at her ear. "I believe one of the males from this farm suggested something similar, but when we checked, it did indeed put too much pressure on our capacities. I remember we were forced to forget about expanding our products this way."

"I have an idea that may work for you. Why not choose a grower in each land, supply him or her with the seeds, and license them to produce the spices for their own land? Possibly you might suggest a fee for each path, or perhaps request a portion of the sales in each path."

"Kat, you are brilliant. Baklai needs to have markets in addition to horses." Gayzella rose, gave Kat a huge hug, and laughed gleefully. "I will make sure I advise the Thane of your suggestion, and promote to him that this idea merits you receiving a new horse. Not only do I expect them to be impressed, but they should consider this plan as payment for the animal." She sat down again.

Kat felt a lump in her throat. "Thank you." *They're so kind.*

A server approached their table with a tray of dishes and beverages.

Mouse announced they had ordered for her. "I noticed

how much you enjoyed the morning meal the previous turn, so we asked for the same thing."

"Thanks." She blinked rapidly, and drank a hasty sip of tea. "This tea is delicious, and it makes me want to dance."

Eestred took a sip from her mug. "It is lowenna tea, most popular on Baklai, and conveys happiness."

"That's interesting. Glowen grows flowers called lowen blossoms."

Gayzella added. "Glowen's flowers and our tea are related. We used the seed of their flowers, and created a hybrid with the seeds of a sweet spice. We send a small amount of lowenna tea to Thane Brennan each path. The Glowens do not request any more, since they possess their own flowers, but their Thane is partial to lowenna tea at each morning meal."

"No offense, Gayzella, but I suspect your own Thane should be drinking the tea as well."

Gayzella snorted as she tried to hide a grin. "I agree Thane Cathked would benefit from lowenna. He avoids the tea because he believes the requirements of a Thane must be accomplished seriously. It is said he decided lowenna would interfere with that process."

They continued to chat as they ate their meal.

Kat was curious. "Gayzella, what do you plan to inspect?"

"The herb and spice gardens and the tea garden need a close inspection. Because I made a thorough inspection of the green vegetable plots and the colored bulbs last quarter path, they will require only a cursory survey. I will spend a little more time on the maize garden, as the silk is browning, and is almost ready for harvesting."

"Will that take you the entire turn?"

"No. Eestred and I will return to the Keep after a mid-turn snack. The Keep is not far, and I have much work to complete. Do feel free to remain here for the balance of this turn, and head for the Keep on the morrow."

"We have not decided when we will leave Losgayrin, so Mouse and I will wait until the mid-turn meal to decide. If we do accompany you, we do not need to do much packing."

"Finish your tea, and we will head for the gardens."

The four rose and, with Gayzella in the lead, walked toward the luxurious gardens.

Kat noticed one of the males of the village following them at a discreet distance. "Who is that following us?"

"He is the head of the gardening staff. He is following us in case I have questions that need to be answered."

Kat's first sight of the gardens took her breath away. Separated sections of land, some in raised plots, some in fenced sections, and some surrounded by tiny hedges, spread before her.

Gayzella turned first to the maize garden, filled with tall green stalks laden with what resembled ears of corn. Gayzella paused to examine the brownish silk protruding from the top of each ear of maize. She tore the ear from the stalk and removed part of the green outer layer to reveal plump golden buds. "They are still small enough to be quite sweet, so I will request some be sent immediately." She exposed more of the golden kernels, and bit into them. A white juice sprayed from them and she closed her eyes and smiled. "Delicious." She stripped off the complete outer layer and handed the ear first to Kat. "Take a bite of this, and pass it on."

Kat bit, and the sweet juice gushed into her mouth. "This is heavenly." She passed the ear to Eestred. "Do you always eat the maize raw?"

Gayzella grinned. "I do personally, but most Baklai prefer to roast theirs."

Mouse accepted the ear from Eestred and nibbled on it. "How wonderful. Might this also be used as food for those traveling through the land?"

"Unfortunately, not. Once the maize is picked, Sire Mouse, the sweetness appears to fade quickly. After three days, we reconstitute the flavor by boiling ears with our sweet spice. We do attempt to preserve many of the fresh ears in water and sweet spices, and sealed in glass containers so we can augment our meals in the coldest quarter of the path."

Gayzella, with the maize in her hand again, handed it to the Baklai accompanying them, who bent down and buried it in the dirt.

Kat walked over to him. "Why did you bury that ear?"

He glanced at her. "It will provide nourishment for the soil and, this way, will not attract the rodents."

Kat peered at the small mound of dirt. "Nor will it attract reekers, right?"

"Correct." He smiled. "Our gardens are very important, and we lavish them with as much care as possible."

Gayzella nodded at him and brushed off her hands. "We will take a brief view at the green vegetation and the bulb gardens." She led them on.

Kat thought the green vegetable garden unimpressive. Mid-sized and small green plants with a variety of oddly shaped leaves grew in profusion. The beds raised on different levels were certainly lush.

When they arrived at the bulb garden, she gasped. Rows and rows of small bushes, vines trailing over pyramid shaped trellises, and masses of mid-high bushes, all covered with bulbs of bright crimson, small purple ones, long green ones, and twisted yellow pods.

"Wow. Do you eat many of these raw as well?"

"Yes. They keep exceedingly fresh in the cold of our food dungeons."

"Gayzella, you folks in Baklai grow the most amazing variety of vegetation. You appear to grow everything you need to make sure your people are self-sufficient. Yet I have encountered some of your people in other lands who left Baklai because they were unable to provide for their families. Why is that?"

Gayzella left the vegetation area and led them toward the spice area. "We are not a perfect people. On occasion, despite their upbringing, some of our males find it difficult to live within the rules of our people. We are a synarchy. We enjoy a joint ruling between our females and our males. Neither group wishes to control the other. As females, we admire and respect our men and we encourage them to experience themselves as warriors. Our males respect and admire us, although I do suspect they tend to sometimes be uneasy around us, simply because we lean toward more spiritual matters. Spiritual matters which they do not understand. Nor do they wish to."

Kat walked beside the Baklai woman, moving through the various plots of gardens. "Gayzella, I experienced a number of interactions with Haydar in Kaylin. Others told me he settled in Kaylin because he was unable to cope with life in Baklai."

Gayzella laughed. "That is true. Haydar is a male who fears females. He would obey all orders from superior males, but was never willing to listen to the insights our females attempted to pass on, without success, regarding the rest of Pridden. He now strongly relates to Kaylin, but we all understand it is his mate who rules the household." She sighed. "To many who visit Baklai, our males are the brawn, and we are the brains. There is no truth to that statement, of course."

Eestred and Mouse followed close behind, listening, Kat believed, to her continuing conversation. "I met a male in Rifella who sold himself in servitude to a Morden, because he claimed this was the only way to earn enough to support his family."

"This does happen sometimes. Those who live close to the Morden border, often live on poor land which cannot sustain them. Instead of requesting help, they struggle and fall victim to Morden raiders. Thane Cathked regularly asks his patrols to move those from land too close to the border to better homesteads in the west. Often these males are stubborn and refuse to admit they did not choose wisely in their place of residence. They move back, and repeat the cycle."

She pointed at the garden ahead. "This is my favorite growing area—spices, herbs, and teas."

Kat gazed across the neatly laid out gardens. The spices and herbs lay row on row, low-growing bushes and small vines hanging over knee-high trellises, all covered in berries and odd-shaped balls in red and green and purple.

Mouse spread his arms to encompass the area. "This is extraordinary. I was not sure what to expect, but I am amazed at how you have arranged your produce."

Gayzella smiled at him and then leaned down to the small bushes, and plucked a leaf. She rubbed it between her fingers, and the air exploded with a spicy green aroma. "If you wish to experience the scent of the various herbs, pluck one leaf, and share it among you. Your challenge will be to remember all the different aromas."

Kat, Eestred, and Mouse wandered together down the

rows, picking the odd leaf and comparing with each other.

Gayzella guided them to the tea garden, but this did not possess the visual excitement of the spices. Most of the tea grew on bushes, none of which were flowering at the moment. "Take a small leaf from near the top of the bush and chew on it. You will not experience the same flavor as you would after the leaves have dried, but it will give you an idea."

Kat sighed. "The herbs, spices, and tea are amazing. I would love to spend ten turns here, simply smelling all the tantalizing scents and tasting these tea leaves."

Mouse smelled a leaf and placed it in his mouth. "Gayzella, I believe this is also my favorite area."

"You are both more than welcome to stay another night. Eestred and I will pack our bags and meet you for a mid-turn snack."

The Baklai gardener smiled at them, waved his hand, and returned to whatever chore he had been performing.

The three women and Mouse agreed to meet at the dining hall.

Kat followed Mouse to their rooms. "I think I will pack as well. It does appear to be an excellent idea to stay until the morrow, but I would prefer to return to the Keep."

Mouse nodded. "I agree. I too have seen enough farms, no matter how interesting. While I am fascinated by the spices and teas, I am more than curious to find if we can obtain a horse for you."

They climbed the stairs to their rooms, and, at his door, Kat paused. "Er, Mouse. We are joining Gayzella and Eestred for a mid-turn meal, but would you mind if we waited until after they leave before we depart Losgayrin? I am so filled with information I only wish silence."

Mouse laughed. "I am in full agreement. I am but a single male. I have traveled a long way with three well-informed and curious females. My ears need a rest."

Kat glared at him. "Rude, Mouse. Rude."

"I did not mean to be rude."

She laughed. "I'm only making fun. I must admit, my ears need a rest too." She walked to her door and entered her room.

She strolled over to the desk, fed Wink, and attached the pyrock cage to her backpack.

Deciding to continue to wear her leathers, Kat packed her robe and everything else and piled her bags on the bed.

She headed to the door and opened it, obviously startling Mouse, who stood with his fist in the air, about to knock.

She raised a brow. "Dining hall?"

He nodded and they set off.

At the entrance, wrapped in the delicious aroma of roasting blick and the sweet smell of some dessert, they paused to search for the two females.

Eestred waved at them from a table with four chairs. Kat joined her and Gayzella, with Mouse trailing close behind.

An apprentice came and took orders for four small bowls of blick stew and more lowenna tea.

Only half filled, the hall was relatively quiet, and they sat in silence. Kat contemplated the extraordinary vegetation and the odors and flavors she had experienced that morning, and she assumed the others were doing the same.

Within minutes, their meals and tea arrived, and they dug in.

Eestred sighed. "This has been a busy morning, and I must admit I am weary from the sun and the walking. I am hoping food will restore my energy.

The others nodded their agreement, and they ate without conversing. The two women finished first, as they had ordered light meals.

Gayzella rose. "Eestred and I must depart. Are you both planning to stay until the morrow?"

Kat stood and hugged her. "We doubt we will stay, but will not depart right away. However, we do thank both of you so much for the escort and the details of these farms. I've experienced so much these past few turns. My thanks, Gayzella." She embraced Eestred who had also risen. "Enjoy a safe trip back to the Keep. We will no doubt meet with you again when we are under Thane Cathked's roof."

Mouse now rose. He bowed his head to both women, and thanked them for their help and information.

The two women left the hall with a final wave goodbye, and Kat returned to her seat to finish her meal.

Mouse pushed his plate aside. "I am sufficiently comfortable with the amount of food I consumed, but I would prefer to tarry a while and enjoy another mug of tea. Can I order some more for you?"

"I would appreciate if you would. To sit here and relax in silence is perfect."

The server delivered a huge pot of lowenna tea and a pair of clean mugs. Mouse poured for both of them, and they sat and sipped the delicious beverage.

After two mugs of tea each, Kat rose and stretched. "I would like to spend this night at the Keep. Should we leave now if we want to arrive before dusk?"

Mouse nodded. "I too prefer to sleep at the Keep. I am most anxious to discover if the Thane has made a new decision about a horse for you."

They left the table and returned to their rooms to pick up

their luggage. They then set off for the stable.

Kat was eager to hear if Cathked had changed his mind, although still uncertain as to why the Baklai blamed her for the horse's death.

I sort of understand their concern. They depend on horses for their lives.

CHAPTER 23

The road from Losgayrin to the Keep lay before them and appeared well-traveled. Kat rode beside Mouse in companionable silence. This part of their journey was not long, and soon the buildings and towers of the Keep appeared on the horizon.

Kat stopped her horse. "Mouse, before we arrive, I wish to discuss our coming meeting with Cathked."

Mouse stopped beside her and raised an inquiring eyebrow.

"I understand a little more about the relationships between males and females in Baklai. So, I will let you communicate with the Thane, and I will attempt to maintain a respectful silence." She pursed her lips. "As I view their way of governing this land, the females are strong-minded, brilliant women. They far outweigh the males in their intellectual smarts. But they understand the males in Baklai need to possess their own sense of power, which is their physical strength and their uncanny ability with horses."

"I agree with you, Kat. Their society is surprisingly balanced."

"Because of this, I believe I will be granted a horse by Cathked, because I have allies among the women. Therefore, I do not need to be in a contest with the Thane. I have used their own rules to bend to my liking."

"I am pleased you do not need to wrest control back from him."

"Mouse, Cathked controls the horses in Baklai. He does

not control me."

Mouse gazed at her his eyes wide in astonishment. "I believe you have assessed the situation accurately. I will follow your lead."

She laughed. "I never thought I'd hear you speak those words."

He shrugged. "You should be aware by now. I always give credit where credit is deserved."

"I must admit, I hadn't taken notice."

Mouse said nothing, but his left eye twitched.

They rode on and shortly arrived at the tall iron gates.

Kat gazed up at the magnificent castle-like structure. She wondered where the Baklai got all the stone for the Keep.

They entered, and headed into the stable area to bed their horses. They unsaddled and removed the bridles, but when Kat picked up a curry comb, a young attendant entered the stall, and took it from her. "We will brush and prepare your horses, Lady Kat. Their water troughs are filled, and if you would prepare the hay net, you may attend your rooms. Healer Caleth is waiting for you both."

Kat relinquished the comb, grabbed her bag and her long bow, and stepped outside.

Caleth stood waiting. "Lady Kat, Sire Mouse, I will escort you to your rooms, and we will discuss your travels on our way."

He led them through the entrance to the inner Keep, and guided them through the stone passages to their rooms. "Gayzella mentioned you both accompanied her and Eestred in visits to Frothan and Losgayrin. I trust you found both farms of interest?"

"We did and, luckily, avoided any confrontations with reekers." Kat shivered. "From what we've learned, the spray from a reeker can be most challenging."

"The odor is unbelievably foul. They requested my help to treat the male progeny of the leader of Frothan. The poor young one was in much distress, and was ostracized for almost five turns."

"What did you do to help him?"

"We gave him many showers. We were most fortunate. Eestred and Makinti had recently returned from Glowen to order Orenberry wine for Thane Cathked. While on her visit, she discovered candles infused with the scent of lowen flowers. We burned two of these candles in the room with him, and we fed him lowenna tea. The candles diminished the odor of the reeker, and the tea kept him from falling into despair."

As Caleth finished his story, they arrived at Kat's door. "Your quarters, Lady Kat." He bowed his head. "Thane Cathked has requested you," --he turned to face Mouse-- "and you, Sire Mouse, attend him in a meeting on the morrow after your mid-turn meal. My bond mate, Layleene, will take you to him. As for the balance of this turn, you may both be at your leisure."

Kat thanked him, and he strode back along the passageway.

Mouse, about to head to his own room, stopped and eyed Kat. "I will not dine in the hall this evening, as I am not hungry, but I need to make some preparations before we meet with the Thane on the morrow. Also, I have not reported to Eduardo for some time. May I request the use of your pyrock after my report is prepared?"

"Of course, Mouse. Knock when you need her." She stretched. "I need to record many things in my journal, so I will call for a light snack and tea rather than attend a full meal in the dining hall."

They nodded at each other, and entered their own rooms.

Kat dumped her baggage on a chair, and placed Wink's cage on her dresser. She extracted some pyrock food from her backpack, and lifted the creature from her cage. "You are going to take a trip for Mouse, so you'd better eat now." She fed the tiny animal, and redeposited her in her cage. Wink licked her paw with a small pink tongue, burrowed in the padding, and fell asleep.

Kat pulled out her pages, cathnog pen, and the Kaylin ink from her diplo bag and laid them out on the small table in her room. She decided to bring her journal up to date first.

The last items she had recorded were her visit to Dinerth Caleesh, and her observations about the interactions between the men and women on Baklai.

She wrote all she recalled about Frothan and Losgayrin farms, although she couldn't draw a picture of a reeker, since she never got close enough to see the creature clearly. But the Hunters were different. She remembered how those magnificent birds soared, spiraling in the thermals. *The freedom to fly like that must be electrifying.*

Her back ached, and she realized she had been bending over her papers the whole time. She straightened and stretched, releasing cramped muscles. She put her pen down, removed her Rifellan leathers, and dressed in loose pants and an equally loose top. She hung the leathers in the open closet, and placed her robe beside them.

A minor pang of hunger reminded her it was most likely close to the time of the evening meal. She tugged the tassel in the corner.

When a young female apprentice appeared at her door, she requested tea and cookies. Kat tried to describe the delicious cinnamon ones she ate in Kaylin. The woman laughed. "My Lady we do not keep those ones in Baklai, but we do possess something similar which I am sure you will enjoy. I will bring them with your tea."

"Thank you. Before you go, could I possibly arrange for my Rifellan leathers, and my robe to be cleaned?"

"Yes, you can. I will send someone from the laundry to bring your refreshments, and they can take your leathers and robe for cleaning."

Still smiling, the woman turned and hurried from the room.

As she waited for her meal, Kat gathered the pages of her journal and returned them to her diplo bag.

By the time she had cleared enough space for her snack, someone knocked at her door. She answered to discover a different female, carrying a tray with a large pot of tea, a mug, a bowl of what appeared to be soup, and two small plates with cookies arranged on them.

The woman entered at Kat's invite and deposited the tray on the table. "You have some outer-wear for cleaning, my Lady?"

"Yes. My Rifellan leathers and my robe."

The woman walked over to the closet, and took the leathers. "My Lady, you do not need this robe cleansed. Because of the extraordinary weave of the fabric by Master Thontook of Kaylin, this robe possesses unusual qualities. To clean it, you only need to shake it well in the shower of your personal to remove the dust. Afterward, hang it in the personal, outside of the shower stall. Turn the shower to the hottest water while you consume your meal. After you have completed eating, turn off the water and let the robe cool and release the creases while you sleep. By the morning of the morrow, your robe will be as clean and as crisp as when you purchased it."

"Thank you for the information. I will do that."

"I will return your cleaned leathers to you after the morning meal on the morrow." Carrying them, she left the room.

Kat took her robe and performed the cleansing the female had suggested. She left the robe hanging while she ran the shower.

She returned to the table to enjoy the soup. She tried the cookies on the two plates. One resembled the cinnamon cookies of Kaylin, but the other possessed a nutty flavor and complimented the soup. She finished both the soup and the thin nutty crackers, licking her lips with pleasure.

She moved the tray with the empty soup bowl to the desk, but kept a large mug of tea and the cinnamon cookies on the table. Before continuing with her writing, she turned off the shower, leaving her robe to hang overnight in the misty heat.

Returning to the table she removed her personal list of cool words, and the translations of Priddanese words Mouse had given her. She sat staring at the page, waiting for a word to surface. As she sipped on her tea, she picked up a cinnamon cookie and chewed it. *I can't eat only one.* Another joined the first.

Cattywampus. The word popped into her head. Her mother had told her the word when Kat was little. It meant that everything was all askew. Usually, her mom used it when examining Kat's incredibly messy room. Smiling to herself, she wrote the word on her list. She placed the list back in her diplo bag and drew Mouse's list of Priddanese words toward her.

She examined it, and considered what other words she might need. She would ask Mouse to supply more words when he arrived to send his missive to Eduardo.

I didn't realize Mouse reported to Eduardo regularly. Interesting.

CHAPTER 24

After Kat entered her room, Mouse opened his door, and deposited his luggage next to the small table underneath a window. He extracted maps of Baklai from his bag and placed them on the table. He sat and studied the terrain through the eastern section of the land. He also pulled out maps of Morden and set them beside the others.

After drawing a route through Eastern Baklai and on into Morden, he stopped and rubbed his jaw.

He wondered if it would be best to cross into Morden and ride through the Merga-Doo up towards the Skinya-Doo, and meet with mostly the southern Mordens. He would stick to the west of the Heer River and would thus be less likely to be seen by Galdin or his guards. He had no idea how he would keep Kat from Galdin's clutches once they were in Morden. Had he explained to Eduardo what Galdin wanted of her? Would it be safe, Mouse wondered, to visit the Assassins' Keep?

He pushed the chair back from the table and paced the room. Mordens that he trusted, populated the lands on the west side of the Heer, but the east side of the river, he was long convinced, told a different story.

The Assassins' Guild was east of the Heer, and he held doubts about them. They had appeared in at least three of the attacks on Kat. Mouse was positive Galdin called on them for help to capture her.

The underground river called the Afon-Asgwin, which some called the River of Bones, lay north of the Assassins'

Keep. The river was home to a minimum of three cenotes or sinkholes, created when the surrounding rock collapsed into the waters far below ground level. To the east of the Afon-Asgwin was the Kennes Doo. He had never penetrated that forest because of its horrifying history. Men entered and never returned. No large animals lived in the place. What else lived in the forest, no one knew.

To the north of this forest lay Galdin's Keep – a place Mouse never wished to guide Kat to.

He sat down to examine the maps again. He specifically consulted those of Morden. If Kat was captured and taken to Galdin's Keep, might she be able to free herself by plunging through a cenote and use the Afon-Asgwin as an escape route? What would her chances be if she entered Morden? Mouse got up and paced the room again, creating a list of pros and cons in his mind. He possessed no answer. He needed to consult with Eduardo.

He pulled out a separate piece of parchment and began to write to Kaylin's Lord. "Sibling, we have a problem. When Kat and I arrived in Baklai, we discovered her horse was killed on board the boat from Glowen. Thane Cathked has not yet agreed to give her a replacement animal, because he fears that someone is after her and any horse in her possession is in danger. Before we left on our initial travel through the western part of Baklai, I asked Makinti, the Rifellan Praetor to Thane Cathked, if he might arrange to confirm the cause of death of her horse. I am waiting to hear if he has further information about this."

Mouse rose and paced the room again. He returned to his seat and continued his message. "Kat has been attacked in each land we visited thus far, and while we cannot confirm every situation, I suspect Galdin is behind them all. I hoped Baklai would be safer, simply because of the number of Rifellans in this land. She appears to be well respected by them because of her resemblance to their royalty."

Mouse paused and rose. Hunger drove him to tug the tassel in the corner. He waited for a server to arrive, and then he requested a light meal. He strode up and down the room, and finally a knock at the door heralded the arrival of his meal.

He devoured the soup and munched on the crusty bread from the accompanying plate. Once finished, he poured a mug of tea, moved the tray to his desk, and sat again to complete his missive to Eduardo.

"As you are aware, Galdin wishes to ensure he possesses Kat in his power so he may gain access to you. Remember I told you about his desire to consume your living heart? Some strange belief that it will bestow on him your Wielder powers. He is convinced Kat is the only one who can accomplish this for him. I have used up most of my excuses to keep her from his clutches, but how can I protect her from him if we are all in Morden? Would you agree to allow us to avoid traveling to Morden and return directly to Kaylin?"

He signed it M.

Mouse read his report again and, satisfied, placed it to the side of his mug and drank some more tea.

He folded his maps, stowed them in his bag, and regarded the note with some trepidation. He hoped Eduardo would not be annoyed that he asked so much in order to protect Kat.

He realized the Lord would not reply, obviously, if Mouse failed to send the note. If he sent it this night, Eduardo would have plenty of time to review the situation before Mouse would need to make the decision to take Kat to Morden or not. He rose, picked up the note, and left his room. Once in the passageway, he knocked at Kat's door.

When she answered, he held the note in his hand. "You promised to allow me to send this to Lord Eduardo via your pyrock."

"Yes, come in." She passed him a tube to hold his message, and then reached into Wink's cage to extract the little creature. "I hope you will help me with some more Priddanese words."

He placed the note in a tube and handed it to her. "I would be delighted. A fair exchange."

He watched as Kat bent her head to the small animal. "We need you to deliver a message."

As if she understood, Wink hopped down to the table and extended a tiny foreleg.

Kat tied the tube to the creature's leg, and looked back at Mouse. "Eduardo?"

He nodded.

Kat lifted Wink up in air. "Deliver this to Lord Eduardo."

Wink flapped her teeny wings twice and with, a pop, disappeared

He moved to the table, and sat beside Kat, who had placed her parchment in front of her. "What words would you like to have the Priddanese for?"

Kat gave him the words, and he wrote them on a spare piece of parchment. He watched as she painstakingly copied them to her own list, and then wrote her runes beside them. Once finished, she smiled up at him. "Thank you, Mouse. I'm heading for bed shortly. Can we meet for the morning meal on the morrow?"

He nodded. "I will call for you." Tired himself, he rose, and exited to return to his room.

I hope Eduardo will allow me to avoid taking Kat to Morden. Only danger awaits her in Galdin's land.

CHAPTER 25

Kat's last thought after climbing into bed the previous night had been about whether or not she would obtain a new horse from Cathked.

She had forgotten to close the curtains on her windows the night before, and Pridden's rising star wakened her with its rays. She peered over at the dresser. Wink was still absent. *What did Mouse say to Eduardo?*

Reluctantly, she left the cozy bed, retrieved her robe from the personal, and she slipped it over her head. The previous night, Mouse said he would come for her, but Kat's stomach gave a grumble of hunger. She humphed to herself, left her quarters and knocked at Mouse's room.

When he opened the door, he raised an eyebrow. "I was on my way to call you to our morning meal."

"I'm so hungry I couldn't wait. Can we go?"

"I too ate only a light meal the previous evening, and I find myself ready for food." He closed and locked his door, and they set off down the passageway.

Kat's stomach grumbled again. "I want to be well fed before we meet with Cathked."

"Layleene will take us to meet with him after the mid-turn meal."

"I know. But I want to eat something substantial now, because I plan to consume something light at mid-turn. One should always eat lightly before a battle."

Mouse stopped instantly his face twisted in obvious horror. "You do not plan to battle the Thane, do you?"

Kat frowned. "Of course not, Mouse. I've got allies to do battle with him." She laughed at his wild eyes and raised brows. "I am only being humorous. It was just an expression. Relax."

He continued to walk toward the dining hall, shaking his head. "I am never quite sure when you are attempting to be amusing."

Kay sniffed the air as delightful odors of cooking food and spices wafted from the open doors ahead of them. The Keep was an odd place. At times, the meals were bland and tasteless and, at others, gourmet driven.

Mouse walked past her, through the doors of the hall and made directly to a table, from which Layleene beckoned them.

Layleene rose and, as Kat, who followed Mouse, got closer, she hugged her. "Welcome. This should be a fine turn."

Kat backed out of the hug, stared at her, and raised both eyebrows. "Horse?"

"We have every expectation of success."

"We?"

"The women of the Dinerth. You conducted yourself well, and I believe you gave Gayzella an excellent idea for another marketable item."

A young serving woman approached their table and took their orders. Kat asked for a bowl of fruits, a plate of Baklai bread, and slices of roasted blick. She also requested a substantial mug of lowenna tea. *Keeping happy is the most important thing I can do today.*

Her stomach growled again. "The women of Baklai impressed me with how brilliant they are in running their land. They were so welcoming." Kat arranged her face in what she hoped was a wry smile. "All, that is, except for the Thane's bond mate. I don't believe Kerdinon likes me. I hope she won't interfere with me finding a replacement horse."

Layleene frowned. "Yes, she seemed oddly confrontational toward you. The only thing which comes to mind is that she may harbor jealousy about you. With Lord Eduardo's backing, you are now an important figure in Pridden and in Baklai. Kerdinon always considers herself of extreme importance. You may be interfering with her view of herself."

Kat peered at the healer. "Truly? I hadn't heard of her before coming to Baklai."

"Few of us are familiar to those outside the lands in which we live. The Lords and Thanes are, of course, recognized by most of the people of Pridden. Generally, we healers of Shendea and the warriors of Rifella are more likely to be well remembered." She ceased talking while the server delivered their food and tea to the table.

They all dug into their meals, and satisfied sounds of pleasure replaced the conversation.

Mouse was the first to finish. "You know, Layleene, Baklai does send some of their equine handlers to other lands to act as Horse Masters."

"They do indeed, Mouse. However, if you examine the number of people from each of the lands who are well known throughout Pridden, only a small handful experience any notoriety. Merchants and those with specific needs do travel but that too, is limited. Visiting another land can be demanding and time-consuming. Most people prefer to be at their homes, raising and supporting their families. Traveling for the sake of simply seeing another land is an undertaking best left to the young."

Kat frowned. "I guess that's why Eduardo sent me on this journey through Pridden."

Layleene squinted at her. "Because you do not possess a family?"

"No. Because I'm still young."

Mouse grinned. "Perhaps he merely wanted you out of his way because you ignore rules so easily."

Kat's mouth dropped open. "Are you attempting to be humorous?"

"Yes."

Kat continued to stare at him. *Mouse? Humor? I'm at a loss for words.*

Layleene stared from one to the other. "You two display an odd relationship." She rose from the table. "Please excuse me, but there are duties I need to perform. I will call for you both at your rooms after the mid-turn."

"Thank you, Layleene. Kat and I will be ready."

As the healer departed the hall, they both left the table to head for their own rooms. Kat decided she would list the items in her mind she had packed in her bigger bag to make sure they were what she wanted to send to Wynneth at Kaylin.

At the door to his room, Mouse faced Kat. "Will you please advise me when your Wink returns?"

"I will." She unlocked her door and entered.

In the corner of the room, stood her biggest bag, packed with the items she decided should be returned to Kaylin. Before she called for an apprentice to arrange delivery to Wynneth, she reviewed what she would need for the rest of her journey through Baklai, and also what Mouse had suggested for Morden.

Her limited clothing included one set of Rifellan leathers and armor, her robe, boots, and a few shirts and pants. As to weapons, all she needed were her dagger and long bow. The only jewelry she took were her pendant with the magnificent green stone, the glass ring from Garren, and her pink bracelet. The rest she packed in the bag for Kaylin. Two other items she kept were her lowen-scented lip gloss and the rainbow scarf purchased in Shendea.

Satisfied with her packing, she tugged the tassel in the corner of the room. When the apprentice arrived at her door, she gave him instructions about where the bag was to be delivered. She had already enclosed a note for Wynneth. Almost all the words she had written were in Priddanese, with the help of Mouse, and she explained the reason for her shipment. Her final words in the letter were, "If something should happen to me, please distribute the items in any way you see fit. My thanks." Kat sighed. *My horse is dead. Am I worried about my own safety?*

The young male bowed his head, assured her he would arrange the delivery to Kaylin, and left.

A sudden flutter of wings and a loud squeak announced the arrival of Wink. She perched on the desk and held out her foreleg. Kat removed the tube, gave the pyrock some food, and settled her in the cage.

Carrying the tube, Kat left her quarters and knocked at Mouse's room. When he opened his door, she passed it to him.

His eyes lit up. "Excellent, Eduardo's reply." He peered back at the window in his room. "I suspect it is almost midturn. Would you consider ordering a light meal and tea for us? After I deal with Eduardo's note, I will join you in your quarters and we will wait for Layleene to escort us to Thane Cathked."

Kat nodded. "I will." She returned to her room. *Why doesn't Mouse want to share Eduardo's note with me?*

❋❋❋

After Kat left, Mouse read the letter from Eduardo. "I am sure you feel Kat is in danger, but you have traveled through three lands with her, and thus far danger has been averted. We both know, Galdin has said many threatening things in the past, but I doubt he is able to follow through. He controls his guards with an iron fist, but we are both aware he has little hold on the rest of Morden. I have received reports he uses the Assassins' Guild often, but I am convinced he does not control them. Ssarff is his own man, and I would not be surprised to learn he distrusts the Thane. Keep to the schedule we discussed in Kaylin. If needed I will send you help."

Mouse sighed. *I hope Eduardo is correct.* He scratched his head. *Is he also accurate about Ssarff?*

Mouse paced the room. He glanced at the bigger bag in the corner of his room, packed and ready to send to his home. He strode across to the tassel and pulled it. When the young apprentice knocked at his door, instead of sending the bag home, he gave him instructions to deliver it to Lord Eduardo instead.

Mouse estimated Kat would have ordered their mid-turn snack, so he tucked away Eduardo's note, and left his quarters. As he closed his door behind him, a young apprentice arrived with a tray for Kat.

She opened the door and glanced past the apprentice. "Mouse. Good timing. Come in."

He followed her to a table, on which the apprentice placed the tray of their noon-turn meal, and sat in the chair she indicated. "Are you ready to meet with the Thane?"

"I am. I know the women of Baklai are on my side regarding a horse. I am confident Cathked will supply me with one."

"I realize you believe in the women of Baklai, and I hope you have judged the situation well." He shrugged. "No matter the outcome. Whether you obtain a replacement animal or not, we should depart the Keep on the morrow."

"I agree." Kat frowned at him. "You're wrong about me, you know. I don't ignore rules. I avoid them when I don't understand the reason for them. My father always said to me, 'At the end, our only regrets are the chances we didn't take because of someone else's rules.' If anything, I try to bend the rules so that they make sense to me, and allow me to function in this strange world." She paused apparently in thought about her next words. "I am sure I will receive a new horse, but as soon as I do, I think leaving Cathked's Keep will prove prudent. I don't want him to change his mind."

"I believe that is a wise decision. We will cross the Keep bridge over the primary branch of the Farralawn River into the Eastern side of Baklai"

"Thanks, Mouse."

He smiled at Kat. *I hope she is this calm in the meeting with Cathked.*

CHAPTER 26

After they finished their snacks, Kat suggested Mouse return to his room, as she needed time to dress in complete Rifellan leathers in preparation for the meeting with Cathked. Both Eestred and Layleene remarked on how much she resembled Rifellan royalty, which would be more likely to gain sympathy from the Thane.

The Baklai apprentice removed the tray from her room, which left her free to dress. Before donning her leathers, she fed Wink and indulged in a shower. Refreshed, she dressed and brushed her mass of red curls.

Kat tucked her wee dagger in her left boot. Although not a skean dubh, it reminded her of her mother's Scots ancestry. She picked up the dagger she normally wore on her belt and eyed it thoughtfully. She decided she did not need her dagger in the Thanes's quarters, and the Baklai might not appreciate her wearing a weapon in his presence. She hung the dagger in the closet.

During her journey through the first part of Baklai, Pridden's star had darkened her usual bronze coloring. Her skin seemed dry, so she smoothed lotion over her face and arms to prevent peeling. Lastly, she spread lowen gloss on her lips.

Infused with the scent of happiness, she smiled at herself in the mirror. *I need to meditate. It's been a long time.* She sat comfortably in the armchair in the room, and touching her first three fingers, closed her eyes. How long she sat mentally drifting, she didn't know. A knock brought her back to reality.

Rising and walking to her door, she opened to find Layleene standing in the hall, accompanied by Mouse.

"Is it time?"

"It is." Layleene hugged her. "You appear happy, Kat. We will head for the Thane's meeting rooms now."

The three walked slowly along the hallway to the Thane's quarters. At his door, Layleene requested the guard announce them. The guard opened the door and indicated to the Thane the three were waiting, then stepped aside and allowed them to enter.

In the center of the room stood an enormous and highly polished round table, seated around which were, Thane Cathked; Galakis, the Master Hunter; Makinti, Praetor to Cathked; and Horse Master Penabon.

A number of important females were also at the table: Kerdinon, bond mate to Cathked; Grayseen, bond mate to Galakis; Eestred, bond mate to Makinti; and Gayzella, Head of House for the Keep.

Kat indulged in an inner grin. The males all sat at one half of the table, and the females at the other.

Mouse sat down next to Penabon, and Layleene and Kat took the empty seats among the women.

Cathked stood. "Welcome to you all. We are here to decide upon the question of supplying the Lady Kat with a replacement horse after the unfortunate death of her own. Before we vote on this question, Horse Master Penabon wishes to convey some additional information to this group." He waved at Penabon to stand, and Cathked regained his seat.

Penabon cleared his throat as he rose. "When we first examined the horse, we considered some unknown person murdered the animal by cutting its throat. We discovered that while the horse did ultimately die from the cut, the animal was in severe respiratory distress prior to this act. We believe someone cut her throat to save the creature from much pain and fear because she was unable to breathe. Further examination revealed grain chaff filled the horse's breathing passages and lungs. We located a broken sack of it in the corner of the stall. As horsemen, we are all aware that chaff is normally mixed with hay and used as fodder. We have no idea how the sack came to be so close to the animal, nor why the mare inhaled it. We would expect her to attempt to eat this but not to breathe it into her lungs. We cannot conclude this as an act of murder without the knowledge of why the horse foolishly inhaled the chaff. The cutting of the throat was an act of mercy, nothing more." He sat down.

Makinti stood. "Horse Master, why was a bag of unmixed chaff stored among livestock in the hold of the ship?"

"Apparently the Glowens did not possess two separate storage compartments in the hold. They stored many other items unrelated to horses there. Lady Kat would not have the knowledge to realize the potential challenges to any animal. She is not at fault."

Kat felt as if a huge weight had been lifted from her. *Poor Fiona. I wish I'd been aware of the potential danger though.*

Makinti sat, and Cathked rose again. "Based on this evidence, Lady Kat, we must apologize for our previous thoughts. We will enjoy a small libation of Orenberry wine to end our meeting. After that time, you will accompany Horse Master Penabon to receive a replacement for your further travels." He clapped his hands, and three male apprentices entered from an area Kat assumed was a kitchen. All bore trays with mugs containing Orenberry wine, which they distributed to the members.

I'm getting a horse. Joy, rapture. I'm getting a horse. Kat took a small sip from the mug. She sighed in relief when she realized the wine had been watered. As they drank, the people at the table chatted with each other. The buzz of conversation was music to Kat's ears. All she could think was that she was finally getting a replacement horse.

At some point, Kat noticed that Cathked and Kerdinon had left the table. The rest of the group rose and dispersed. Cathked's departure was obviously a signal the meeting was over. As they left the Thane's quarters, Eestred and Layleene both hugged and congratulated her on being given a new horse.

Kat waved at Mouse, and ran to catch up with Penabon. "Horse Master, may we view a replacement horse now?"

"Lady Kat, normally your guide would discuss this with me, however I do understand your eagerness. So, of course, you may follow me."

Penabon led her to a series of paddocks filled with horses of every color and size. "I suspect you may prefer a slightly smaller animal. Am I correct?"

Kat nodded, too overjoyed to speak.

"We will go through this paddock to the next. The horses are all well trained. Simply push them aside."

Kat peered up at the enormous beasts, and gulped. "They are huge, even compared to the ones my Guide and I have been riding."

Penabon turned and eyed her. "These animals are our largest and are those who are most often used for heavy-duty work."

All she managed was a "Wow." Intimidated by these horses, she tentatively pushed the rump of the animal closest to her and he moved at her touch. She relaxed. *Penabon is right, they are well trained.* Moving the sizeable beasts aside as she needed to, she followed the Horse Master through the crowd of massive animals to the next paddock. She gazed back at the cluster of enormous horses behind her, admiring them. She straightened her spine and sighed with pleasure.

The paddock they entered contained mares which were at least three hands shorter than those in the primary enclosure. She stood in awe, gazing at the beautiful creatures ahead of her, acknowledging the horses on her world were still smaller. One mare, a lovely rich brown with a brilliant white star on her forehead, ambled toward her. "Oh, Penabon, this one is choosing me. Is she available?"

He stared at the horse. "I believe you are correct. The mare has made her choice. We will take her to the stables where Sire Mouse's horse and your baggage animal are kept." He tied a rope bridle around her head, and led the mare from the paddock.

They walked the horse past the collection of paddocks toward the Keep, and through the gates to the inner stables. Penabon led her into a stall and handed Kat a curry comb. "She will need a hay net, but the water trough is filled." He stared at Kat. "Treat her well. She is a fine animal." He turned on his heel and left the stable.

Kat thought her smile would split her face in two. She rushed to the feed bin and grabbed a handful of hay to fill the net. She patted the mare on the nose. "I'm going to call you Starlight." Kat began to groom her, and Starlight nickered softly.

Horse groomed and the stall tidied up, Kat reluctantly left the stables to locate Mouse. She made her way through the inner Keep to Mouse's quarters and knocked.

He opened his door and grinned at her. "You appear incredibly pleased. I assume you now possess a new horse?"

"Yes, she's fed and watered and groomed. I need to wash the dust from me, but would appreciate heading after that for an evening meal. Will you join me?"

"I will indeed. Do what you need to, and come when you are ready."

"Thanks, Mouse." She entered her room and peered at Wink as she passed her cage. The small creature lay curled in a tight ball, breathing tiny snores.

Kat took off her leathers and shook the dust from them in the personal. After a quick shower, she donned her robe, left her room, and crossed the hall to Mouse's quarters. A knock and his door opened.

His map bag hung over his shoulder, and they needed no words as they strode the passageway to the dining hall.

Once in the hall, Mouse chose a table for two, and as they sat, an apprentice approached them. They ordered food and tea.

Kat smiled at Mouse. "Did you know you were supposed to come with me when I got my new horse."

"I did not, I must admit. I assumed since Penabon had advised you that you were not at fault, you could follow him on your own."

"I think they still prefer to deal with other men, but he seemed convinced I was so eager about a new horse, that I could be forgiven this minor break in protocol."

"Good." Mouse patted his map bag. "Once the meal is over, I will go over our next route on the maps I obtained from Makinti."

"Mouse, I'm curious about what happened to my original horse. According to Penabon, whoever brought her life to an end did so as an act of mercy. So, I can't feel anger toward him or her."

"I suspect a male was the one who helped her to die. She was a strong animal, and it would have been difficult to handle her."

"You're probably right. But I am even more curious about the sack of grain chaff. Someone left it in the corner of her stall, with the top open. I do not believe she would breathe it in rather than eating it. Does that truly sound like an accident?"

"When you put it in those words, it does not. Someone who travelled on the ship must have left it there, and perhaps did something to entice her to inhale the chaff. Accident or not, I doubt we will ever know the truth."

***

After the meal was over, as he promised, Mouse traced out the route they would take on the second part of the journey through Baklai. "We will meet early for our morning meal so we can depart in plenty of time for our first stop at the Eastern hut. We will spend one night at the hut before moving to the village of the Mating of Horses." He raised an eyebrow at Kat. "Are you packed for the journey? Remember, we will not be returning to the Keep once we leave on the morrow."

"I'm packed, and I sent my largest bag, loaded with the items I will no longer need, to Wynneth in Kaylin."

"I too sent my extra baggage on. I suggest we retire to our rooms so we are refreshed for riding on the morrow."

"I will sleep well, Mouse. This day contained much stress, but the outcome was perfection. I will come to your rooms on the morrow to meet for the morning meal."

"I will be ready."

They both left the table and walked the passageway to their rooms, murmuring goodnight at their doors.

Kat entered her room, lightness in her step. *A horse. I have a horse!*

CHAPTER 27

Kat woke from a deep sleep to the sounds of growling and squealing outside her open window. She sat up, yawned and stretched. Curiosity forced her out of bed to peer out the window and discover what caused the fracas. Below her, a mowzer had caught a blick, which fought for its life. Kat, fond of the little blicks, yelled at the feral cat-like creature to stop. Both animals, startled, tore off in separate directions. *Probably shouldn't interfere with nature.*

She stretched again before preparing for her day. Once clean and clothed in leathers, she attached Wink's cage to her backpack, gathered her bags and her long bow, and left her room to call on Mouse.

He answered his door at first knock and, carrying his bags, walked with her to the dining hall.

Once seated, they enjoyed a light meal of a grain mixed with a red fruit that tasted of nuts. The meal was both filling and delicious. The apprentice offered lowenna tea, but Kat was so happy about her new horse, she chose karri-san instead.

"You do not need to eat so quickly, Kat. We are early enough to reach the resting hut with plenty of time to spare."

"Sorry, Mouse. But my new horse is ready to ride, and I'm incredibly excited to do so."

"Ah yes, the new horse. Our baggage animal will be most pleased to carry a much lighter load."

Kat glared at him. "Are you saying I'm too heavy?"

He raised his brows in shock. "No … um … its only …

baggage horses do not normally carry passengers."

Kat grinned at him. "I'm pulling your leg, Mouse."

A look of horror crossed his face. "No one is pulling on my legs. And it would be most improper if you did so."

"Good grief. This is an expression from my world that means I am teasing you."

He shook his head and sighed. "Humor, correct?"

Kat simply raised an eyebrow.

Mouse rose. "Fine, we will leave now." He waited while she collected her bags, and they headed for the stables.

When they entered the stables, Kat brought Starlight from her stall and presented her to Mouse. "Isn't she beautiful? Her name is Starlight."

"Yes, she is a fine-looking animal." He shook his head. "I still find you odd that you insist on giving names to animals."

Kat shrugged.

They each saddled and bridled their horses, and Mouse loaded their luggage on the baggage animal.

Kat pulled a small stool beside Starlight and using it, stretched to put her foot in the stirrup and hauled herself into her saddle. "This is going to be a terrific ride. My saddle fits well on her." She wheeled the horse around to face the Keep gate. "She responds well too."

"I am glad you are happy with your new horse." He turned his animal and headed toward the outer gate of the Keep.

With Mouse in the lead, they rode past the docks, along the Farralawn River to the Thane's Keep bridge. The bridge was broad and well-constructed of wooden planks tightly set and reinforced with thick wooden pilings on either end. The sound of the horses' hooves clopping over the bridge soothed and relaxed Kat.

As they left the bridge, Mouse turned right, once again

riding beside the Farralawn, but this time southwards.

Kat gazed across the expanse of the river to the cliffs closer to the Keep. The waters below rushed headlong over massive boulders, grinding away at the earth on either side. The Farralawn, she had learned, was the longest and roughest set of waters in Pridden, flowing from the headland located near Clog Arth at the most northern end of Rifella. By the time this river flowed through Baklai, it became a violent and dangerous body of water.

They rode for some time when Mouse stopped on the road ahead of her. "The Keep provided us with a noon-turn meal, but we are not far from the resting hut, and I suggest we wait until we arrive and can eat in comfort."

"Fine. The noise of the wind blowing through these tall grasses sounds so much like waves crashing on a beach, and it's loud. Hopefully, the hut will be quieter." She realized she was so caught up in thoughts of the river, she wasn't aware of how much time had passed.

"If you lean to your left, you can catch a glimpse of our accommodation for this night."

Kat leaned and peered in the distance. A brown roof beckoned above the waves of rippling golden grasses. "Yes, I do."

Shortly, they arrived at the hut. Kat dismounted and led her horse into an attached stable, complete with individual stalls. She removed and stored Starlight's bridle and saddle. She filled a bucket with water from a full-sized trough outside and lugged it into the stall. She wrestled with an armful of hay and, after she filled the net, seized a brush and groomed her beautiful horse.

Mouse, somewhat quicker with his mount, was now bringing water to the baggage animal.

Kat filled its hay net and helped Mouse brush the dust

from the horse.

Their animals taken care of, they entered the wooden board-and-batten hut, chose rooms, and dumped their bags. The interior was similar to many other travelers' rest-stops they had paused at—clean, plain, and utilitarian. Kat set Wink's cage on the dresser and fed the pyrock two pieces of food.

She left her room and saw Mouse had set out a container of food, supplied by the Keep's kitchens. "Is there sufficient food for this evening's meal as well?"

Mouse nodded at her. "There is. However, I saw some edible red berries on bushes beside the hut. We can expand our later meal with some of them for dessert."

"Wonderful. I've had them before and they're delicious." She prepared tea from crushed lowenna leaves and placed two filled cups beside the food on the table.

They both sat to enjoy their meal.

They had barely completed cleaning up the eating area when the clop of two horses trotted up to the hut.

Kat strode to the door and opened it. She glimpsed Makinti and Eestred as they entered the stable to bed their horses for the night.

Eestred turned. "We are so glad to catch you both. Once we take care of our animals, we will join you."

When the two Rifellans entered, Kat, seated on a comfortable sofa, rose and hugged Eestred. They both sat back down, while Mouse performed the usual Rifellan handshake with Makinti.

The Praetor lifted Eestred's bag and his own and claimed a third room for the two of them.

He and Mouse located well-stuffed armchairs, and Kat refilled the pot and added wood to the fire to produce more tea. She poured additional water into Mouse's mug and her own, and Eestred prepared mugs for her and Makinti.

They sat and chatted about the Keep and their journeys thus far. Makinti imparted excellent news. "The Keep handed us the makings for blick stew, so our evening meal will be delicious."

Kat sighed in relief. "Thank goodness. I am so ready for a change from journeyklim. And Mouse has found red berries outside the hut. We should have a delightful feast."

"Cathked requested I attend the Mating of Horses two turns hence, at which he will also appear, and he asked that I invite you to view this as well, Mouse."

"I am most flattered. I will be delighted to attend."

"We will all stay for two nights at the Eeglos village. Kat, Eestred will show you the gardens at the village, and no doubt you will shop in their small market."

Kat peered at Makinti. "Can't we attend the Mating as well?"

He raised his eyebrows. "Absolutely not. No female is ever allowed to view a Mating."

She glared at him. "Oh, come on. Why not? Horses mating is a perfectly natural occurrence. Unless there's something weird about the way the Baklai horses perform."

"Kat, that is the way it is in Baklai. Males and females each have their place."

She snorted. "It doesn't have to be that way."

Makinti shrugged. "You must come from a strange world. You do not appear to possess differences in what males and females may do." He smiled at her. "The only ones who attend a Mating are the males known as the Hunters. You may have noticed some of them from time to time. They wear two hawk feathers entwined in their hair, which are always worn on the left side of their heads.

Kat pursed her lips, but said nothing.

Makinti and Eestred glanced at each other, and Eestred shrugged.

Makinti turned again to Kat. "No matter what else, we shall all enjoy a delightful meal thanks to those little blicks. Eestred always travels with a package of herbs and spices to enliven any meal, and, we have a half bottle of Orenberry wine." He grinned, mischief on his face.

Well. I can pretend to be diverted. Kat clapped her hands. "A feast it will be indeed. Thanks, Makinti."

Mouse asked Makinti some questions about horses, and the two headed for the stables. Eestred settled with Kat on the sofa, and armed with additional tea, passed a pleasant afternoon filling her in on some a Rifellan warrior's duties in Baklai. Finally, they both excused themselves and headed to their rooms for a brief afternoon nap.

❋❋❋

After a delightful evening of a luxurious fire, excellent conversations, gourmet food and fine wine, Kat yawned. "Forgive me. I believe my bed calls to me."

At that, they all began yawning, and mumbled good night to each other. Makinti, one of the last to head for bed, dimmed the globe lights in the seating area, and taking the waiting Eestred by the hand, headed for their room.

Kat, listened to their murmurings and the creak of beds, and closed her eyes.

Her father wouldn't suggest she allow rules to prevent her from seeing a mating. She was now more curious than ever. She snorted. *Why do they really want stop me?*

CHAPTER 28

The following morrow, Kat woke to the sounds of the others moving about, and their soft speech as they began their day. She left her bed and completed her morning stretches, easing cramps from muscles and limbering up for a day in her saddle.

The hut, although plain, contained a luxury she'd not encountered before -- a personal in each room. She entered the shower and ran warm water over her body. Once dressed in her leathers, she fed Wink and packed her bags. She carried them out to the common room, dropped them near a table, and called a greeting to the others.

Mouse indicated a chair at the table. "We served you some breakfast grains." He appraised her. "You appear in excellent spirits this morrow."

"I am. Starlight is a remarkable animal. She is so comfortable to ride."

Makinti's raised eyebrow almost formed a question mark. "You refer to your horse by name?"

Mouse rolled his eyes at Makinti and nodded slightly.

"Of course. She chose me as her rider. Since we must communicate with each other, she requires a name."

Makinti shook his head and frowned. "She does?"

"Of course."

"Kat, surely you do not believe your horse must have a name."

Kat rolled her eyes. "I dislike it when you patronize me." She glared at Mouse, who grinned at Makinti's obvious discomfort.

Eestred glanced up at her mate, an odd expression on her face. “I often think of my horse by name as well. In my mind, I refer to her as Warrior.”

He glanced at her, askance. “You never told me this before.”

She partially hid a grin behind her hand. “I was afraid you might think me odd.”

Makinti shook his head back and forth. “I do believe, Sire Mouse, females *are* odd, and we males should be on our guard around them.”

Both Kat and Eestred burst out laughing.

Mouse and Makinti stared at them with eyes wide open and foreheads wrinkled.

Makinti peered at his mate. “Why do you laugh?”

Kat, her expression sympathetic, patted him on the arm. “You are not aware of how true your statement is.”

The Rifellan woman rose. “Our meal is complete, and before we begin a war between the four of us, we are supposed to leave the hut as clean as we found it. I suggest we tidy up behind us and set out for the Eeglos village near the Mating arena.”

Kat stood and walked toward her room, calling back over her shoulder. “A wise idea, Eestred. I am most anxious to ride Starlight again.”

Eestred batted her lashes and gave the two men a coy smile. “Perhaps you males would clean the dishes from our meal?”

Both men rose, and Makinti stared at her again. “Eestred why are you acting so far from your normal behavior. This is new. I do believe Kat is not the best influence for you.”

She shook her head pityingly. “Bond mate, women possess many different sides." She smiled sweetly at him. "I will pack our luggage." With those words she strolled slowly to their room, her hips moving rhythmically.

The Rifellan stared again, his mouth open. He shook his head and blinked. Without another word, he helped Mouse carry the dishes to the counter to be washed and stored back in the cupboard.

***

With conversation back to what the men considered normal, all four carried their baggage to the attached stable. Saddles and bridles in place, and the baggage horse loaded, Mouse, map in hand, conferred with Makinti about the route.

"I agree, Mouse, the pathway you marked is the shortest and most comfortable. We will not travel as close to the cliffs, but we may view those later when we head to the training grounds."

They swung into their saddles, Kat with a little help from Mouse, because Starlight was still taller than the horses she normally rode. They set off, Mouse and Makinti in the lead, with Eestred and Kat following.

Kat sighed. "I love traveling through Pridden's lands. I may complain on the odd occasion, but everything is so new and fascinating. Baklai possesses weird creatures, even though the land itself is rather dull." She smiled. "I am particularly comfortable on Starlight. Her gait is so gentle."

Kat's animal nodded its head up and down and nickered.

"You're welcome, Starlight."

Eestred chuckled. "I always suspected horses understand us. You and your Starlight appear to be able to converse better than most."

"I think she's extremely intelligent."

Starlight nodded again and nickered some more.

"She is certainly aware when you are complimenting her."

"I believe most horses are much smarter than we give them credit for. When I was about six ye… er paths in age, my female parent introduced me to riding. The stable wanted to make sure I would be safe, so they set me on an old horse, who only wore a rubber bit. They had no idea he was a mean, cantankerous beast, whose sole joy in life was exasperating riders."

"That does not sound like a fine way to introduce young children to horse riding."

"It wasn't. The more I hated him, the more horrible tricks he tried on me. He would trot toward the manure pile and refused to change direction should I attempt to turn him. I had my fingers in the ring attached to the bit in his mouth, his head actually touching his side, and he still would head in the same direction. At the manure pile, he would stop abruptly, hoping to throw me over his head. He never managed to, but it was a constant battle between us."

Starlight snorted.

"Thank you, Starlight, I appreciate your sympathy."

Eestred grinned at Kat. "I must admit you have more conversations with your horse than I ever did."

"I usually didn't indulge in many out loud conversations with my poor Fiona. They were mostly thought words. I decided I would prefer to speak to Starlight more freely, and may anyone who thinks I'm crazy go to hell."

"That's an odd word. Hell? Where is it?"

"Sorry, an expression from my world. It's a mythical place where criminal people go after they die, to experience torture and everlasting pain."

"Your world sounds quite violent."

"Perhaps. But I have also experienced violence on your world of Pridden." Kat shrugged and smiled. "Although I believe your Lords and Thanes are better leaders than we possess. We have a saying on my world. 'Power corrupts, and absolute power corrupts absolutely.' I suspect many of our leaders begin with the best of intentions, but the possibility of financial and personal gain and the frustration of dealing with systems that are seriously flawed, become too heavy a burden to carry. They falter and fail." *Best not mention assassinations.*

"I find it pleasant to hear your world is not perfect. Your way of viewing our world is different from how we view ourselves, and I often wonder what type of people you lived with."

Makinti and Mouse stopped their horses, and waited for the women to catch up. Mouse approached Kat. "Makinti indicated the Eeglos village is ahead, and if you look carefully, you can see the buildings from here. He suggests we do not tarry but ride a little swifter, so we can be settled in our rooms before Thane Cathked arrives with his party of guards."

The women agreed, and they picked up their pace and soon approached the stables on the edge of the village. Greeting the Stable Master, they descended from their horses and led the animals into the stalls the Master indicated. Three additional apprentices helped them prepare their horses for the overnight stay.

The Stable Master directed them to the closest wooden structure. "Ask for Ragvenoos, and he will arrange for rooms for you and a tour if you wish."

They walked to the largest house and enquired for Ragvenoos.

A very brown Baklai with fine strong features stepped from his door, and greeted them with a huge smile. "Makinti, and Lady Eestred. Welcome again. We have not experienced the pleasure of your company for almost a full path."

Makinti indicated the other two with a wave of his hand. "Ragvenoos, please welcome the Lady Kat and her traveling guide, Sire Mouse."

Ragvenoos bowed to them both. "Follow me, and I will conduct you to your rooms." He reached back and withdrew four keys from a board inside his house. He set off ahead of them toward a long, two-storied building, which Kat thought appeared similar to the log long-houses of some of the First Nations people in Canada.

Ragvenoos told them that the main floor of the building contained a substantial kitchen and an enormous dining lounge. The second story, he advised them, consisted of ten individual rooms. As he led them up the stairs, Ragvenoos kept up a running commentary. "You are in luck. We are only beginning the noon-turn meal, so once you leave your luggage in your rooms, you may join us. You may wish to spend some time in our market. Lady Eestred, you are familiar with the market, so perhaps you would provide a tour for Lady Kat."

"I will. My thanks."

He arrived at the doors to the rooms and handed them the keys with numbers imprinted on them. The Rifellans were given two keys with the same number.

Makinti exchanged a Rifellan handshake with Ragvenoos, and the Baklai male departed.

Makinti paused at his door. "Shall we all meet here in a few moments to head to the dining hall?"

Eestred stopped. "Bond mate, may I suggest you and

Mouse attend the dining hall." She turned to Kat. "Would you prefer to join me at the market place? We can enjoy a light snack at one of the stalls, and then indulge in some shopping." She grinned and faced her mate. "I assume you two would prefer to avoid shopping?"

Both the males appeared suitably horrified at the prospect. "My dear mate, I would be most grateful to avoid attending the market place with you."

They all laughed, and entered their rooms.

In her quarters, Kat placed Wink's cage on the dresser, and the pyrock shifted a little, squeaked, and dropped back to sleep. Kat tossed her bags on a chair, removed her leathers, which she shook to free them of sand. She splashed water on her face and dressed in light pants and her Rifellan leather uppers.

She left her room and knocked at Eestred's door. The Rifellan female answered. "Perfect. You are ready. Let us go to the marketplace."

They walked together, exited the long house, and Eestred led them to the small but active, marketplace.

Kat breathed in the luscious odors of food on the air.

I'll quiz Eestred about how to attend a Mating. Will she be as against it as the Baklai are? I still don't understand why the Baklai are afraid for their women to view a mating.

CHAPTER 29

Although Kat had spied flags in the distance, she had no idea what a bustling, hectic marketplace she would encounter.

The stalls were not grouped in sections related to their specific products. Instead, food, art, clothing, and flowers jumbled together in a higgledy-piggledy fashion. The market was a mass of color and laughter and conversation. Children squealing with delight, ran among the stalls adding to the glorious chaos.

Caught up in the energy of the area, Kat wanted to run amok as well.

Eestred touched her on the arm. "Relax Kat. We will be able to experience almost everything. We have plenty of time, and the marketplace is not that enormous."

"I'm sure you're correct, but the excitement of the place is catching."

"The first thing we should do is consume a mid-turn meal. I enjoy the unusual dishes that my favorite stall keeper prepares. We can finish with kossil-kweth tea."

"That's the calming tea from Glowen. Do you import much kossil-kweth?"

"Kat, Baklai is in the position on Pridden where they need to import goods from most of the lands. All the inhabitants of Pridden are fond of tea, but the Baklai, more so."

Eestred raised her head and sniffed the air. She grinned at Kat. "We are in for a treat. I believe Dibron obtained wullawerth meat. He uses both Glowen and Baklai spices, and he created a stew for which he is famous. His dessert is a delicate type of pudding, over which he pours a sauce made from crushed cantobeans, mixed with golden river."

"I adore the flavor of golden river. I sent some ahead to Wynneth, the healer in Lord Eduardo's Keep."

Eestred quickened her steps and soon directed Kat to a seat at a nearby table, and she entered Dibron's stall to order their meals and tea. Then she returned to sit beside Kat.

Kat licked her lips. "The delightful odors of the food are making me drool."

Eestred laughed. "You are a true sensualist. I messaged Bardu's mate, Irina, and she related many things you did which surprised even her. You will never be content with living life safely or easily, will you?"

"I suppose I won't. But Eestred, I wasn't always like this. I was living my life quite well -- when without warning, I found myself on Pridden. I'm completely blank about how I got here. But because of my travels through Pridden, I'm reminded again of how short and precious our lives are and how unexpected situations can occur without any prescience. My male parent always encouraged me to take advantage of any opportunities that presented themselves. He never had the ability to accomplish all he wanted. I sometimes forget I had vowed to never again take life for granted."

"Is this why you often act in a precipitate manner?"

"Eestred. Have you been talking to Mouse?"

"And Irina."

"I don't consider myself rash, but sometimes, if you hesitate too long, the opportunity passes, and is lost. Mouse is, in my opinion, a hesitant man. I suspect he loses many opportunities."

"And I suspect, you underestimate your Mouse."

A young apprentice brought a tray to their table, and deposited plates of food and dessert, and massive mugs of tea.

Kat laughed. "I'll not allow the opportunity to consume this delicious meal pass without tasting everything."

She took a mouthful of the wullawerth dish, and moaned in pleasure when the flavor exploded in her mouth. "This is glorious."

"I told you this would be worth a visit."

Kat savored each mouthful, interspersing her nibbling with appreciative comments.

When they completed their meal, Eestred picked up her mug of tea. "I hope you will consider drinking our tea in a leisurely manner. If you wish, we can indulge in shopping afterwards."

Kat hesitated. "Er … I would first ask a question of you."

"Yes?"

"Eestred, you and Makinti were sent to Baklai to be stationed here for a number of paths, weren't you?"

Eestred nodded.

"And Makinti is well known among the horsemen of this land, is he not?"

"Yes." Eestred leaned forward. "What are you asking, Kat?"

"Can you help me to, or make a suggestion how, I can view the Mating of Horses?"

Eestred backed her chair away from the table, her mouth open and eyes fully dilated. "By Caleesh, Kat. You truly do not expect to be able to attend a Mating?"

"I truly want to. To me, it is weird to surround what should be normal with such secrecy."

"You cannot, Kat. It is forbidden for any female to be present."

"This is one of those things I find out of sync. Do your Baklai males truly believe females are too sensitive to view one? Is there something horrifying about this act in Baklai?"

"Everyone told you clearly, males see and do certain things, and women do others. This is the way things have always been in Baklai, and are not likely to change in the near future."

"What's the worst that might happen if I did sneak into the arena? I'll avoid being seen. It's unlikely they'll ever find out, but if they do, the males would be angry. So? I'm not afraid of their anger."

"What might happen?" Eestred shook her head. "May Caleesh stop you from this madness." She clasped her hands together. "Thane Cathked himself would be involved, and the males will be far more than angry. Their fury might ultimately lead to violence. If you press on in this madness, you could be subject to a trial, and the penalty for breaking any of the iron rules of Baklai is prison. And, after a certain length of time, you would also be ejected from the land. All Pridden would be apprised of your transgression, and you would be welcome in no other land. You might well be removed to the unknown areas beyond our mountains. These areas, unexplored by anyone, are called Air Wyth. No soul ever banished to Air Wyth, has ever returned."

"I simply don't understand why they would have such an extreme reaction. I have seen horses mating on my world, and it's quite clinical. Naturally, I'm eaten up with curiosity as to what is so different about this in Baklai. When I was a young child, my father told me there was nothing I could not do or see if I put my mind and training to it. He also said that most people came up with rules as protection for themselves, because they lived in fear. If that is the case here, I need to understand why the Baklai live in such a state of fear about horses mating."

"I beg of you, Kat, do not attempt to attend the Mating. Please heed my warning."

Kat stared at the Rifellan woman in silence, and blew out a frustrated breath. "I understand your warning, and I'm disappointed. Forgive me, Eestred, but I don't feel much like shopping. I need to think some more."

They both rose, and Kat, puzzled by what she considered animals acting in a natural way, strode from the marketplace back to her quarters, her mind boiling over with questions.

Thoughts raced through her mind. *Do they make such a secret of this because it's horrifying or dangerous? If it is, why would they let Mouse attend? He's an outsider.* She wondered if she could trust him enough to tell her if there really was something unthinkable going on. And, she asked herself, was this one of the things Eduardo wanted her to learn about Baklai? If she didn't pursue it, would she be failing her assignment and breaking her agreement with him? She had no idea what exactly was at stake here. *I will have to enter the arena unseen. No one must ever know.*

Back in her room, Kat paced the floor. *They tell me it's forbidden and there are ghastly punishments for breaking this rule. But no one explains why.*

CHAPTER 30

Kat remained in her room and ordered something light for her evening meal. Mouse called for her to join him in the dining hall, but she demurred. “I’m not feeling well. I may have overdone my noon-turn meal. I suspect I simply need an early night.” She hoped Mouse would accept her excuse.

After the young apprentice delivered her meal, along with a further massive pot of kossil-kweth tea, she extracted her journal and writing instruments from her diplo bag.

While she didn’t wish to deliberately break the Baklai rules, her desire to understand what she considered incomprehensible about their Mating of Horses was too strong. She needed to know more about the ritual, and if it was something that Eduardo needed to know about. *Why has this aroused my curiosity so strongly?*

Kat pulled her journal toward her and dipped her cathnog pen in the Kaylin ink. She needed to know what was fueling her desire to attend the Mating. Was the answer in her early years, or was it really her current suspicion of something more unpleasant? She penned a line in her journal. ‘I think I was lucky. My early education qualified as different. Much of which I learned was thanks to my father who was a man ahead of his time.’

Was this the reason she questioned everything? Perhaps also the reason she willingly took risks to ignore the rules? Rules needed to be explained, she thought, otherwise they simply were put in place to control people. *Baklai is so strange. Women appear to run the land, but they are barred from attending a Mating. Why*?

She recalled another line her father always used. "It is other people's rules that make us regret the chances we didn't take, and therefore the opportunities we missed."

Writing about her early childhood reminded Kat of the awful night of the accident. It was a memory that would haunt her forever.

❋❋❋

They had visited her brother, who was in his first year of university in northern New York State. As they left her brother's dorm, he ruffled her head. "Take care of yourself, peanut, and stop causing so much trouble." She bristled at him. "Stop messing my hair, I'm not a kid any more. I'm twelve now. I'm almost a grown up." He laughed and gave her a hug.

They only realized as they drove a few miles the weather had become hideous, with huge snowflakes whirling around the car, falling thickly in layers on the unplowed road.

Kat, nervous about the unknown dangers of the snow, wrapped herself in a blanket and curled up in the back seat, shivering When the seat belt dug into her side, she loosened it, giving her room to lie down on the seat. "Are we going to be alright, Dad?"

Her father, called out to her. "Yes, we'll be fine." He avoided the secondary roads, and followed the well-travelled highways.

Her mother leaned back between the seats, the highway lights shining on her bright red hair, the only color in the white blanket of the thickening snowfall. "We'll be fine honey. Keep yourself wrapped in the blanket and get some sleep."

Within minutes, her father spoke to her mother. "I'll stop

at the first available motel. Its madness to continue on in weather like this."

Without any warning, a wave of lights blinded them, as a huge truck crested the hill ahead, sliding over the road toward them, the load behind the cab lashed like the tail of an angry cat.

With no options to escape the inevitable collision, The truck and its load ripped into their car. Metal crunched and groaned. Brakes squealed. Her mother screamed for her father. He made no sound to further disturb the muffled blanket of the blizzard. Instantly, silence reigned.

Kat, on the floor of the back seat, had slid under the front seat which had shifted over her, trapping her. Her mother moaned and called to her father. All that disturbed the night was the ticking of hot metal cooling.

Kat obviously lost consciousness. She woke later in a hospital bed, crying for her parents. Her entire world came to a crashing halt as the police and doctors gently explained that both her parents had perished in the wreck.

***

After all this time, the memories still brought tears. She felt again the urgent need to take advantage of opportunities that arose. For her, life must be lived in the now.

Caught up with the emotions of that time, she had finished her meal without actually being aware of the flavors. The kossil-kweth calmed her. She put away her journal and walked to her dresser to feed Wink, who squeaked plaintively from her cage.

Before she made the final decision about viewing the Mating, Kat thought she should explore the path to the arena.

The night, dark and moonless, with the stars providing little illumination, blanketed the landscape. Quietly and carefully, Kat moved through the trees toward the arena, a dark shadow of a building. She walked silently around the outside, to determine the location of all doors, and found a possible entry point at the rear of the structure. Silently, she established that the door at the rear was unlocked. She peeked in and saw a dozen places which would help her conceal herself. Luckily, no windows graced the building.

Armed with the information she gathered, Kat reached a decision, and returned stealthily to her quarters.

Her curiosity about the Mating was acute, but she was torn between her desire for knowledge, particularly as it applied to Eduardo's request, and the need to honor the Baklai rules. Her father always encouraged her to settle any queries hovering in her mind, by looking for answers. Bound by the rules of diplomacy, he never followed his own dream by speaking out against the treatment of women in his own country. He was positive he would have time in the future to pursue this. Now, of course he never would.

After recalling these memories, she realized she would regret it if she did not view the Mating. If this Mating concealed challenges for Baklai, she must at least know whether or not to report it to Eduardo. She was convinced she could conceal herself so that none would know she attended. *I will not tell Mouse or Eestred or anyone else.*

She prepared for bed, and slipped beneath the padded comforter for a restful night, clear in her mind how cautiously she must act.

❋❋❋

The din raised by birds fighting over food as they left their nesting sites to greet the new day, forced Kat awake. She tried to sleep in a little more, but the noise of her avian tormentors made it an impossible to relax.

Sighing, she rose to prepare for her day. Mouse had mentioned they would remain one more turn in the Eeglos village.

She had agreed to meet Mouse along with Eestred and Makinti for a morning meal. Her research informed her the Mating was to take place after the noon-turn in the arena, which nestled among trees at the edge of the tall fields of grasses. Her reconnaissance of the previous night assured her she would be able to gain entrance to the arena unseen. She planned to enter well before the beginning of the ceremony to locate a perfect hiding place within the walls of the building.

Happy she had everything worked out to the last detail, and smiling to herself, she dressed in leathers, and left her room to catch up with Mouse.

He opened his door when she knocked and greeted her. "Your timing is excellent. I am eager to eat. Shall we go?"

The two walked down the hall and descended the stairs to the dining floor. She followed Mouse to a table for four. He waited until she seated herself to call an apprentice to take their orders. Eestred and Makinti entered the hall and headed in their direction.

Once their meals were served, the four enjoyed conversations about Mouse's time with the Baklai men, and Kat's tour of the extraordinary marketplace.

Makinti patted his bond mate on the arm. "What are you planning for today? I ask because I must meet with some of the guards to examine any challenges that occurred during the past quarter path."

Eestred grinned at him. "I intend to meet with two of the mates of your guards. We plan on discussing the many failures of our mates, and we will no doubt imbibe too much

Orenberry wine."

Makinti laughed. "You are such an unruly mate. What did I ever do to deserve a female like you?"

"Which is, of course, why you find me so attractive."

He snorted.

Eestred turned to Kat. "Would you enjoy joining us for a noon-turn meal and female conversation?"

"I would love to, Eestred, but I must spend most of the day writing in my journals. It is such a long while since I updated them. I also wish to complete a number of the illustrations I began at the Keep. Might we meet for an evening meal instead?"

Eestred eyed Kat, a slight frown on her face.

"Are you sure you do not wish to join us?"

"Truly, I would love to join you, but I must update my journals. If I get too far behind, it becomes a dreadful chore and takes ages to catch up."

Eestred laughed. "You are correct. When I neglect things, they become burdensome problems. We will meet you for the evening meal."

Is she suspicious?

CHAPTER 31

Once they completed their morning meal, the four headed out to follow their plans for the day.

Mouse chatted to Makinti as they left the dining hall. "I must return briefly to my room to obtain my maps. I suspect your guards may be able to supply me with additional information that may prove valuable. May I meet you at the entrance to this building in a few moments?"

"By all means, Mouse. I wish to dress in my leather uppers, in case I need the protection."

Kat, walking behind them, was startled by his words. *Protection?* She queried Eestred. "Surely no person would attack him. Why would he need protection, and who from?"

Eestred laughed. "Kat, they may appear to be fully grown males, but often when they meet, they believe they are still young. They indulge in foolish games." She chuckled. "I am not positive that males ever achieve full adulthood."

Kat grinned. "I understand. On my world, men often act like children too."

Eestred appeared thoughtful. "Capturing one's younger years is not necessarily a bad thing."

Kat peered at her. "You may be correct. The one who protects and defends your mate, your progeny, and your land against fierce odds perhaps deserves the opportunity to relax in child-like pursuits."

At the bottom of the staircase Kat turned to Eestred. "I must get to work. Enjoy your time with your friends."

Eestred thanked her and exited the long house.

Kat walked up the stairs to her room, where she shed her leather uppers and sat down at her desk to work. The shirt she wore allowed for air to circulate and kept her cool. She extracted her journal and her writing materials, but paused when Wink decided she needed to eat.

Kat removed the pyrock from her cage and fed the hungry creature two pieces. Wink stretched her wings and hopped around on the desk. "You're full of energy today. A good time to check in with Wynneth." Kat found a blank piece of parchment, and, consulting her list of Pridden translations, she wrote a simple note. 'Hope you received my extra clothing which I sent to you at Eduardo's Keep.'

She inserted the parchment into a small tube and motioned Wink over to her. The pyrock extended her foreleg, and Kat tied the tube to the fragile limb. She hoped this would keep Wink occupied while she headed to the arena. "Take this to Wynneth, please, Wink." The small creature extended her wings, flapped them twice and, as she raised off the desk, disappeared.

Kat opened her journal, pulled out other pages of illustrations she had prepared, and put her list of excellent words to one side. She would add to them later.

She wrote for some time, until she decided she needed food. She gazed out the window and estimated it was almost the noon-turn. She yawned and stretched her back, hearing the muscles pop and then, someone knocked.

She rose, and opened the door, startled to find Eestred waiting. "Kat, I thought you might want to join me for a noon-turn snack." Eestred peered in the room.

Kat smiled at her. "Thanks for the invite, but I'm considering calling for tea and perhaps a cookie. As you can see" --she pointed at the pile of parchment-- "I'm in the thick of things. I've got enough to keep me busy until the evening meal.

"Are you sure you cannot take a brief break?"

"No. I am doing so well, and everything is flowing in such a perfect way. So long as I don't stop, I will be finished in time to join you all this evening. If anything, I may have to indulge in a short nap."

"Fine. If you still need to work." The Rifellan woman appeared reluctant to leave, but finally turned and walked down the hall.

Kat suspected Eestred was checking up on her. She headed to the window, and peered out. Eestred was walking toward a building that housed the workers in the village, although she did glance back at the long house, a frown on her face.

Kat decided not to eat now but to order something when she returned from the arena. She took off her bright clothing, picked out a black shirt and pants, and donned her brown robe over her outfit. Soft black shoes made sure she could walk silently.

Once ready, she left her room, locked her door and headed toward the rear entrance to the long-house. Cautiously she descended the stairs and slipped out the rear door, entering the thick copse of trees.

The previous turn, she had snooped around the arena as she headed back from the marketplace. She approached the barn-like structure which stood, separated from the village by fields of grain swaying in the breeze from the Hyal Sea and a lush growth of small trees. Kat stopped behind a tree. At one end, two tall doors allowed access to the interior, and, both stood open. A pair of Baklai males approached, leading a mare who whinnied and tried to kick her captors.

The thick growth concealed Kat all the way to the rear of the arena. She slowly opened the door and sneaked inside. The rear of the building, piled high with hay bales, wooden panels, and extra rails for temporary stalls, appeared to be a storage area. Cupboards and shelving that contained hobbles, straps, shields, buckets, and more extra rails for creating smaller enclosures lined the walls. Also stored here were supplies for protecting the men from aggressive stallions, including body shields, heavy leather gloves, leg protection, and prods.

Kat wormed her way among the bales, and behind some boards, one of which sported an empty knot hole. *Perfect, s*he breathed to herself. She could stand or sit perfectly concealed, and yet have a clear view of the main entrance.

The mare the men brought in was now enclosed in a temporary stall, contentedly chewing at her hay net.

Kat sat for some time, drowsing slightly, until four men entered from the huge doors at the front end of the arena. All wore heavy shin pads, long substantial leather gloves, and chest shields similar to Rifellan armor on their upper bodies. They also sported two hawk feathers in their hair, hanging on the left side of their heads. They carried additional lines, coiled over their arms. Several guests entered the arena, including Makinti and Mouse. She was surprised that Cathked was not among them. The guests were guided to stand behind rails on the opposite side of the arena from where the mare was located.

Two of the men, whom Kat recalled were known as Hunters, approached the mare, whose ears pricked up at the sound of the whinny of a stallion, and they grasped the reigns on each side of her bridle. The other two removed the rails of the stall and set them aside. The mare was now held in place only by the men at her bridle.

Three more men entered the arena through the huge double doors, leading the stallion. All wore the same type of heavy gloves, shin pads, and chest shields. All maintained a safe distance from his rear, avoiding any danger of him kicking them. They held onto lines leading from either side of his harness, maintaining a modicum of control over the massive animal. After all were in the appropriate positions, the Hunters closed the huge double doors.

The mare, in heat, whinnied at the sound of the approaching stallion, her tail held high, as she stood firm, waiting. She was at the mid-point of the normally empty arena, on the opposite side of where the guests stood. The mare shook herself, whinnied again, then urinated, releasing pheromones to add to her scent to tantalize the stallion.

The stallion nickered and curled his upper lip, sniffing the air, inhaling the pheromones, and approaching the mare to nudge her. He pranced around, snorting and nodding his head up and down. Moving closer to the female, he bit at her rear end, her sides and her back.

The mare screamed and kicked backward, narrowly missing the courting male.

This appeared to inflame the stallion even more, and he snorted again and pawed at the ground, approaching the mare from the rear.

The mare nickered, raised her tail higher, and backed toward the stallion. Again, he pawed at the ground, sniffed at her, and finally raised himself up and on her back, biting at her neck.

Kat opened her mouth and gulped when she caught a glimpse of his enormous erection.

With a further scream, the male thrust into the mare and

bit at her neck, seemingly preventing her from escaping him.

The room, heavy with the funk of sex and the scent exuded by the mare, drove the stallion to double his efforts. After what appeared to be only a few additional thrusts, he screamed again and slid from the female, his forelegs dropping back to the ground.

Kat stared at the scene. *I forgot how brief it could be.*

The men, holding the mare's bridle relaxed the extreme hold on her, and she walked to a substantial pile of straw and lay down, breathing heavily.

The men who controlled the stallion, indicated the guests were to leave immediately by a side door near the front entrance, which they did, moving hastily from the building.

The heat in the arena and the miasma of pheromones, affected Kat. Her knees weakened, her mouth dried, and she experienced a rush of heat. A movement at the far end of the arena startled her. One of the males sniffed the air. "A female is in here."

The Baklai men turned as one and glanced around the arena, eyes dark and glazed and fixed on the rear end of the building. Each exhibited an astounding erection.

Kat already creeping toward the back exit, flinched at his words, turned and fled from the rear door. She tore through the trees to the back entrance of the long-house as soundlessly and swiftly as possible.

Crashes of barriers and bales being pushed aside and metal stall pieces overturned spurred her on as she pulled open the outer door of the long-house leading to her quarters.

She fled up the stairs and, fishing the key from her pocket, entered her room. The rear door of the arena squealed and slammed against the outer wall as the remaining Hunters poured from the Mating building. *How could they smell me?*

Without wasting a second, she shed her robe in the personal and shook it out. She stripped off the black shirt and pants, and donned the blue one with beige pants that she wore earlier. She spread highly scented lavender lotion on her skin before putting on her Rifellan leather uppers. *This should conceal my scent.*

She hastily hung the robe and her discarded clothes in the personal, poured some scented lotion in the shower, and briefly turned on the hot water. Aromatic steam enveloped the room.

Kat closed the door to the personal and rushed to open the window to air out everything. Finally, she flung herself into a chair at her desk, and slowed her breathing. She picked up her pen and began writing in her journal again, her heart thumping like a steam engine. She waited, listening, barely breathing.

The rear door of the long-house squealed open to the clump of male feet. Their forceful treads traversed the hall and paused outside each room. Heavy knocks at some doors made Kat's heart beat faster. Someone stopped outside Kat's room, and she held her breath when she detected sniffing outside her quarters.

A long pause, and the man at her door continued on without knocking.

Was the smell of lavender strong enough?

CHAPTER 32

Kat's heart still pounded as she left her desk to tug on the tassel. When the young apprentice arrived at her door, she ordered kossil-kweth tea.

"Do you carry any cookies you might bring with the tea?"

"I will ask for something from the kitchen, Lady."

He left, and she returned to her desk to record more in her journal. Nervous and with a strong sense of guilt, she refrained from recording anything about her trip to the Mating arena. Instead, she wrote about some of the best meals she had enjoyed, and ended by indicating that she spent the entire day writing and drawing. *I had no idea the males might detect my presence.*

The young apprentice delivered her tea and cookies. Delighted to discover these cookies were much like the cinnamon types she used to consume in Kaylin, she ate them with pleasure. Her heart calmed.

She breathed a long sigh of relief, but at the sound of a loud knock at her door, she jerked in her seat, and her heart jumped in her chest. "Who is it?"

"Mouse. I am here to escort you to the dining hall. Makinti and Eestred are seated, and we wondered if you forgot to join us."

"Mouse, my apologies. I lost all track of time. Would you wait a minute or two while I change my shirt?"

"I will wait outside your door."

Kat nipped into the personal, which still retained the odor of lavender, and brushed her hair. She draped the shirt she had worn to the morning meal over a chair, and kept on the fresh yellow shirt she had dressed in after her return from the arena. It was perfect with her leather uppers. She made sure to appear in the same pants which she'd worn at the morning meal.

She walked over and opened her door, allowing Mouse the opportunity to peer inside her room. She wanted him to see she'd been occupied with writing the entire turn.

His glance toward her desk, and his words proved her correct. "You have certainly been extremely busy with your writing."

"I'm aware it's messy, but since I'm late for our meal, I'll tidy when I return to my room." After locking her door, she followed him along the hall. *He seems OK. But he's not a Baklai.*

❋❋❋

Mouse led her through the doors of the dining hall, and over to the table where Eestred and Makinti sat drinking mugs of liquid.

Eestred laughed at something her mate said. "I did not consume any Orenberry wine, so I am enjoying one at this meal."

Kat peered at her. "From what you told me earlier this turn, I expected you would've indulged in a wild time with your friends."

"I did say I intended to. However, I sensed disquiet this day, and preferred to avoid the wine. Did you manage to write down everything you planned?"

"I did. My poor hand is quite cramped." She stretched it and wiggled her fingers.

An apprentice appeared at the table and took their orders for their meal. Kat ordered karri-san tea to accompany the blick stew, which was the special. She grinned at Eestred after she placed her order for the tea. "Your mate is beginning to appear too delightful to me."

Eestred laughed. "Make sure you drink plenty of karri-san."

Makinti murmured something to Mouse.

He widened his eyes. "What?"

Makinti nodded. "Apparently."

Eestred touched his arm. "What are you two muttering about?"

"I told Mouse about a rumor floating among the males that someone detected a female in the Mating arena."

His words felt like a blow to Kat's chest, and she tried her best to seem shocked. "A female? How do they know? I thought females weren't allowed to attend. Who was she?" *Eestred's eyeing me suspiciously.*

"No one has any idea. Mouse and I both attended, but we were required to leave quickly after the Mating was complete. They did make us exit unusually quickly, but we saw no female there. Apparently, she disappeared so fast they do not possess a proper description. They thought she wore a robe. They believe she escaped to the long-house in which we are staying. However, when they searched, they found no sign or scent of anyone who had been in the Mating building."

Kat caught Eestred staring at her curiously, and a trickle of sweat rolled down her spine. *It's good I wore Rifellan leathers tonight.* She was terrified the other three could hear her heart thumping in her chest. She hoped if her face appeared red, Eestred would think it was because of the need for karri-san.

Their meal arrived, and Kat downed a huge gulp of tea.

Makinti is staring at me. She swallowed. *I know he didn't see me.*

The blick stew was delicious, with spices added with which Kat was unfamiliar.

Eestred leaned toward her and whispered to her. "Did you go?"

Kat furrowed her brow. "Did I go where?"

She murmured. "To the arena."

Kat gazed at her, aghast. "Eestred. You told me not to." Another cold drop of sweat dribbled down her spine, and her stone grew cooler. She shook her head, hoping she conveyed disbelief.

They chatted aimlessly, and when they completed their meal, Kat yawned. "You need to excuse me. I'm tired of sitting over a desk most of the day." *I've got to leave before they question me further.* "I believe I will take a hot shower to ease the kinks in my back and after, collapse into my cozy bed."

Mouse called the apprentice over and ordered an additional mug of Orenberry. "I am not tired, and I have much to discuss with Makinti about the Rifellan operations at the border keeps." He turned to Eestred. "Will you join us? You can advise me on a female point of view."

"I will. We will meet you on the morrow, Kat."

Kat nodded, left the hall, and headed up the stairs to her quarters. She locked the door behind her and packed away her writings and materials in her diplo bag. *I have to avoid Eestred's company.* She brought her robe and other clothing from the personal, now dry, and packed them in her regular luggage. She disrobed, and hung the clothing she intended to wear on the morrow, on a hook to air overnight. They included her leather uppers, a light shirt, and the same beige pants.

She packed everything else.

She put aside a light night dress, and was about to head to the personal for a hot shower when Wink fluttered to the desk and held out her foreleg.

Kat removed the tube and withdrew the message from Wynneth. It was brief. Wynneth agreed to store what Kat had sent her. Luckily, most of the words Mouse had taught her. She fed Wink and deposited her in her cage. A sense of urgency suggested to Kat she needed to return to Kaylin sooner. *What if I asked Mouse to leave now?*

She thought if she asked Mouse to leave immediately, he would be suspicious as well, if he wasn't already. She would be better to wait.

After Kat indulged herself in a lengthy soothing shower, she slathered herself in the lavender scented body lotion, donned her night dress, and sank into bed. Exhausted, she slept almost as soon as her head hit the pillow.

❋❋❋

Despite the fact she fell asleep so quickly, Kat spent a restless night, frequently waking up, plagued by worry about how the males had detected her at the Mating arena. Could she have emitted pheromones of her own?

When the birds outside began their morning songs, she gave up and rose from her bed. She completed her packing, dressed in the clothes she had put aside the night before, including her leather uppers. She piled her bags on her bed.

She was about to pull the tassel to place an order for a meal when a knock diverted her attention, and she caught her breath. "Who is it?"

"Mouse. I am here to collect you for our morning meal."

Whew. She opened the door. "Come in. I would prefer to eat my meal in my rooms. Will you join me?"

"I was under the impression we would join Makinti and Eestred."

No. How do I explain this? "Mouse they really seem to appreciate being with each other. I thought about this, and I feel we should perhaps allow them more time to be alone."

"I thought they were friends of yours?"

"Of course, they are. That's why I'm suggesting we allow them to sleep in and relax. We don't need to wait for them. Plus, I'm anxious to see the training village."

Mouse eyed her, brows narrowed, curiosity written all over his face.

"What?" Kat eyed him with a frown.

Mouse sounded suspicious. "You are acting oddly. You seem to be in a hurry to leave?"

"Oh, Mouse. You're reading reasons into nothing. I'm weary of always traveling." She yawned. "I want to complete this journey for Lord Eduardo, and go home. A delay anywhere means a delay in my return." She strode to the tassel and tugged.

"What is going on Kat? Why do you want to leave so hastily?"

"I told you, other than nasty creatures, Baklai is not intriguing. I've spent too much time visiting boring farms, and I've had quite enough of traveling on horseback. I want to go home to my own world." *Does Makinti suspect me? And does Mouse also?*

A knock, and Kat opened the door to a young apprentice. "Ah thank you. I would like a meal of your grain cereal with the red fruit, and karri-san tea." She gazed back at Mouse. "And you?"

"I will order the same, except I prefer kossil-kweth tea."

The young male bowed his head and headed down the

hallway.

Kat walked over to the dresser, picked up Wink's cage, which she fixed to her backpack. She glanced at Mouse. "Are you packed for the journey to the training village?"

"I am." He walked over to the small table and sat in one of the chairs.

"What do you believe we'll experience there?" She rolled her eyes. "Other than more horses, of course."

Mouse eyed her again. "I expect we will discover how they train their animals to be so pleasing to all who ride them."

"Yes. No doubt you are correct."

"Kat, you are not yourself. What is wrong?"

"Everything's fine." She shivered. *I should have heeded Eestred's warnings.* She asked herself if she should have contacted Eduardo to confirm this was part of her agreement.

Mouse shook his head, and opened his mouth to ask more questions, but a knock indicated their meals had arrived. He opened the door, took the tray from the young apprentice, and carried it to the table.

Kat began to eat her meal at once.

"We do not need to rush, Kat. The training village is not far and, should we leave later, we would still arrive before the mid-turn."

Despite his observations, Kat ate, and drained her tea. She gathered her luggage, and hustled him out the door.

I want to avoid Eestred and Makinti.

At his room, Kat urged him to hurry. "Get your bags, and we'll go straight to the stables."

Frowning and pushed by Kat, Mouse grabbed his small bag and the messenger bag he used for his maps. At the stables, they saddled and bridled their mounts, assisted by one stable hand. When ready, Mouse helped Kat into her saddle and scrambled up on his own horse's back.

Kat set off, with Mouse forced to follow her, trailing the animal that carried their baggage.

"You do not need to ride so fast, Kat. We do not have far to go, and it is unnecessary to tire your animal for such a short trip."

Mouse was correct. The trip was short. Not long after he spoke, Kat spotted the buildings of the training village. She gazed at the sky. It was still well before the noon-turn. This village was almost the duplicate of Eeglos. Mouse led them to what was obviously the stable, and an apprentice helped them remove the saddles and bridles from their mounts, and store them in an adjacent stall. The horses were not tired and required no grooming. Kat was too preoccupied to speak to Starlight.

When the horses were settled with water and food, the apprentice directed them to the village leader, who he said would show them to their rooms.

Kat realized Mouse was determined to spend the night, and the thought unsettled her.

Twelve rooms were on the upper floor of what resembled a long-house, similar to the one in Eeglos. On the lower floor were the dining hall and a couple of meeting rooms.

Mouse stopped beside his door. "Shall I call on you when it is time to attend the noon-turn meal?"

"That would be fine, Mouse." *No. It wouldn't be fine.* She did not want to spend the night, but what could she say to him? She rubbed at her forehead. "You know, I don't really need to see any training. I've seen horses trained before. If we left right after the meal, would we be able to reach the first Guard's unit before dark?"

Mouse frowned and peered curiously at her. "I will check the maps, and let you know."

As he entered his room, Kat unlocked her door and deposited her bags inside.

She fed Wink, and sat in a comfortable chair to settle her anxiety until Mouse came to collect her for the noon-turn. She tried to slow her heartbeat. She wondered if they suspected she was the woman who attended the Mating. She was determined to appear relaxed.

She succeeded in bringing her heart rate down and was stretching to ease her muscles, when she heard a knock. *Mouse?*

She rose and went to the door. As she suspected, it was Mouse. She joined him to head for the dining hall. When they arrived at the entrance, Kat, delighted to discover that Makinti and Eestred had not yet arrived, breathed a sigh of relief. After they were seated, Mouse pulled out a map from his bag, and Kat waited anxiously to discover if they could leave immediately after the meal.

"Kat, unfortunately, if you will view the distance of the first guard's unit from this village, you will realize we cannot arrive before it is too dark to travel."

Her heart sank. What would happen when Eestred and Makinti arrived?

She and Mouse ordered and consumed a meal, and Kat drank a substantial pot of kossil-kweth tea, which helped to calm her. She reluctantly agreed when Mouse suggested they head to the training ground to observe how the Baklai schooled their horses.

A trainer stood in a paddock, working an enormous horse. He began by walking up to the animal, approaching him from the front, and extending his knuckles, with his hand wrapped around a fruit of some kind. The horse nudged and bumped at the trainer's hand, pushing at him in an attempt to expose the fruit.

The Baklai rubbed his knuckles over the nose of the horse, and murmured inaudibly to him. Still whispering, he slid his hand down under the animal's nose and opened his fist. displaying the fragrant fruit. The horse nuzzled at the hand and delicately wrapped his lips around the fruit, mumbled it into his mouth, and chewed. The Baklai continued to murmur and, stretching up, placed his forehead on the muzzle, as if he and the animal were exchanging thoughts.

Kat stared, fascinated, as he moved closer to the creature, rubbing the shoulders and chest. She realized the trainer was gaining the confidence of the horse and would continue to do so until the animal fully accepted him.

A muscular Baklai approached the trainer and whispered to him. Both turned to stare at Kat, and her heart skipped a beat. *What now?*

At the sound of people approaching, Kat turned. Eestred and Makinti walked toward her. Their expressions were fixed and cold. *They know.*

Her stone turned icy, and her pulse hammered in her throat as the trainer, the muscular man, and three other Baklai headed toward her.

Oh God, they all know. Kat turned to hide herself somewhere … anywhere. The Baklai yelled out. "Stop her. She is a criminal. She broke the rule of a Mating." They ran toward her, and the biggest male caught hold of her arm. He growled out a threat. "It is prison for you, female."

Kat yelled and tried to pull away, sweat forming on her upper lip, when Eestred grabbed her other arm. "No. You cannot imprison her. She is under our protection."

Without warning, all was chaos. Kat's stone still lay frozen on her chest, Eestred shouted, as did the various Baklai, and the horses, startled, neighed and thrummed the ground with their massive hooves. As she tried to free herself, she searched for Mouse. *Can he help me?* She saw him on the periphery of the action, his face screwed up in horror.

In the middle of the noise and confusion, Thane Cathked rode up and bellowed for all to stop. Pointing at Kat, his lips stretched in a straight line, he growled at her, "You." His face was black with fury. "You attended a Mating in secret?" His face darkened further, and he twisted his brow in anger. "Is this the way you repay us for our courtesy toward you?"

I'm done for. They'll take Starlight. Or worse.

He swung his horse toward her and stopped inches in front of her. He hauled his bulk off his animal and stormed the few steps toward her. "You are in deep peril. The penalty for any woman viewing a Mating is a prison cell."

Prison? What else?

"What we will do with you later, we have not decided. We will hold a trial to determine if Air Wyth is your punishment, or if you should be cast into the Hyal Sea."

The sea? Kat felt a momentary stab of relief. Could she call for help from the Sha-hee?

He stomped back to his horse before issuing orders to his countrymen. "Take her away."

The men pulled her from Eestred's grasp, and dragged her off.

Kat stumbled. She tried to resist by pulling away, but a pain in her shoulder forced her to cooperate.

A trial? How will I escape them?

CHAPTER 33

Kat's heart thudded as the Baklai males frog-marched her to the home belonging to the leader of the training village. They thrust her in a windowless room and locked the door. She stumbled as she entered and kept herself upright with difficulty. The tiny dark room had a bare earth floor. In one corner sat a cot frame, with a thin straw pallet and a single folded blanket. A bucket perched in the other corner.

Kat limped over to the bed and sat, but jumped up again. This was no softened mattress prepared by the young of the straw farm but untreated stalks that protruded from the thin sack and stabbed her in every part of her body. She covered the pallet with the threadbare blanket, which helped a little.

The door handle jiggled, and a metallic click echoed through the room as it opened.

Kat, too exhausted with fear to rise, stared as Mouse entered the room. Her captors relocked the door behind him.

He came over and sat down. "Kat, what have you done?"

She swallowed, and lowered her head to conceal her face. *I will not cry. I will not cry.* "How did they find out?"

"Did it not occur to you that they would ensure their security was tight?"

She shook her head "No." She raised her eyes to him. "What are they going to do to me?"

"Eestred and Makinti, who, by the way are both furious with you, are doing their best to find a way to protect you from Cathked's wrath. I used your pyrock to send a message to Eduardo, requesting ideas on how we may aid your defense."

Kat started at the mention of Wink. "I forgot all about her. Is she OK?"

"Do not worry about Wink. I took extreme care not to touch her, and I fed her by simply leaving food on the desk near her. I will make sure she is taken care of."

"Cathked mentioned a trial."

"Yes, but this will take place two turns hence. He is allowing time for witnesses and for those who wish to defend you, to arrive here."

"I am terrified, Mouse. I don't want to die. I don't want to believe they will really follow through with a death penalty."

"I cannot believe you thought the Baklai are not deadly serious about their rules." He cleared his throat. "Many do support you, Kat. We will do all we can to save you." He shook his head. "Not because you are innocent of the charges, but because we suspect you, as usual, acted upon your instincts without thought to the consequences."

He gazed around the room. "This cell will be cold at night, so I will attempt to send your robe to you so you may keep warm. It will also make lying on this cot more comfortable." He patted her hand. "We may not be able to give you luxuries, but at least we will give you some comfort." He shook his head. "I hoped I was wrong, but I suspected you were the woman who broke the rules about the Mating."

"Thank you." She swallowed again, wanting desperately to scream at the situation she caused. "I am sorry, Mouse. I hope I didn't cause you problems as well."

"Only that Eduardo will be displeased that I have failed to protect you from yourself." He sighed. "I am angry, but more at myself than you. We have traveled together long enough that I should be aware of your tendency to ignore rules, and that you often act without considering the results."

Kat hung her head.

Mouse rose. "I will visit you each turn to make sure you are receiving adequate food and drink. On the third turn, you will be taken to the large hall in this village to stand trial, and I will accompany you as your trial representative."

Kat, unable to speak because she was so grateful to Mouse for standing by her, simply nodded.

He walked to the door and rattled the handle to be allowed to exit.

❋❋❋

In the evening, the males brought Kat a meal and water to drink. Mouse accompanied them and gave her the robe.

Kat quickly undid her Rifellan leather uppers and handed them to him. "Leathers are too uncomfortable to sleep in, so can you please place this with the rest of my baggage?"

He nodded. "These men have brought you food and drink. Is it adequate?"

"I'm not hungry."

"You must eat, Kat. You need to keep your strength up."

"I will try." Overcome by the sensation of being trapped in a treacle-like cloud of black mist, Kat trembled. "Waiting for the trial is intolerable. You have been my only visitor. Am I a pariah now?"

He sighed. "No, Kat. No one but I am permitted to visit, because I am your trial representative."

The two Baklai males who delivered her meal stood waiting for Mouse to leave with them.

"You are not forgotten. We are working on your defense." He stood to leave with the Baklai males, and turned back to nod at her when he reached the door.

Kat tried to eat some of the food, but gagged on it, and

instead, drank deeply of the water provided. She pulled the robe over her head and wrapped herself in its folds, lay down on the cot on top of the thin blanket and tried to sleep.

❋❋❋

For two turns, Kat ate, drank water and met with Mouse briefly each time he came. He quizzed her about her reasons for secretly visiting the Mating arena and about her home world, in an attempt to build a case to help her. His questions urged her to consider her reasons. Did she ignore another culture's customs because she considered only her own desires? Did she use Eduardo's assignment as a reason to satisfy her own curiosity? *Have I disrespected the Baklai?* Most of the time she slept, wrapped in her robe.

Disturbing dream-like visions of trudging through barren lands, searching for an escape, caused her to toss and turn. Sometimes she relived her drowning in the sea when she visited Glowen. Each time she woke sweating, her heart pounding and her mouth dry. Depression began to overtake her, and she slept longer and longer, hoping to avoid thinking about her life or possibly her death.

On the morning of the third turn, two Baklai women entered her cell with warm water, a washcloth, a towel, and a fresh set of clothing. They helped her remove her robe, shook it out, and hung it on a hook while she washed herself. One of the women removed some clean smelling lotion from her pocket and handed it to Kat to smooth over her skin. Finally, she donned her clean clothes and put on her robe again. Kat was so grateful to be clean and refreshed, she burst into tears.

Neither of the women showed any emotion, and Kat gained control of herself and dried her eyes.

The women left, and Mouse entered holding her Rifellan leathers. She mouthed a silent thank you, handed her robe to him, and donned the leathers. He stood beside her as four Baklai males arrived to escort her to the trial arena.

Kat entered the huge hall, flanked by the four Baklai. At least they were no longer physically holding her, and she did her best to hold herself tall. Mouse walked beside her.

The inside of the hall was paneled in wood, burnished to a sheen of light sienna. Set out were a number of chairs, upon which sat Baklai males and females, and the first two rows of chairs contained people she recognized. She suspected they were the witnesses for and against her. Two tables, each with two chairs stood in front of the crowd. Mouse moved to the table on the left, and she saw Hunter Master Galakis seated at the table on the right.

A raised platform at the front of the room appeared reserved for Cathked. To his right, on the level with the rest of the spectators and witnesses, sat a Baklai female, table in front of her, equipped with parchment and writing materials. Kat guessed she sat at the front to record the proceedings.

The males conducted her to the seat beside Mouse.

She gazed around at the makeshift courtroom. Her heart thumped. She was really on trial.

The female recorder stood and motioned for all to stand. "Please rise for Thane Cathked."

All rose, and the Thane strode into the hall, and seated himself at the raised platform. The recorder motioned for all to return to their seats.

A knife with a heavy hilt lay on the table in front of Cathked. With a dark glowering expression on his face, he hammered it on the wooden table in front of him. "We are here to judge the guilt or innocence of Lady Kat. Hunter Master Galakis, please read out the charges against this female."

Kat shivered at the scowl wrinkling his forehead.

Galakis stood, and bowed to Cathked. "Thane Cathked, the Lady Kat is charged with unlawfully making her way in secret to view a Mating in the arena at Eeglos. By doing this, she broke the most sacred rule which disallows women to view such an act." He cleared his throat. "The penalty for this transgression is serious and demands either banishment or death. We will present to you, Thane Cathked, witnesses, before you rule on the case.

Kat gulped and turned to Mouse, narrowing her eyes.

He placed a cool hand on her arm, and murmured. "Show no fear or any other emotion. Nothing is carved in stone as yet."

"My Thane, we call Horse Master Penabon as our first witness."

Penabon stepped to the front of the room and, when questioned by Galakis, he said the males from the Mating arena told of a disruption by a woman. He further testified that when they gave him the limited description, he suspected Kat, because to his knowledge, she was the only one who possessed a brown robe.

Cathked glared at Kat.

Galakis asked how the males recognized that a woman hid in the arena. Penabon suggested they question Fraglan, the leader of the Mating crew.

Penabon returned to his seat, and Fraglan stepped to the front and advised the crowd he had inhaled the scent of a female. He further noted, as soon as he announced what he had detected, a female ran from the building and disappeared. He advised they immediately worked their way from the arena and, when finding no person nearby, headed for the visitors' rooms. However, once in the long-hut building, they detected neither the odor of the Mating arena nor of any female who had recently attended that building. At that moment, they were unsure of where the woman had fled.

Cathked stroked his chin and peered at Kat with interest.

Galakis next called Makinti, who testified Kat was indeed the only person he knew who was the possessor of a brown robe. After discussion with a number of the males of Eeglos, he admitted his only conclusion must be that Kat was the woman who had breached the sanctity of the Mating arena.

Galakis then called Kerdinon to the front of the room.

Cathked's mate advised him she was positive Kat knew that she would not be able to attend a Mating, and by breaking the Baklai rules, she should be given the maximum penalty. "The female is obviously a liar and flouts our land's rules."

At her words, Kat stiffened and grabbed Mouse's arm.

Cathked startled, it appeared, by the testimony, stared at Kerdinon, and then turned to glare at Kat.

Although Mouse was able to ask questions of all the witnesses, he had not examined any of the previous ones, but rose to question Kerdinon.

He bowed to her. "Lady Kerdinon, what convinced you that Lady Kat was aware of the penalties of attending a mating?"

"I overheard some of the other females advising her."

Mouse thanked her and returned to his seat.

Kat whispered to him. "She's lying. She was nowhere near me when I was told about the rules."

He murmured to her from the side of his mouth. "But we cannot prove it."

Cathked banged the hilt of his dagger on the wood and rose, and the entire hall rose as well. "We will take a recess for the noon-turn refreshment and return here afterwards for

Lady Kat's representative, Sire Mouse, to present her side of the trial."

He glared at both Kat and her council.

The four Baklai stepped forward to escort Kat back to her cell. Mouse followed. "Kat, while we eat, we will need to discuss what occurred thus far and decide on the best way to defend you."

What can I possibly have as a defense?

CHAPTER 34

Back in her cell, she and Mouse discussed her defense over their noon-turn meal. "Mouse, Kerdinon was lying. She was never around when anyone discussed the rules of the Mating ceremony. I cannot understand why, but for some reason she disliked me from the first time I met her."

He frowned at her.

"I was polite and used all the honorifics, but she was rude to me, so much so, other women at the Dinerth were aware of her dislike of me."

Mouse shook his head. "We might never understand why she shows such antipathy toward you. However, the damage is done, and hopefully we must find enough positive thoughts from our witnesses about you for the Thane to overlook her damning words. Let us not forget, you did know about the rules." He rubbed his jaw. "I believe we should take the chance of allowing you to be your own witness. No one can explain why you always act in a certain way better than you can. Remember to present your actions as they might benefit the Baklai."

"I will do my best. I hope Cathked will deign to hear me out."

"He will listen. You will be acting as a witness, and he needs all the information possible to decide on your guilt or innocence."

Keys jangled in the lock, the door opened, and the four Baklai returned to escort her to the trial.

❁❁❁

Back in the arena with all seated, Mouse rose and called his first witness. Gayzella, the woman with whom Kat toured the spice and tea gardens, rose to provide a character witness. She reminded the Thane how Kat had suggested a new way to expand the Baklai sales outside their land. She said she was convinced Kat had the good of Baklai in mind in her various actions.

When she stepped down, she was replaced by Grayseen, the Master Hunter's bond Mate. She assured the Thane she had found Kat to be an intelligent woman, who valued horses and who, she was sure, had never intended to insult the Baklai by her actions.

Cathked showed no emotion to any of the testimony, but he did lean forward when Eestred stepped up.

Kat clutched at Mouse and leaned toward him. "Cathked is definitely not sympathetic."

Eestred reminded the Thane that Kat was herself a horsewoman, and a warrior, similar to most Rifellan women. She said she and Kat had discussions about how Kat, in her younger years, had helped with horses on her own world.

She also told Cathked that Kat was familiar with mating between horses in the wild. Eestred testified that Kat was incredibly curious about Matings on Baklai and why they were so secretive. She conveyed that Kat felt by attending the Mating, she might learn about additional dealings about horse coupling that she could take back to her own world.

Eestred's mate, Makinti, indicated that Kat was an accomplished horsewoman, similar to those in Rifella.

Layleene, when called to the front, told the Thane she had found Kat to be an honorable woman. Although she made errors, they were usually because of lack of understanding, not through any desire to cause problems.

Mouse stood and addressed Cathked and advised him that while he had journeyed with Kat through five lands, he had found her odd viewpoint often contained much sense, and thus she would be his last witness.

Cathked frowned and admitted this was unusual, and as such, he would question her.

When called upon, Kat stood almost directly in front of Cathked so he would be able to question her while watching her face. The Thane was direct in his enquiries. "Why, Lady Kat, were you so obsessed with viewing a Mating?"

Kat shook her head, and spread her hands in a pleading gesture. "If I might speculate, Thane Cathked. My visit here is replete with strange happenings around horses. Someone killed my own horse, and although your advisors discovered whoever cut her throat performed an act of mercy, I am convinced she was murdered. But who forced her to breathe in the chaff, which appears was the real cause of her death? Who did this and why?"

Cathked raised an eyebrow, but nodded his head.

She took a deep breath. "For some reason, a hissar appeared close to the primary branch of the Farralawn River, where they never appeared before. How and why? So many strange happenings seem to revolve around horses. Is it possible some of these happenings lie at the door of the Mordens? I was worried that the Mating Ritual held clues, or perhaps indications of unseen danger."

Cathked's eyes widened, and blinked.

She stared directly at him. "It astonished me to discover the extent to which your males avoid letting females understand the specifics of horses mating. I was unable to resist viewing the Mating, even though I realized what the consequences could be. Why would you hide this from your females?"

Cathked raised an eyebrow. "Many things exist which females do that we males are not privy to."

"Perhaps they are keeping a measure of power for themselves because you prevent them from knowing about horses."

Cathked frowned. "I admit the males are totally fixated on their horses, but they are dedicated to their jobs with them."

"I understand, my Thane. However, many males are delighted to be involved in growing things when they are guided by the females to do so." She held out her hands. "Might some females appreciate being involved in horses? I do realize most of the females do not show that sort of interest."

Cathked frowned. "Go on."

"Are there not some men who would enjoy being involved in commerce other than horses? Rifellan warrior women are all most attached to their horses and are interested in every part of their welfare. Only in Baklai are they required to relinquish the health and care of their own horses to your males."

Cathked stared at her, unblinking. "Do you wish to add anything more?"

"Yes. I am beginning to understand why Eduardo sent me on this journey. I never understood this before, and for some time I thought he was punishing me. Might he have sent me because I can view the lives of those on Pridden with a different viewpoint? I worry, my Thane, that because your males and females keep secrets from each other, that this might prove a weakness in the future. When I decided to break a Baklai rule, for which I now apologize, I wondered if this was part of the challenges Eduardo requested that I examine."

She cleared her throat. "If the males and the females were each represented by a single stick, those sticks are easy to break. Bind them together, and they are stronger."

Cathked sat back in his seat and stared at her, eyebrows raised and questions in his eyes. "Your words about our land are certainly different, and many things you say do make sense. One more question, Lady Kat. Did viewing the Mating supply you with the answers you sought?"

Kat lowered her head. "No, it did not, my Thane. I must admit I was more than wildly curious. I was concerned there was something quite dangerous about your ritual. Maybe I was not intended to satisfy the extreme curiosity I felt. Whatever the reason, this discussion with you is a result. That may be reason enough. Whatever I did, I apologize for breaking this Baklai rule. I do not believe I ever realized how important this was to your land. I now see that the Baklai seem to view this as a sacred ceremony."

Cathked shook his head. and stared at her again, a puzzled expression on his face. He cleared his throat and banged the hilt of his blade on the wood. "Do you, Sire Mouse, wish to say anything further in your summation?"

"I do my Thane. I am well aware Lady Kat's knowledge of horses is equal to many males, and I believe her testimony is truthful and that her sin was curiosity and perhaps some hint of fear. She comes from a world much different from Baklai. Haydar found her behavior strange for a female, particularly those from Kaylin. But he trusted her enough to give her a horse. My Lord Eduardo trusted her enough to suggest she visit all of Pridden so she would understand the people of the lands."

"What you say is true. However, her transgression with Baklai protocol is serious."

"My Thane, during our journey, Lady Kat often made what appeared to be errors, to my increasing dismay. However, I am beginning to look at those errors from a different viewpoint and realize she uncovered oddities that might not have been beneficial to the people of the lands in which she travelled, and thus they caused changes for the better."

Cathked nodded at him, and rose, as did everyone in the hall. "I have heard all that has been spoken in this place, and we will rest for the balance of this turn. I will give much thought to this, and we will meet on the morrow after the morning meal for my decision."

He left the hall.

❋❋❋

Escorted back to her cell, Kat waited for a meal and the appearance of Mouse. He walked in with the males bringing her meal. "You did well. I do believe your words made an impression on the Thane."

"Do you truly think so?"

"I contacted Eduardo, as I told you, and asked for suggestions from him. It was he who told me to allow you to testify on your own behalf." Mouse nodded to himself. "Eduardo is an astute leader."

Mouse handed her the robe, and took her leathers with him when he left.

Kat donned her robe, wrapped herself in it folds, and lay down on her cot, too caught up in thoughts to eat.

I hope ... I hope.

CHAPTER 35

Kat woke during the night, her stomach grumbling with hunger. The globe in the cell emitted only a faint light, and she was barely able to see the meal from the night before, which still stood on the small table her captors allowed her. Insects with multiple legs and hard shells crawled over the food but avoided the journeyklim that rested on a separate plate. Shaking a piece of the bread-like klim to ensure no creepy crawlies clung to it, she swallowed some and drank from the canteen.

Is Mouse correct? Did Cathked find my words logical?

She moved the small table away from the cot, wrapped her robe around herself and lay down again, determined to sleep some more. She had to be alert on the morrow. She yawned, tossed a few times, and finally tried to meditate.

❋❋❋

The metallic click of a key in the lock roused her, and the males guarding her entered with a fresh meal. They removed the insect-ridden plate from the evening before.

As the guards exited the cell, two females bearing water, soap, and a towel entered. Mouse followed them in, holding her leathers, which he placed on the cot and turned his back to her. Dressed in only a minimum of underwear, Kat eagerly washed as much of herself as she could reach. Once dried with the small towel, she donned the leathers. She cleared her throat, and Mouse faced back toward her.

She handed him her robe, which she knew he would return to her room. “Thanks, Mouse.”

The women left, taking the washing supplies with them.

Mouse waited until the clank of keys indicated the door had been locked. He waved Kat toward the cot and he sat beside her. “Did you sleep well?”

“I am well rested. But I am anxious.”

“I urge you to keep calm outwardly. We will shortly be called to enter the hall to wait for Cathked to hand down his decision. As I mentioned the previous turn, you made a fine impression. However, he cannot find you totally innocent. He must extract some form of retribution for your actions. His people would stand for nothing less.” Mouse stood and paced around the cell. “Whatever his decision, Kat, you must accept this with good grace, or at least appear to. Some form of punishment must be given to you. Can you keep your temper, no matter what the circumstances?”

“If I can avoid Air Wyth or drowning or any other kind of death, I will be relieved, and I will behave with propriety.”

Mouse smiled at her. “It will serve you well.” He sat again. “Now eat.”

Kat ate as much as her stomach would hold and drank more water. She and Mouse sat in silence, each immersed in their own thoughts.

At last, the click of metal on metal, and the door opened. The four Baklai males assigned to escort her to the hall, stood waiting for her. Mouse preceded them from the cell, and Kat followed, flanked by the males.

The hall, filled with spectators murmuring to each other, appeared more crowded than the turn before. They ceased talking when Kat appeared. She made her way to the table she had occupied before and sat in the chair beside Mouse.

Galakis rose from his seat, and all within the hall stood. From the doorway behind the dais, Cathked appeared, carrying a leather case. He walked toward his chair, seated himself, and motioned for all to sit. He thumped the wood in front of him with the hilt of his blade. "I am calling this session of the trial to order."

Kat's chest emitted a thump from deep within. The silence seemed acute. She held her breath.

Cathked hammered on the wooden table top again. "I spent much time considering all the facts of this trial. I also read the notes written by my aide." He gestured at the woman below him and off to the side. "I found this a most difficult decision."

He removed a parchment from the case he brought to the hall. "Much of what Lady Kat spoke about was logical and certainly presented a different point of view." He straightened in the chair. "However, while it appears to me her actions were not truly a deliberate flouting of our rules, nevertheless, she did break them. I decided that, while she does not deserve banishment or death, and despite the fact our ways may change in the future, she still broke a stringent rule of the Baklai."

He stared at her. "Lady Kat, please approach."

Kat stood and walked toward the platform, and faced Cathked.

He stared severely down at her. "I have decided, after much discussion with my advisors, that you may continue on your journey. Frankly, we would prefer you depart Baklai at the earliest possible time."

A buzz ran through the hall.

He thumped the table-top with his blade again. "However, we need you to be monitored continually until you depart our land, which should be in a few turns. To this end, we will assign you an observer who will view you closely until you cross the bridge into Morden. This observer will be with you constantly and will accompany you everywhere. Each night, he will lock you in your room." He stared down at Kat again. "All your actions and words during this period will be closely observed and controlled." He glared at her. "But do not for one moment think, Kat, that you will escape totally unscathed. You seem to be more than curious about horses, and you suggest that females should be more involved in their care."

Kat swallowed. *Uh oh.*

His grin was feral this time. "We will allow you the opportunity to prove this to us. Until you leave Baklai, you will work as a stable hand. Your task will be to feed, water, and groom all animals brought to the stables where you are located. You will do this without help from any of my men. You will no longer be considered a visiting Lady, but only a common stable hand. Do you understand this?"

Kat gulped. "I do, my Thane."

A triumphant spark lit up his eyes, and he banged the table top again. "I have always encouraged the citizens of Baklai to express themselves to me. Thus, I ask, does anyone disagree violently with this punishment?"

Kat turned and looked at the audience. Heads shook, and no outcry came from any person. Her shoulders relaxed, and she breathed out in relief, particularly when she saw a number of the women who smiled and nodded at her.

Cathked raised his eyebrow at her. "Remember Kat, your movement in our land will be controlled and under close scrutiny during the balance of your visit to Baklai. Do your work and prove you are worthy to work with and care for horses." He turned to the rest of the spectators. "This trial is now concluded." He rose and left the hall.

Makinti approached Kat accompanied by Eestred, who hugged her. “We were so furious with you about taking such a stupid risk, and so worried the Thane would demand that you pay the ultimate price for what you did. I cannot believe he was so lenient. I have always admired his leadership, but now, more so. Something you said must have been of great importance to him.”

Kat frowned slightly. “Lenient? I suspect the work he demands will not feel lenient when I have to take care of all these horses. At least though he did not banish me or demand my death.” She rubbed at her forehead. “I don’t know what he felt about my words, but I do wonder what he thought when his own mate demanded I be banished.”

Eestred laughed. “He is smitten by her. He would accept anything she says. I suspect that your words and the logic with which you presented them were the reason he found in your favor.”

Kat glanced around the hall, and caught Kerdinon glaring in her direction. “If he is so smitten by her and she knows it, why did she ignore my punishment? Why didn’t she ask for a stronger sentence from him? I didn’t change Kerdinon’s mind about me.”

Eestred swiveled her head to gaze at the woman in question. “No, you did not. Her murderous expression clearly indicates she hates you. I suspect though she enjoys the thought of you laboring in the stables. To be treated as a stable hand most likely indicates a serious fall from grace. The Baklai are formal people and she thinks you would be devastated by the loss of the term Lady.” Eestred grinned. “She has no idea you prefer not to be addressed as such. Still, I wonder why she exhibits so much animosity toward you.”

Kat frowned. “Who knows.”

Makinti stepped closer to Kat. "Despite the fact I was so angry with you breaking such a sacred rule, my apologies for the need to testify against you. I would not lie about what I believed I witnessed."

"Makinti, you told the truth. No one should ask for more than that." She hugged him, and he stepped back startled. "Please pardon me. I am not in Rifellan thrall. I am so grateful I have you and Eestred as friends."

A man appeared at Kat's side. He bowed. "Lady Kat, I am Kesiad. I will be accompanying you for the balance of your journey in Baklai."

"The Thane did advise me of this. And Kesiad, you cannot call me Lady."

"My thanks for the reminder."

"I am not sure what I should do next."

"Thane Cathked is in this village to watch his new horse being trained. His current animal is aging, and will soon be retired and put to pasture in the enclosed area surrounding the Keep. He has not indicated that you may not attend the training. Would you wish to view it?"

"Will any of this training be held after the noon-turn?"

He nodded.

"Thank you. I would like to attend." She was curious if this would afford her more time to learn why Cathked had made this decision about her fate. She turned to Mouse. "We will be departing this village on the morrow after our morning meal, will we not?"

"I see no need to remain longer."

Kat faced Kesiad again. "Do we need to tell you ahead of time when we are leaving."

Kesiad grinned. "No, my ... er Kat. I will always be aware of your departure because I control when you are allowed to leave your room."

Kat's gazed at him, soured by his words. "Oh yes. I almost forgot. You will also need to release me when I am required to take care of horses in the stables." She sighed. "Well, it is the noon-turn, and I'm hungry. I guess you'll be accompanying us to the dining hall."

Eestred stepped up to Kat for one more hug. "We must leave you. Makinti needs to head directly for the Border Keep, where many chores await him. Keep safe, Kat."

❋❋❋

After the meal, Kat, her monitor, and Mouse headed for the training ground. Standing at the fence of the actual training ring were Cathked and his mate, Kerdinon.

Kat stood next to Cathked, and Kerdinon shot dagger glares at her. Kat cleared her throat to attract the Thane's attention. "Hunter Cathked, I wish to thank you for your willingness to listen to my explanation of my behavior. I am so sorry I caused you such challenges, but I do now understand why your people refer to you as Hunter."

Kat saw the faint smile and the glint of pride in his eyes.

"You are skilled in flattery, Kat. Understand, I did not make my decision because of pity. Much of what you said was logical and sensible. Many discussions will occur among my close advisors about your words, long after you have departed Baklai. You taught us new ways to view people. I shall remember these lessons."

She smiled at him and moved away from him to join Mouse further along the fence, and Kesiad moved with her.

The three of them viewed the training of the Thane's new horse in silence. The instruction was similar to what Kat had seen when they first arrived in the village.

At last, Kat announced to the two males, "I'm going to

retire to my room and pack my belongings. I'm looking forward to continuing our journey along the east Farralawn River. Mouse, I'm going to order a light evening meal in my quarters. I need to regain my sense of focus. Can we meet on the morrow for our morning meal? And, after eating, can we leave for the Guards' unit? This is where the first bridge to Morden is located, is it not?"

Mouse smiled at her. "It is. I also will eat a meal in my room. We have spent a few challenging and stressful days."

They left the fence, and strolled toward the long-house, and Kesiad accompanied Kat to her room and double-locked her door. The arrangement of the locks fascinated Kat. Two locks were on the door, one that Kat's key worked, the other only locked the entrance from the outside. Once inside, Kat was unable to leave, and Kesiad couldn't enter because of the lock on the interior, which she controlled.

In her room, Kat fed Wink, who uttered a hungry squeak. She packed all her clothing except those she would be wearing the following turn.

She removed her writing materials from the diplo bag, and settled to record the Mating, the happenings of her trial, and Cathked's subsequent decision.

She completed her writing and tugged the tassel. Kesiad allowed the apprentice to enter, and she ordered the recommended meal and a substantial pot of karri-san tea. When it arrived, Kesiad again allowed the young male apprentice entrance.

While not extremely hungry, she finished off her meal, and then sat silently, drinking her tea and meditating on her good fortune to be allowed to continue her journey in Baklai.

Kat yawned and readied herself for bed. After indulging in a hot shower, she slathered herself with lotion and slipped under the cozy covers. The last thing she thought about as she sank among the comfortable folds of her mattress, was how well all had turned out.

I told Cathked the truth. Thank Caleesh he listened.

CHAPTER 36

A bright beam of sunlight woke Kat the following turn, and she slipped out of bed and walked over to the window. Leaning out, she breathed in the clean, green scent of dawn, mixed with the faint tang of horses.

She chuckled to herself. *They never considered I could sneak out the window, or send secret messages.* She shook her head. She would not consider doing so, given the circumstances. *They let me off so lightly.* Following Cathked's directorate was worth having her freedom.

She fed Wink, washed, dressed, and set her bags on the bed. With everything ready, she plonked herself in the padded armchair and waited for Kesiad and Mouse to collect her for the morning meal.

Mentally, she reviewed the route they would take to enter Morden—the Guard building at the first bridge, then the resting hut, and finally the guards' Border Keep at the second bridge over the east branch of the Farralawn. She estimated three or four turns at the most.

The jangle of keys and the click of the lock and finally a knock indicated Mouse had arrived. She rose and opened the door.

"Good morrow, Kesiad. Mouse. I'm ready for my meal."

The three set off along the hall, and down the stairs to the dining center. When they entered, Kesiad directed them to a table for six, and summoned the apprentice to take their orders.

Kat eyed her observer. "Kesiad, are you expecting someone else?"

"Healer Caleth and his mate, Layleene, advised they would like to join you for the morning meal."

He no sooner finished speaking when the two healers appeared at the entrance to the hall.

Mouse waved at them to join their party, and they hurried over.

Caleth smiled at Kat. "You appear less stressed than when I last met with you, Lad … er, Kat."

"I am. However, I realize I must admit I am solely responsible for many of the challenges I encountered. I'm sure Mouse would say I should be more thoughtful before I act." She saw Mouse raising his eyebrows and nodding in her direction. She rolled her eyes at him.

Puzzled, Kat asked the healers if they were both headed for the Border Keep.

Layleene smiled at her. "Caleth always accompanies Thane Cathked when he travels through Baklai on his once-per-path inspection. He will leave this place on the morrow, but I will return to the Thane's Keep." She patted Kat on the arm. "I only attended the training ground village for the trial."

"Thank you. The number of females who attended and who told me they supported me gave me such hope. Baklai females are amazing."

"Kat, in my experience, females are amazing in all the lands."

Kat laughed.

Once their meals arrived, the four friends chatted about all that occurred during the preceding three turns.

Kesiad said little, but he watched the others with interest.

Mouse rose and suggested he and Kat should set out for

the Guards' unit at the chasm end of the Farralawn's eastern branch.

❋❋❋

Mouse and Kesiad followed Kat to the stables where she prepared their horses for the journey. They tried to object, but Kat reminded them this was Cathked's order. She did gratefully accept their help with the saddling

Kat took the opportunity to feed and water the other horses in the stable as part of her new duties.

"Mouse, can we allow Kesiad to make use of the baggage horse, because we truly do not need that animal any longer? The bags we each carry are small enough to fit on the back of our own saddles. What do you think?"

"An excellent idea. I planned on leaving the animal with the guards at the Border Keep, as I would prefer to journey as lightly as possible once we enter Morden." He glanced at Kesiad. "We would appreciate it if when we leave the Border Keep and cross the bridge to Morden you would request that Makinti contact Haydar in Kaylin. The horse is rightfully part of his herd to manage. I am sure Haydar would wish the animal to be returned to Kaylin."

"My thanks for the use of the horse, although Cathked told me to choose one from Penabon. However, I will follow your wishes and request that Makinti offer to return this animal to Haydar.

"We appreciate you performing this task."

Kesiad turned to Kat. "Are you ready to leave?"

Kat smiled. She enjoyed the sense of accomplishment in caring for all the horses. "I am." She searched for a stool. "I think I need help mounting Starlight. Despite the fact that Penabon considers her small, she is still many more hands than the horses I used to ride in my world."

He hurried over so she placed her foot in his cupped hands, stepped into the stirrup and hauled herself aboard Starlight. She murmured thanks to him.

Both Kesiad and Mouse stretched their legs to place their feet in their stirrups and pulled themselves up in their saddles.

The road toward the Guards' unit near the chasm bridge was wide and clear, and the three rode abreast most of the way.

As they neared the eastern branch of the Farralawn after riding for most of the morning, Kat stared in awe at the deep cliffs created by the river. Although a considerable distance lay between the sides, she glimpsed the waters roiling over boulders far below. "That's a long way down."

Mouse surveyed the scene. "The Heer River, as it nears the coastal cliffs of Morden, by the Hyal sea, is similar."

Kat peered at him. "I almost forgot. You are from Morden, aren't you?"

"I am. But I am not from this immediate area. I am considered a southern Morden." He chuckled. "Although if truth be told, I am from the north western part of Morden. All the people on the western side of the Heer are counted as southern Mordens, even those of us who live in the northern part of the land. Much about Morden is strange."

"I met many people from Morden during my journey through Pridden, and the ones called the southerners are people whose company I enjoyed. Many of the ones I encountered from the north were not pleasant."

Mouse grimaced. "That is true, Kat. Our people are much divided. This is why we must travel lightly and be wary when we journey through Morden. We will discuss this further when we stay for a couple of turns at the Border Keep."

Kesiad raised his eyebrows. "You are both definitely traveling into Morden after leaving the Border Keep, correct?"

Mouse sighed. "Yes, we are. This is part of Lord Eduardo's plan."

Kat's stomach rumbled. "Mouse we've been traveling for some distance now. How far are we from the Guards' unit?"

"We do not have too much further to go, but since you are expressing hunger, I believe we should stop for a noon-turn snack. The kitchens at the training village prepared us meals and gave each of us an extra canteen for water for our horses."

Kesiad pointed to his left. "A small clearing with a few trees and places to sit is over in that direction. Follow me."

They entered the clearing, which contained some short grass and a number of boulders, many of which had depressions carved into them.

Kesiad led his horse to one of the boulders and after removing the cap on his canteen, poured the contents into a depression in one of the rocks. He dropped the reins over the head of the horse, which he led to the rock. The creature dipped his mouth in the water and drank his fill.

Kat followed his lead, and glanced over at Mouse who was also watering his animal.

Kesiad kept an eye on his horse. "When they are finished with the water, tie them to one of the small bushes so they can crop the grass near them."

The other two did so.

Mouse retrieved two packages for him and Kat, and Kesiad brought one for himself from his saddle bag. They sat and munched in silence.

The Keep kitchen had wrapped their sandwiches in large green leaves, and once they finished their meals, they buried the foliage to leave the rest stop clean.

The three retrieved their horses and mounted them, Kat with help from Mouse. They returned to the road and continued to head for the Guards' unit.

They travelled without talking until Pridden's star lay low on the horizon, the silence only broken occasionally by the clop of a hoof on stone, or the odd snort or nicker from one of the animals.

Kesiad raised himself to stand in his stirrups and smiled. "The following bend in the road indicates we are close to the Guards' unit. We will have time to settle in our rooms before the evening meal."

Kat sighed. "At last."

Sure enough, as they rounded the bend, a fortress-like building stood in a clearing amid the stalks of grains. An edifice, built of stone and walled on all sides, had a massive gate barring the entrance. Crenelations adorned the tops of the walls, providing protection for archers firing upon any attackers.

Kesiad pointed to the battlements. "Most of those are more for show. The Mordens have never attacked us this far south. If they run into our effective force, they can find no quick escape on the Morden side of the border. The Border Keep is the one which requires the most effective security against attack."

"I trust we can sleep soundly."

Kesiad grinned. "Yes, Kat, you can."

They arrived as the entrance gate rolled up and when they entered, the guards inside directed them to a stable in the far corner of the fort.

A young man ran out to meet them. "Lady Kat, welcome, and also welcome to you, Sire Mouse." He gave Kesiad a solid punch. "I have not seen you in many a turn."

Kesiad explained to Mouse. "This is my male parent's brother's progeny. We grew up together." He murmured separately to the man. "You cannot call her Lady."

He opened his eyes wide.

Kat called to him. "Kesiad is correct. Thane Cathked has ordered all to cease referring to me as Lady."

The young male directed them to the stables, and two helpers stood ready to handle their horses.

Kat stopped them from dealing with her animal. "I must take care of these horses myself. It is what Thane Cathked has demanded."

The three young men stared at her, but stepped aside when Kesiad indicated to them her statement was true.

Kat prepared everything for Starlight, but Kesiad and Mouse handled their own animals. When she tried to stop them, Kesiad advised her that Cathked had not forbidden them to feed and water their own horses. "Sire Mouse and I are not under orders from our Thane."

"You both paid attention to his ruling at the training village."

Mouse smiled at her. "Kesiad and I discussed that our saddles are heavy, but we will allow you to provide water and fill their hay nets. The regular stable hands do not normally unsaddle or groom our horses, so this should meet with the Thane's approval."

By the time Starlight was bedded for the night, Kat had also topped up the stable hands' horses' water troughs and hay. She wiped a gritty hand across her forehead. *Did I leave a streak of dirt on my face?*

One of the young men stepped forward and handed her a rag. "Please … er … Kat, this is sufficient. If you will bring your bags, I will show you to your rooms."

Kesiad's cousin spoke to him. "We were told about your monitoring of Kat, but not about her caring for the horses." He handed Kesiad extra keys. "You will be in the room next door to Kat."

Escorted to their rooms, they left their bags and were headed gratefully to the dining hall, guided by Kesiad's cousin, when Kat halted.

"Kesiad, can you wait one minute? I must feed my pyrock."

He nodded.

Followed by her minder, Kat ran back to her room, unclipped the cage from her backpack, and put it on the desk. She extracted pyrock treats from a side pocket of the pack and popped them into Wink's waiting mouth. The little creature swallowed and dropped off to sleep again.

Kat caught sight of her sweaty face in the mirror and strode to the personal and washed and dried her face in the basin. She locked her door and followed Kesiad, his cousin, and Mouse to dine in the hall.

At the door to the hall, the cousin advised he would leave them, as he knew Kesiad was familiar with the fort.

They ordered meals and drink, and once everything arrived at their table, they sat and ate, barely conversing. Weary after their long ride, they rose, ready for their beds when a clatter of footsteps at the door attracted their attention.

Kerdinon stood, surrounded by a dozen or more personal guards. She indicated two would stay with her in the hall, and she dismissed the rest with a flick of her fingers. As she turned to occupy a table, she set her gaze on Kat.

She walked over to the three standing at their table. "You." She sniffed as if at a bad odor. "You deserve to be imprisoned for breaking our rules." She pivoted in place and headed to a table further away from Kat and her party.

Kat blinked, and she, Mouse, and Kesiad headed toward their rooms. As they walked along the hall, Kat shook her head at Mouse. "I wonder why she rode ahead of Cathked? Isn't that weird?"

Mouse frowned and twisted an eyebrow. "I am not sure weird is the best word, but it certainly is odd."

Kat stopped in the middle of the hall. "Oh no. Kerdinon and all her men just arrived. I suppose I must go to the stable and bed their horses."

Kesiad shook his head. "No. You do not need to. If any visitor arrives after dark, the stable hands will only help with water and food. Visitors must take most of the care of their mounts themselves in such cases."

"Are you sure, Kesiad? I don't wish to ignore the Thane's rules too quickly."

"I am sure, Kat. Lady Kerdinon cannot demand you service their animals this late in the turn."

"I still better make sure their horses have been fed and given water. Kerdinon was present when the Thane gave that order." She turned and left for the stables followed by Kesiad.

Mouse trailed after them, reluctance in his steps.

When they arrived, all were relieved to find the horses had plenty of water and hay in their nets. They had been unsaddled and groomed as well.

Kat breathed a sigh of relief. The three returned to the hall and entered their rooms. Kesiad locked Kat in.

Does Kerdinon being here mean more trouble?

CHAPTER 37

Ssarff sent an apprentice to summon Ssestin to his quarters. A rhythmic knock prompted him to open the door and usher his second-in-command into the room.

"Master Ssarff, how can I be of help?"

"Galdin summoned me again. I assume this time to obtain my agreement to enter Baklai and also to reveal who his ally is there." He groaned. "I need you to manage the Guild while I am absent." He flashed a grim grin at Ssestin. "Unless of course, you prefer to attend Galdin in my stead?"

Eyes open wide, and forehead twisted in horror, Ssestin held up his hands as if to fend off an enemy. "Sire, I hope you are jesting?"

"I am." He shook his head slowly, and peered at him under his brow. "However, I cannot understand why you would not be delighted to place your head in the cathnog's maw to help your master avoid danger."

Ssarff was grinning again, and Ssestin laughed. "Some things even the most loyal of assistants cannot perform."

"Were we not more than friends in addition to you being my most trusted assistant, I would not make such weak jokes."

"I am honored by our unique relationship, Master Ssarff. I have no greater desire than to act as your assistant." He gazed at his leader, a worried frown crinkling his forehead. "So Galdin called for you again?"

Ssarff nodded and grunted.

"Does he wish you to attend him soon?"

"The messenger moth mentioned the words 'at once'." Ssarff gestured to a chair. "Please sit. We should discuss the upcoming meeting. Any suggestions you might make as to how this must be handled would be most welcome."

"If I may, Sire, since this could take some time, will you be agreeable if I order tea?"

"By all means. Although I might wish to choose Orenberry wine, tea is more appropriate since we need to keep clear heads."

Ssestin walked to the corner of the room and tugged the corded tassel.

They both sat at the small table, and when the sound of a knock echoed through the room, Ssarff called out, "Enter." He ordered clear-focus tea from the apprentice.

Ssarff reached back to papers on his desk and withdrew parchment and writing implements, which he handed to Ssestin. "We should make a list of the best ideas we envisage. First though, write down the traits which we are aware Galdin does possess. Also include any rumors that exist about him." He grimaced. "Some of these may give birth to ideas on how to handle his obsession over the female called Kat."

Ssestin dipped the pen in the ink, paused, and held the pen at ready. "Master Ssarff, do you have insight as to what is occurring in Morden? Thane Galdin has always been known as a cruel man with little regard for the people. We have always been the Assassins' Guild, available for hire when someone was deemed to require dismissal from life. But all is changing."

Ssarff leaned back in his chair. "What do you see as changing about us?"

"If anyone came to us for our services, but our Guild viewed the assignment as lacking a valid reason, we refused.

We worked for Galdin a number of times and accepted his assignments because he is the Thane. Recently it appears he is acting without what I might call leadership skills."

"I tend to agree with you. Galdin all too often seems to act without wisdom. When he hired us to capture the woman Kat and eliminate Lord Rhognor, we assumed the Lord was acting foolishly. Instead, it became apparent Hesginn desired the Lady Halfin as his mate. Galdin considered this a valid reason for dispatching Rhognor, but the gentle Lady Halfin died in his stead. That was an error on my part. I have since regretted this. When we discovered the capture of the woman Kat was tied to the intended elimination of Lord Murwenna and her heir, I now believe we should have ceased working with the Thane."

"Sire, his errors in judgement about his allies seem to be increasing, and his assignments appear to be increasingly unruly. He is becoming more dangerous and more irresponsible each day."

The scratching of Ssestin's pen on the parchment held their attention until a knock indicated the arrival of their tea.

Ssestin rose to take the tray from the young apprentice and, before locking the door behind him, advised him to ensure that Ssarff should not be disturbed until the noon-turn. He poured out two substantial mugs of clear-focus, handed one to Ssarff, and placed the enormous pot on the table

Securing the second mug for himself, he sat at the table and regarded his list again. "Are you aware Master of the rumor that Galdin prefers the company of prepubescent males?"

Ssarff grimaced. "I am aware of it. Why?"

"I dislike bringing this forward, but would we avoid his reprisal if we supplied him with a present of one?"

Ssarff's mouth dropped open. "Ssestin! Such suggestion is beyond the pale. I cannot believe you uttered those words."

Ssestin hung his head. "Neither can I, Master Ssarff. Desperation sometimes utters words of desperation."

"To give him a young male? If your son was as young as those he is said to prefer, would you present him to Galdin?"

"Please Sire. Please forget I said that. Such a thought causes my skin to wish it could creep from my body."

"It should. We all fear the direction Galdin is pursuing. He becomes a more dangerous individual daily. All Morden is in a state of despair. I know you too well, Ssestin. I am convinced you would never truly consider such a vile action."

"What if you attempted something totally different?"

"Such as?"

"When Galdin offers you a pre-payment, is it possible you might refuse it and tell him because of your failure to bring the woman to him previously, you will forgo an upfront fee this time. If you do not accept his coin and you fail again, he can hardly fault you."

Ssarff stroked his chin. "I hate to admit previous failures, but it was due to Galdin's lack of success by his supposed allies that we were never able to deliver Kat to him before this."

"Perhaps you should advise him the previous failures were because his allies betrayed him. I suspect that would turn his anger against them and away from our Guild.

Ssarff smiled. "Excellent. I do believe your suggestion is a valid solution. You have also exonerated yourself for your previous suggestion." He gulped the rest of the tea in his mug.

Ssestin bowed his head. "My thanks. I assume you will

not capture the Lady Kat for Galdin?"

"You have already made a case that we should protect this Kat from Galdin rather than assist him in capturing her. I also believe the woman will be of advantage to us in the coming turns."

"It certainly seems that Galdin is so obsessed by needing her to defeat Lord Eduardo that all of Pridden may be safer if he is foiled in this endeavor."

"Ssestin, I will gather everything I need for the trip. Will you please make sure my horse is saddled and fed and send two of the best Assassins to shadow me to Galdin's Keep? I will attempt to arrive between meal times, so I will not be required to stay for any length."

"And I, Master, will advise the same two males to accompany you as before, since they are familiar with the route."

"Fine. Request the kitchen to prepare at least three meals for me and the two Assassins so we will not need to stop often, unless our horses require it."

"Yes, Sire." Ssestin bowed his head and left the quarters.

❁❁❁

Shortly before the noon-turn meal, Ssarff and the two Assassins rode out from the Guild, with the Master remaining on the west side of the Heer. The Assassins crossed the Heer and traveled through the forests. Their minimal abilities with magic were sufficient to shadow Ssarff from across the river.

After the noon-turn, Ssarff stopped briefly beside a riverside pool of the Heer to water his horse. He ate his meal, and drank from his canteen, which he refilled from the pool.

He continued to ride, carefully enough to spare his horse. By the time Pridden's star began to dip below the horizon, Ssarff had watered his animal, and crossed the Heer to rest for a short time inside one of the doos or forests. The closest, the Skinya-Doo, supplied him with needed concealment. He attached the reins of his horse to a small tree to allow it to graze, and then cut branches of leaves to act as bedding. Finally, he wrapped his robe around him and sank on the branches to rest briefly. Calming his mind, he set his internal clock to wake him well before dawn.

Ssarff opened his eyes, wide awake after his refreshing nap, rose from his bed of branches, and shook out his robe. He listened carefully, not able to see his shadows, but mentally aware of them deeper in the forest. He scattered the branches of leaves to obscure the traces of his journey. A quick drink from his canteen, and he mounted his horse, also refreshed from the short rest. He headed back across the Heer, leaving the protection of the Doo, to continue his journey through grasslands. Taking his respite in the confines of the forest gave him confidence he was alone except for his Assassins, who shadowed him from among the trees.

He stopped briefly for a noon-turn meal and watered his horse. On the following turn, as Pridden's star rose full in the sky, he approached the gates of Galdin's Keep. Galdin's guards recognized the powerful leader of the Assassins' Guild and admitted him. "Thane Galdin awaits you in his reception area, Guild Master."

"My thanks for the information. Would you see that my horse is fed and watered? You will not need to remove his saddle, as I will not be long with the Thane."

***

The two Assassins, followed the same route as last time they accompanied Ssarff to the Thane's Keep, and on the morning of the second turn, waited under cover for their leader to appear.

❁❁❁

Galdin, as usual, hooded and glowering, waved the Master Assassin to sit. "I confirmed a contact for you in Baklai. My ally in Baklai is a female named Kerdinon, who is the bonded mate of Cathked."

Ssarff's brows climbed up his forehead. "The Thane's mate? Are you sure you can trust her?"

Galdin's smirk was secretive and oily. "She is not happy in her current position and is an ambitious and calculating woman. Her male parent haled from Morden, while her female parent birthed in Baklai. She wishes to rule Baklai and requested my help to remove Cathked from his Thaneship." He laughed. "She also suggested we should bond and rule both Baklai and Morden together. She is convinced that in this way, we would gain control of the horses in Pridden, which would ensure our power. Naturally I did not disavow any intent to bond. Although, I doubt I could ever trust the woman."

Ssarff, horrified by the possibility, remained outwardly calm. "Do I gather, Thane Galdin, you wish us to seek out Kerdinon and work with her to capture the woman you wish to use?"

"Indeed, and you will be aided by the personal army she brings with her, a mix of Morden and Baklai males. Furthermore, I will send a small contingent of my own guards." Galdin rose from his chair and asked Ssarff to follow him. "Come. I will take you to my Coin Master, and he will provide you with a first payment for the capture of the woman."

"Wait, Thane Galdin. Your initial payments were always most generous, but due to the failure on the part of your allies, we have not been able to complete any of your previous requests." *Does he realize I have not yet agreed to the task?* "We feel in the interest of a successful mutual business, we will waive the advance payment and only require compensation when the mission is completed successfully."

Galdin's eyebrows raised. "That is most generous and unexpected of the Guild, Ssarff. I accept with thanks."

"You are most welcome, my Thane. I must leave you immediately so I can make arrangements for us all to gather at the appropriate place in Baklai. I must ready my Assassins." He suspected Galdin would be incensed when he discovered that no contract existed between himself and the Assassins. Ssarff chuckled internally. The official coin was, after all, Galdin's own rule. All assignments had to be sworn to and confirmed with the exchange of a single coin. Actually providing a partial pre-payment was strictly an option.

He departed the Thane's Keep as fast as he was able and, in less than half a turn, crossed the Heer and rode into the Skinya-Doo to meet with his Assassins at their previously arranged rendezvous point.

The two males greeted him. "Master Ssarff, our horses have only rested briefly. We suggest we walk the horses to the upper end of the Merga and spend the balance of the night camped among the trees. We should travel the length of the Merga-Doo in the predawn, cross the Heer River and ride directly for the Guild. We suggest we travel while the star is risen and be able to arrive at our Keep prior to the darkening of the sky."

"I agree. My discussion with the Thane was complicated, and if he fully understands what I did, we will be safer within the confines of the forests."

❋❋❋

The three men exited the Skinya-Doo as the star sank below the horizon, and when they entered the Merga, the forest to the south, they stopped, exhausted, having been without sleep for nearly two turns. They watered their horses at a pool immediately inside the forest, and tied their reins to bushes to allow the animals to crop the grasses.

Settling their saddles on the ground as pillows, they cut leafy branches to cushion the sleeping area. The two Assassins set traps for the small animals of the forest, and all three wrapped themselves in their cloaks, lay down, and fell asleep. They decided against keeping watch, because this forest's reputation was one of being benign. The Thane would wait to hear about the results of the raid by Kerdinon and the Assassins before he pursued anything further.

The following morrow all woke as dawn displayed her palette of blues, golds, and pinks. The two Assassins prepared a meal from the contents of their traps. They ate, cleansed the area of the remains of their meal, and re-saddled their horses.

❋❋❋

By the time the three arrived at the Guild, Ssestin, his second-in-command, stood waiting anxiously to meet with Ssarff.

Ssarff entered his quarters, and ushered his second-in-command ahead of him. Ssestin immediately tugged the tassel and, when the apprentice arrived, ordered tea and a snack for his master.

They sat, and Ssarff yawned broadly. "It was urgent that I return quickly, though I must admit I am short on sleep."

"What happened at your meeting, Sire?"

"I am surprised it went so swiftly. Galdin never appeared to understand that I had not agreed to perform the task he requested, despite the fact he is normally so suspicious. Also, according to ancient Morden custom, with no coin changing hands, no contract exists. He has used this tactic many times himself; therefore, I was expecting him to see through my plan."

Their tea arrived, and they waited until the apprentice left before resuming their conversation.

"Ssestin, you must leave for Baklai as soon as we finish our tea. You will be meeting with Kerdinon, Thane Cathked's mate. You should meet her after dark at the resting hut between the two Guards units."

"Cathked's mate?"

"Yes. I believe Galdin was so pleased with himself when he hinted that he had agreed to bond with Kerdinon and rule both Baklai and Morden with her that he did not pay attention to whether or not we accepted his task. From his body language and the way in which he spoke of her I am also positive he holds no intention of fulfilling his agreement with her."

"I will meet with the Thane's mate, Master Ssarff. How many men should I take with me?"

"None."

"None?"

"Correct. You do not need to reveal to Kerdinon that you are the sole Assassin in attendance." Ssarff grinned. "She is expecting to meet with the leader of the Assassins, and I doubt she will even consider that you are on your own. Make sure you protect yourself at all costs. I suggest you also make contact with the woman named Kat to offer your aid as we discussed previously. Make sure she understands we support her against the Thane."

Ssestin shook his head. "We are heading into dangerous ground, Master. Might this be the beginning of the end for Galdin?"

"Pray to Ssayleese it is." He stared at Ssestin. "Go now, and be safe."

His second nodded, rose from his seat, and left the room.

Ssarff rubbed his brow and growled to himself. *This could prove complex. I pray this Kat will be of help to us.*

CHAPTER 38

The rattle of metal on metal, penetrated Kat's consciousness, and a knock on the wooden door woke her completely. She staggered over to the door. "Mouse?"

"Yes." He called back through the door.

"How long will it take us to arrive at the hut?"

"Less than half a turn."

"If we leave this unit at the noon-turn, will we reach the hut before twilight?"

"Yes. Why?"

"I didn't sleep enough. You and Kesiad should head for your morning meal. When I am ready to wake. I will check to make sure Kerdinon's horses and those of her men are fed and watered. Then I will call for a meal, and the apprentice can find you to let him into my room. I need more sleep."

"I understand. Sleep more if you need to. You do not need to concern yourself with Kerdinon's horses, as she and her guards have departed already."

Mouse and Kesiad's voices faded as they walked away from her room. *Joy. I don't have to see the bitch again.*

Kat stumbled back to her bed and slid beneath the covers. One yawn, and sleep claimed her.

❋❋❋

Kat stood, unable to move, and stared as hundreds of guards, clad in black, rushed over the bridge toward her, the hooves of their horses thrumming on the boards as they galloped. In the lead, a huge man mounted on an equally enormous black horse, eyes red with fire, aimed his lance at her.

The horse, clad in armor, bit and reins rattling, it raced directly at her, roared and squealed as if enraged. The mounted man bellowed "You!" Terrified, she tried to retreat but her limbs refused to obey.

Straining to yell for help, she sat up, sweating and terrified. Her stone lay warm between her breasts. There was no danger. She breathed and hugged herself in relief. *Only a nightmare*. Kat sat on the edge of her bed for a moment, waiting for her heart to slow. She shook her head, rose from the bed, and moved to the window. In the courtyard below, men and their horses wheeled and rode in formation, performing what appeared to be usual army exercises.

Grateful she'd only experienced a dream, she removed her night clothes and forced herself to take a cool shower. Now well awake, she dressed for the day, completed her packing, and fed a demanding Wink. She popped her diplo bag in her backpack, and attached Wink's cage to the outside. She deposited all her bags on her bed, ready to leave after the noon-turn meal.

Kat tugged at the tassel in the room, and, when the apprentice knocked at her door, she asked him to call Kesiad to release her. She knew that despite this inconvenience, these restrictions were much preferable to prison or banishment. Despite what Cathked thought, Kat knew she was free and in control of her own attitude.

The rattle of metal keys at the door alerted Kat of her minder's arrival. She opened the inside lock, and, when the door swung free, both Kesiad and Mouse stood waiting.

She pasted a smile on her face. *Kesiad is only doing his job.* "Good morrow. I'm so hungry I could eat an entire horse."

Mouse winced at her words.

Kesiad stared at her, mouth open in horror. "No one in Baklai would ever consider consuming a horse, Kat."

Oops. "Nor would I, Kesiad. On my world, we sometimes use expressions so outrageous as to indicate the depth of our hunger." At that moment Kat's stomach sent forth a deep and lengthy grumble.

His mouth closed at once, and he blushed. "I understand. My apologies for causing you to wait for your meal."

"Relax. I, myself, am to blame. I ate little at last night's turn, and I truly needed to sleep late this morrow. Remember, Kesiad, I am only a commons table hand."

Kesiad blushed again. "I know Thane Cathked ordered this, but I am unable to view you in that light."

Kesiad led the way to the dining hall, and Mouse leaned down to Kat and murmured. "Your body possesses an uncanny knack of reacting when needed."

She eyed him with a bare turn of her head. "I truly am hungry. I didn't order my body to react like that."

Mouse's mouth curled in a slight grin.

The three entered the dining hall, and Kat immediately ordered karri-san tea. She knew she'd be among many Rifellans before leaving for Morden.

"Mouse. Whatever you're having, order me the same, please."

A young female server waited for their orders, and Mouse discussed the menu for this noon-turn. He raised his eyebrows in appreciation when she mentioned blick and ordered for both himself and Kat.

Kesiad brightened at the sound of blick stew. "Bring three orders if you please."

Another serving woman brought tea, which they sipped while waiting for their meal.

Kat did not notice Cathked's mate in the dining hall. "Mouse, did Kerdinon appear for the morning meal?"

"Briefly, yes, but left with her guards long before us."

Kat frowned. "I remember you telling me. I still can't believe she didn't wait to travel with Cathked. I think it's weird. I'm also surprised she didn't wait for me to prepare her horses for departure. I thought she would enjoy lording it over me."

Kesiad piped up. "The Lady Kerdinon is a strong female in her own right. Some of us suspect she considers herself an equal ruler of Baklai along with the Thane."

"Interesting. I suppose she is in a way. The Thane is probably more concerned with the business of horses in Baklai, and she, like the other females I met, are more concerned with the rest of the commerce of your land."

"You are no doubt correct, Kat. I must admit she does not appear to support you. I suspect if she were to make the decision about your future, you might be fighting your way through Air Wyth at this particular moment."

Kat laughed. "I don't understand her intentions. She has demonstrated great antipathy toward me from the first time we met. The reason why, eludes me."

Kesiad frowned. "That is strange."

Their meals arrived, and the trio applied themselves to the task of eating and fell silent, except for occasional murmurs of appreciation.

So hungry, Kat needed to force herself to eat slowly. When she finished, she drank more tea, reveling in the happiness of a satisfied stomach.

Mouse rose. "We should depart now if we want to arrive at the hut before dusk."

Kat stood. "All my bags are ready."

Kesiad joined them, and they returned to their rooms to gather their baggage, and then headed for the stables.

Kat, with help with saddling, prepared their horses. Once saddled and bridled, they mounted their animals, Kat with Mouse's help, and left for the hut on the way to the Border Keep.

❊❊❊

Pridden's star lay low in the sky as they rode up to the hut. Because of the number of trees surrounding the building, Kat didn't see it until they reached the entrance. The word "hut" was a misnomer. Rather than being a small edifice with a few rooms, the strong building, constructed of a blonde wood, closely resembled a fortress. It stood with two substantial wooden gates, propped open, indicating no other guests currently stayed there, and the entire building appeared spread over a large area.

She turned to Kesiad. "This is no hut. It's almost a fort, with gates and walls surrounding an inner courtyard."

Kesiad laughed. "You are not incorrect. We call it a hut, but all the buildings along this border are well fortified." He shrugged. "Morden is across the river, after all."

Passing through the gates, she gazed toward the guest area. and realized guest rooms were arranged in the center of an inner courtyard. In one corner nestled a sizeable stable, able to hold at least a dozen horses, and the travelers immediately moved their animals to stalls. A young apprentice ran from the lodge.

"Lady, Sires, I am Maregiti, and I will help you with your horses."

"Thank you for the offer, Maregiti, but I am ordered by your Thane to service all the horses on my own. Plus, he has ordered that you cannot refer to me as Lady."

Maregiti opened his eyes wide and mouthed an oh.

Starlight nickered at Kat as she unsaddled her in the stall, while Kesiad and Mouse unsaddled their mounts. Kat brought water and hay for all the animals. She stopped and stood still. *Do I hear other horses?* "Maregiti, are any others staying here?"

"No, my Lady, only one other resides here." He gestured at another young male standing at the entrance to the stables. "This is Gweer, and he will show you to your rooms for this night."

Gweer bowed. "If you would follow me?" He led the way into the lodging area and, handing them keys, showed them to their rooms.

Kesiad obtained a second key for Kat's room, which operated her door from the exterior only. "My thanks, Gweer."

"When you are settled, please come to the general room, and I will show you where we keep the food to nourish our guests."

They thanked Gweer and carried their luggage into their rooms.

Kat dumped her bags, separated Wink's cage from her backpack and placed it on the dresser. The pyrock slept on, so Kat decided to feed her after her own meal.

She was assigned a simple room that includeda narrow cot with limited bed linens and a tiny personal tucked in the corner. Kat removed her robe, shook and hung it outside the personal, and donned her Rifellan leather uppers.

A knock indicated the arrival of Kesiad and Mouse to escort her to the general room for a meal.

Gweer met them in the room and showed them where they might find dishes and food stuffs to create an evening repast. The food, limited to fresh produce that would keep without being cooked, filled a cool cabinet. They each chose ingredients to satisfy their hunger, and after placing bowls and eating utensils on one of the tables, sat to eat.

"Mouse, Kesiad, did either of you hear other horses when we were in the stables?"

Mouse raised an eyebrow at her. "My horse kept snorting at me when I removed his saddle, so no, I caught no sounds of others."

Kesiad shrugged. "I am around so many horses daily, I rarely pay attention to their noises."

"I'm sure I heard something."

"It is quite possible, my Lady. So many herds roam the grasslands on the other side of the tree line."

"Perhaps those were the sounds I detected." She stretched tired muscles. "I have eaten sufficient food, and I encountered so much stress lately, I'm heading for bed."

Mouse nodded. "A wise idea, Kat. We can leave immediately after our morning meal for the Border Keep. We will stay at the Keep for two turns so we can plan our journey through Morden. By that time, Thane Cathked will have joined us so we may bid him, and Baklai, farewell."

"Fine."

They all rose and followed Kesiad to their rooms.

Kat entered hers, and listened to the clank of keys in her lock as Kesiad secured her door. She walked over to Wink, who chirped and opened her mouth, waiting to be fed. Kat grinned at her and offered two treats. Wink stretched, circled in her cage, and plopped down among her cozy little blankets.

Kat stood, deciding whether to change into night clothes, but an uneasy sensation made her bed down wearing her Rifellan leathers, even though she knew they were uncomfortable to sleep in. She pulled a light comforter over herself and yawned.

Did I really hear horses? Why am I so restless?

CHAPTER 39

Kat had barely fallen asleep, when she shot up in bed, instantly awake, at the thud of horse's hooves on packed earth, and the hammering of fists on wood. She jumped from her bed, and ran to the window to peer outside. She had not been asleep long and blinked to clear her head. Beyond the outside walls of the hut, an army of men were riding toward the gate. Those who had already arrived at the entrance, hammered on the wood, as they tried to break through the barred gates.

I'm safe until Kesiad arrives. She grabbed some parchment and hastily penned a note to Cathked. "Danger. Help. Males attack hut. Kat." She wrote in the few Priddanese words she could replicate. She snatched a tube off the desk and inserted the note.

Reaching into Wink's cage, she withdrew the pyrock, who blinked and held out a foreleg. The creature obviously understood the urgency of her request. Kat tied the tube to Wink's leg and lifted her from the desk. "Go to Cathked, Wink. Hurry." The small creature rebounded from Kat's hand, spread her wings and popped out of existence.

Kat, trapped inside her room, returned to the window again and again to track the progress of the attackers at the gates of the hut. *Who are they?*

She gazed at the courtyard when a robed figure crossed to the stable and came out a moment later, treading soundlessly and leading a dark horse toward the rear of the building. She thought it might be Mouse. He disappeared from her sight, but a creak of wood echoed from beyond her view.

❋❋❋

Mouse woke at the sounds of males and horses and bounded from his bed to catch sight of the invading force. With only five people in the hut, he understood at once how much they were outnumbered.

He rushed to Kesiad's room and found him at his open door. "Kesiad, you must hide and do not, under any circumstances, unlock Kat's door. This is the only way she will be safe from the invaders." He grabbed at Kesiad's arm. "I am serious. Keep her confined. I will ride immediately for the Border Keep to gather Makinti and his men to come to our aid."

Kesiad nodded at him. "Go swiftly. You are our only hope. Quickly retrieve your animal and leave by the gate at the rear of the building. I will hide in the forest."

Mouse ran to the stable and led his horse stealthily from the stall toward the rear gate. He unlatched it without a sound and, once out, leaped on his horse and galloped bareback from the hut area toward the Border Keep. He clutched the mane with two hands. Ignoring his natural instinct to conceal himself in the role of the frightened man, he gripped the horse with powerful leg muscles. He urged his horse to move as fast as possible, hoping the animal would survive the swift journey, which, if he were to preserve his horse's energy would take more than half a turn. He had to cut that amount of time by one third. Kat needed help from Makinti and his Rifellans, and quickly. He had seen the army at the gates, and he suspected the woman he had glimpsed among them was Kerdinon. *Kerdinon? Why?*

He stayed off the well-travelled trail, riding instead through the grasses, and ducking to avoid the occasional tree branch. He had seen both Baklai guards and recognized

Galdin's personal army. Mouse wondered if Galdin was also here, and had Kerdinon formed an alliance with him*? Why?*

The fear that Galdin might already be at the hut spurred Mouse to kick his horse into a faster pace.

❋❋❋

At last, the soldiers smashed open the gates and poured into the courtyard. A woman was among them, but Kat did not recognize her. She put on her boots and hid her small blade in her left one.

Maregiti and Gweer emerged from the residential area of the hut and when confronted by the attackers, stopped in their tracks and held up their hands. The horde, consisting of a Baklai contingent and a group of males who resembled northern Mordens, shouted questions at the woman, who shrugged, and waved her hand. Two of the Mordens thrust their spears into the two males, who seemed to cry out as blood flowed from their bodies and they dropped to the ground. The stable hand, Maregiti twitched once and lay still, but Gweer, writhed in place, obviously moaning in pain.

Kat, horrified by the violence, her face squinting at the sight of the dying men, continued to follow the movement of the various males. They dragged a man from the shadows. Her heart sank as she recognized him as Kesiad. She surmised he had most likely been trying to hide.

The woman laughed in glee as she spotted him, so loudly, even Kat heard her words. "Keep hold of that male. He possesses something I want." *Kerdinon. Oh no.*

They dragged Kesiad into the building.

Kat waited, heart beating wildly, her mouth dry, hoping desperately that Kesiad had rid himself of the key to her room. The pounding of feet echoed down the hallway.

She held her dagger at the ready as the keys clinked at the

doorway.

Kerdinon and six of her men threw open the door, holding Kesiad as their prisoner.

The Baklai woman held her sword at his throat. “Drop your dagger, or this man dies.”

Kesiad shook his head. “Do not give in.”

Kerdinon smiled with teeth bared. “I repeat, your dagger or his life. Your choice.”

Kat dropped her blade.

“Kick it over here.”

Kat did so, and waited for Kerdinon to release Kesiad. But she slit his throat open with her sword, and his blood gushed out and sprayed the room.

Kat cried out in horror. “You said you would spare him if I dropped my blade.”

Kerdinon sneered, her lip curling in triumph. “I lied.”

She motioned to her men, and they grabbed Kat and secured her hands behind her back. “Take her to the room further down the hallway. We will lock her in, as I need her for some additional business.”

As they muscled her down the hallway, one of the Mordens stopped to converse with Kerdinon. She snapped at him. “I am well aware of what your Thane and I discussed. I will personally turn her over to him. All I require now is your silence.”

The men hauled Kat to another room propelled her through the entrance which knocked the breath from her when she landed painfully on the floor. They double locked the door from the outside.

Kat elbowed herself upright and, clinging to a chair, scanned the room for something with which to cut her bonds. The rope cut off her circulation. When she tried to sit up, pain shot through her arms and back.

She waited for her heart to slow down, then walked to the personal. She turned her back to the basin, and fumbled for the faucet handles. They twisted slightly, and water flowed into the basin. She reversed and bending down, drank from the faucet. She twisted her body once more, and turned off the water.

She needed to sit, but with her hands bound, sitting proved difficult, so she returned to the cot and lay on her side to rest and ease the strain on her arms. The noise and commotion created by soldiers drinking and carousing, eventually died down. She assumed most had fallen asleep in drunken stupors. She searched the room for something to help free herself.

Kat started at the faint sounds of keys. The door creaked open, and a shadow crept in the room. *Mouse?*

A black-robed figure walked smoothly across the floor, and a male put his hand across her mouth. “Quiet. We do not want to disturb anyone, although most are so drunk, almost nothing will wake them.”

Kat barely whispered, “Who are you?”

“Ssestin. We met on the boat from Glowen.”

“I remember you. But, why are you here?”

“I am a member of the Assassins’ Guild, and Thane Galdin hired us to help on this mission to capture you.”

Kat stared at him. “Why?”

“You are aware the Lady Kerdinon is here?”

“Yes.”

“She made a pact with our Thane to help capture you. We doubt his plans for you will be beneficial, and we wish to foil his intentions.”

“So, you don’t want to take me to Galdin? Do you have

men to help me escape?"

Ssestin shifted without meeting her eyes. "I am the only Assassin who came. My Master does not wish to aid the Thane."

"You're alone?" She winced as she tried to get more comfortable

He withdrew a knife, and Kat tried to back away, tripping over the cot. Ssestin reached around her and cut her bonds.

She sighed in relief. "Thank you. Being bound so tightly proved painful." She breathed out. "Sorry, I feared at first you planned to kill me with that knife."

"Of course not. Now, before I leave your room, I will give you a set of bonds that will be loose and easy to slip into. That way no one will realize you are free to use your hands. I will also leave this knife in case you need to defend yourself." He slid the knife up her sleeve so the hilt rested in her palm. "I am sorry I cannot take you with me. Kerdinon must not know I released you."

Kat rubbed her sore wrists. "Are they all asleep? I can sneak to the stable and take my horse."

Ssestin shook his head, continuing his whispered conversation. "Do not. You would not be able to escape. Kerdinon would hear you and would be further angered, which would not bode well for you. I believe you need only wait until the morrow for help to arrive. I saw your guide head for the Border Keep. I suspect he will return by mid-morning with the Praetor and his Rifellans."

Kat breathed a soundless laugh. "We think alike. I sent my pyrock to call Thane Cathked to my aid. I'm sure he will arrive about the same time."

"Excellent. We will prevent Thane Galdin from capturing you. But I am vastly outnumbered, so I must leave and return to my Guild. I cannot be seen by Kerdinon or her men to be aiding you. I also cannot be here when Cathked and Makinti arrive. Our Guild will instantly be suspect. If you find the opportunity, please advise the Baklai Thane and your guide, that our Guild took no part in this fiasco."

"I will, and my thanks, Ssestin." She held up her hand as he turned to leave. "Ssestin, did you kill my horse?"

He stood in silence. "Lady Kat, I did indeed cut her throat. She suffered so badly, desperately trying to breathe. I perceived such fear in her eyes, and she collapsed on the floor of the stall. I disliked to see such a beautiful animal suffer. So, yes, I did cut her throat to put her out of her misery." He hung his head. "Please forgive me. This is something I have told to no one else, not even my Guild Master."

"I do not need to forgive you, Ssestin. You saved her from additional pain." Kat sighed. "I do not understand why she inhaled the chaff."

"She did not do it deliberately. I caught a Baklai man forcing her mouth into the chaff bag. He was responsible for her problems."

"Did you know him?"

"I had not seen him before, but he has appeared again."

Kat faced Ssestin and raised her eyebrows in enquiry.

He shook his head at her. "I have just viewed the same male in company with Kerdinon."

He stood still, staring at her for a moment, before he turned and left the room.

A key turned in the lock.

I was Kerdinon's prey even before I arrived in Baklai. Why?

CHAPTER 40

Dawn was imminent by the time the Border Keep appeared, and Mouse breathed heavily, while his steed was lathered in sweat. He arrived at the gates and bellowed for the Rifellan Praetor. "Makinti, Kat needs your help."

Lights began to appear, and soon, Makinti was yelling out instructions. "Open the gates. Saddle my horse, and Rifellans, prepare to ride. We are needed at the halfway hut."

Mouse rode through the gates as they opened, leaped off his horse, and led the exhausted animal toward the stable. As a stable hand appeared, Mouse handed over the reins. "Please take care of him. He has ridden hard and needs rest."

Makinti appeared from the courtyard area. "Mouse. I was up in the tower and heard you roaring. I had no idea you could command such volume." He headed toward his already saddled horse, being led by another stable hand.

"Makinti, can you lend me a horse to accompany you back to Kat? Mine cannot travel another step, and only fear for Kat's safety is giving me energy to keep going."

"Yes." Makinti turned to the stable hand holding his horse. "Bring another animal for this man." He mounted his horse and turned back to speak to Mouse. "I assume we are travelling to the halfway hut. What has happened?"

As he spoke, about twenty Rifellan guards joined him, ready to ride.

Mouse glanced around, anxious for the new horse. "The hut has been attacked. I saw Baklai guards, whom I believe look to Kerdinon."

"Kerdinon?"

"I suspect she is in league with Galdin, because I also glimpsed a contingent of his personal army."

"Is Galdin with them?"

"I do not know. I did not see any Assassins, but they may also be riding with the attackers."

The stable hand brought a horse to Mouse, and he leaped to the saddle. He and Makinti, led the group of Rifellans at full tilt, in the direction of the hut.

With the massive amount of adrenaline still coursing through his system, Mouse drove his mount mercilessly in his desire to rescue Kat. The Rifellans he rode with were just as anxious to foil any attack Galdin planned to make upon the land of Baklai.

Makinti moved up beside Mouse calling loudly over the sounds of hooves and panting horses. "How many men were there?"

Mouse coughed from the dust thrown up by the animals racing along the pathway. "Between Kerdinon's Baklai warriors and Galdin's guards? Twenty or thirty."

"We will be outnumbered."

Mouse sneered. "But Makinti, they are not Rifellans."

They galloped in silence, with no energy to spare in conversation.

By the time the hut hove into view, Pridden's star was well on its way to mid-turn. All the horses were lathered up, and their riders breathed heavily. The men slowed to keep the noise of their approach to a minimum. Finally, Makinti held up his hand to stop the group. He waved at them to indicate silence.

The Rifellans dismounted and, leading their horses, melted into the trees surrounding the outer walls of the hut, their mounts tethered among the trees, and approached noiselessly. The wooden walls around the courtyard sported sharpened points every three feet, and one man, holding a looped rope at ready, crept toward the walls near the rear of the hut and, tossed the rope upwards. He hooked one of the sharp points on the first try. Swiftly he climbed up and threw the rope over the other side. He slid out of view, and reappeared as he opened the gate into the courtyard to allow Mouse and the rest of the Rifellans access. He put his finger to his lips and pointed at two men snoring in a corner near the stable. It appeared they had fallen asleep from an excess of drink.

Makinti silently pointed his men in various directions, and they moved as a unit to cover all the entrances to the lodge, and capture and gag the two drunkards. When ready, with a wild war cry, Makinti launched his men at the invaders inside the hut.

The clash of weapons, the squeals of horses coming from the stable as they reared and kicked at the wood of their stalls, and the screams of pain from men as they died, woke all within the walls of the hut sending many to aid in the fight in the courtyard. Mouse, who had joined in the battle, wielded his sword as fiercely as the Rifellans. Makinti's men swept over the unsuspecting Baklai and Galdin's soldiers and knocked most of them unconscious. Those who woke and fought were the unfortunate ones whose blood soaked the battle ground.

At the sound of more approaching horses and additional battle cries, the Rifellans opened the gates fully, recognizing Thane Cathked as he and his guards approached and joined in the fighting, achieved from the advantage of horseback. Those who remained of Kerdinon's Baklai army threw down their weapons and bowed before the Thane.

Galdin's guards, however, refused to drop their weapons. When they threatened Cathked, his guards thrust and slashed with their swords to end their lives without any qualms.

The Thane dismounted and faced Makinti, almost as tall and equally as broad, his sword dripping red upon the earth. He swung around to Mouse. "Where is your Lady Kat?"

"We have not located her yet, Sire." *He called her Lady. Has this challenge to Kat's safety changed his mind?*

Cathked pointed at a man close to him. "Search the building."

❋❋❋

The man ran into the guest house and, within minutes returned with Kat, who was holding the loose ropes Ssestin had left her.

The barrel-chested Thane growled. "Who is responsible for this? Where is Kesiad?"

Kate stared at him, for once momentarily at a loss for words. "I am so sorry, Thane Cathked, but Kesiad has been murdered."

"How did he die?"

Her voice trembled. "They cut his throat."

Cathked whirled on his own men and the Rifellans. "Tie those Baklai in a line and leave them enough freedom to remove the dead and dispose of them in the Farralawn. Prepare Kesiad for the trip back to my Keep. He will be dealt with in honor as a hero."

He pointed at a figure creeping toward the rear entrance. "Who is that female? Bring her to me."

Three Rifellans ran and captured her before she escaped.

They brought her before the Thane, and he raised puzzled eyebrows. "Kerdinon? What are you doing? Why are you here?"

She stood boldly in front of her mate. “I was on my way to meet you at the Border Keep, and I was taken prisoner by these males.”

Kat gawked at her. *The lying bitch.* “That’s not true. Kerdinon is the leader of the group of Baklai soldiers here.” Kat pointed an accusing finger and glared at her. “She was the one who cut Kesiad’s throat.”

Cathked’s face twisted in horror, and he grew pale. “What?” The word spewed from his mouth like fire from a volcano.

Kat stood silent, waiting for the eruption.

CHAPTER 41

Kat stared at Cathked as he stood stock still, glaring at his mate, eyes black with thunder. "You?" His face had paled when he discovered Kerdinon was responsible for the attack, but now twisted in a grimace of pain and disbelief. "How can you betray your own people?" He roared, flecks of spittle at the corners of his mouth. "How could you betray me?"

Kerdinon reached toward him, fear in her eyes. "Cathked, this is all a misunderstanding. I would never betray you."

Kat froze in place and stared at the two of them. *He can't possibly believe her.*

"Liar." He waved his hand around the courtyard. "With Kesiad's blood on your hands? All this death and the presence of Galdin's personal guards? How can you deny your treasonous actions?" He turned to Galakis who stood beside him. "Arrest this female and hold her for trial."

Galakis motioned to two guards to follow Cathked's orders. They grabbed Kerdinon and, despite her pleading screams and her struggles, secured her hands behind her back.

They led her toward the guest quarters as she cried out to Cathked for mercy.

Nostrils flared, he regarded her with dead eyes. "Shut the traitor up."

One of the guards pulled a piece of cloth from inside his armor, and gagged Kerdinon. She continued to struggle as they wrestled her inside the building.

Kat, horrified at what Kerdinon's punishment might be,

saw Cathked's face darken with anger.

Cathked summoned Galakis. "Galdin's personal guards have been disposed of in the Farralawn. Is this correct?"

"Yes, my Thane."

"The Baklai who followed Kerdinon. Have you had a chance to question any of them?"

"I have, Sire. While they were loyal to Kerdinon, I do not believe they understood she was plotting against you. I suggest you separate them from each other and assign them differing duties. I would also suggest you have them monitored closely."

"A wise move, Galakis. You are advocating for mercy, which, if these males are still loyal to us, is deserved." He frowned. "This change might give them an opportunity to learn the value of being less naìve as well." He nodded at Galakis. "Will you make sure this is done?"

Cathked allows mercy for the Kerdinon's Baklai guards. Kat's thoughts kept returning to words about him being smitten with his mate. *Will he show any mercy to her?*

Galakis nodded. "I will, my Thane, and will you continue your journey to the Border Keep?"

"I intend to. First, we will remain here to complete the trial of Kerdinon and, after her sentencing, will proceed with Makinti and his men to the Border Keep. I would request you return to my Keep, taking the Baklai males with you." He sighed. "I would also wish you prepare Kesiad for his journey back to my Keep. Make sure he is ready for the warrior's fire."

"I will, Sire."

"When I return, we will hold the Rifellan ceremony for Kesiad's journey to Calanta's domain."

"I will be honored to accompany Kesiad back to your

Keep, my Thane. I will return there as soon as you depart for the Border Keep."

"Assign a guard to remain at the hut with one of the Bak-lai males. We will hold Kerdinon's trial shortly and complete it by the noon-turn. I promise you it will be brief. Most brief." He clenched his fists and blew a hot breath toward the building. "Finally, we will depart this place after a quick meal so we can arrive at the Border Keep before dusk."

***

Kat scanned the men in the courtyard to locate Mouse. He was speaking with Makinti and she was about to join him when a horn sounded. The group assembled in the courtyard, this time for Kerdinon's trial. A single chair was set near the gates for Cathked, with the rest of the spectators standing before him. Kat, noting the lack of any other seating, was sure this trial would be short. She joined Mouse.

Cathked announced the details. "Bring the female here." He took his seat.

The guards brought Kerdinon, still bound and gagged, to stand at the left side of Cathked. He had already announced to all, that their joining was dissolved. She would no longer be referred to as the Thane's mate.

Kerdinon, stood shoulders bowed, defeat enveloping her.

Cathked glared at her. "You are brought here before this court to answer for traitorous actions. What is your defense?"

She could not answer because of the gag, but her eyes burned with anger, and her body trembled in fear.

Kat assumed that the Thane kept Kerdinon gagged because he no longer wished to hear from her, not even in her own defense.

He called for Kat to step forward. "I have been told this female captured Kesiad and threatened him with death to force him to surrender the key to your quarters. To your knowledge, is this correct?"

"I was not present, but I suspect it was so."

"You held her off with a knife. Did she agree to allow Kesiad to live if you handed that knife to her?"

"She did, Sire."

"When she obtained your knife, what did she do?"

"She slashed Kesiad's throat, my Thane."

He dismissed Kat with a wave of his hand. "Kerdinon, you have been found guilty of the actions of a traitor, of murder, and inciting a rebellion within Baklai. Your punishment is to be thrown to your death in the Farralawn chasm."

Kerdinon's eyes rolled up into her head, and she struggled to speak.

Cathked stared at her, his face still simmering with fury. He motioned to his guards. "She has been found guilty. Rid me of this traitor."

Standing at the entrance gate, Kat saw three guards grab Kerdinon, lift her up, walk past where she and Mouse were standing, and exit out the walls of the courtyard. Carrying Kerdinon as she fought to release herself, they walked to the edge of the cliffs, and threw her to the intractable fate of the raging waters.

Kat, dumfounded by the speed and cold efficiency of the so-called trial, did not move a muscle. She stared, open-mouthed, as Kerdinon flew through the air toward the torrent below. The woman screamed, even though gagged, as she fell.

Kat had been told the Thane was all powerful. *All powerful? He's a despot.* She shook her head in bewilderment. At that moment, she understood how fortunate she had been. Only now did she grasp how terrifying the Thane could be.

Her heart thumped loudly in her chest, her mouth so dry and desperate for water that she blindly reached out to Mouse beside her and grabbed his arm.

He patted her hand and murmured to her. "I tried to warn you. Baklai is a harsh, cruel land. Cathked is regarded as close to godhood by his people. The three Lords of Pridden are the only people he respects without question."

Kat nodded, completely preoccupied by the Thane's actions. "I had no idea."

Cathked walked toward the guest building of the hut, and waved at Kat to accompany him. She flashed a nervous glance at Mouse.

"Relax. I believe you are safe from his ire."

"I hope you're right." She held her breath, waiting anxiously for more potential onerous reactions from Cathked.

She followed him into the lodge's dining hall. The guards had hastily set up tables for most of the group to be seated for a meal. The Thane placed himself at the head of the largest table.

He beckoned to her to sit beside him. "Lady Kat, you have seen our land at its most cruel and least merciful. I am the Hunter of Baklai, and I am the executioner of the guilty. I hope this has not colored your vision of us. The iron fist with which I rule is necessary. We live beside Morden and the hated Thane Galdin. Do not think ill of us. Our lives are in constant peril. I must always be resolute."

"I must admit, Thane Cathked, your actions took me by surprise." *Surprise? More like shocked and terrified.* "I do understand that living beside a bully is a difficult life. I'm grateful you refrained from punishing me in a similar way."

"I might well have needed to."

A silent scream of anxiety bubbled up inside her, and she

understood how close she had come to death.

He regarded her, a speculative look on his face. "However, your speech and your attitude saved you. You were bold. And, quite disrespectful, I might add. But your words were thought-provoking, and your stance was that of one who believed in her ideas. You interrupted my desire to punish you. My advisors and I now see much benefit could lie in what you suggested. I hold an enormous vision for the path of my people, and the thoughts you expressed appeared to fit. However, change takes time and needs to be accomplished gradually. Despite your tendency to ignore rules, I understand why Eduardo sent you on this journey."

"My thanks, Sire." She coughed. "I have always thought I needed to take action to maintain control of my life. From you, I have seen that freedom comes from within. No one else can live my life for me, so I am the only one who can control it without the need for battle." She regarded him nervously. *I need to ask him for his help to get me home*. She knew she might not see him again before she left Baklai. It was now or never if she was going to ask for help.

Kat cleared her throat. "Sire, I have one last favor to ask of you."

"I will release you from your job as a stable hand. Is that what you were about to ask?"

"No, something quite different, my Thane. While my time on Pridden has been full of new experiences, I still long to return to my home. Lord Eduardo has promised he will do all he can, but requires others with power to achieve my return."

"Lord Eduardo is a Wielder, but I am not, Lady Kat, if you planned on asking for my help."

"Thane Cathked, I suspect you have a lot more power than

even you know. Will you help me when the time comes?" She waited for his answer, adrenaline still coursing through her veins.

"If you truly believe I can be of help, I would be honored to be of assistance."

Kat smiled to herself. *Sometimes the most helpful people are also the most dangerous ones.*

CHAPTER 42

Kat left the dining room and headed for her quarters. Her stomach felt like a pound of lead sat in it. She had gobbled. She needed time to sit and relax and digest her meal without more stress. When she left the dining hall, she had requested red-leaf tea to take with her, hoping it would help relieve her discomfort. The night had been chaos for her, and she had no idea whether she would live or die. The morning when Cathked and Makinti arrived had not been much better. She shook her head and shivered as she remembered the blood and the screams of dying men. *I put stuff like this in my games, but seeing them in real life is abhorrent.* She ached to go home and leave all this violence behind her. She had been told how smitten Cathked was with Kerdinon. His actions against his mate had shocked Kat to her core. She found it difficult to imagine that a man could love any woman so strongly but treat her in such a gruesome manner. All she wanted at this moment was to gather her belongings and find Mouse. The urge to leave prompted her to sprint down the corridor.

She unlocked her door, and when she entered, she was overjoyed to find Wink curled up on top of her cage. She brought the creature to her face and snuggled her fur. "Wink, you must be hungry." She offered food to the little pyrock. Poor Wink, exhausted from her journey to summon Cathked, consumed only one piece of food. She cheeped at Kat, who settled her inside her cage among warm bedding. Wink chirruped once more and curled up to sleep.

Kat had packed almost everything during the early evening of the previous turn, with the exception of her robe, which she folded and tucked inside her current bag. After she gulped her tea, she attached Wink's cage to her back-pack, gathered her luggage and sped to the stable to meet Mouse.

As she entered, she discovered not only Mouse, but also two of Makinti's guards waiting for her. The spare horse used by Kesiad stood waiting, with Mouse's bags already loaded.

Kat glanced around. "I didn't expect to see any guards here. Am I still being monitored?"

One of the men brought Starlight to her, already prepared for the journey. "No, my Lady. Praetor Makinti has requested we escort you and Sire Mouse to the Border Keep."

"Isn't he going to return to the Keep himself?"

"Indeed, he will. However, he and the rest of the guards will attend Thane Cathked and his men. Journeying with so many, means he will travel at a reduced speed compared to us." The man smiled. "He suspected you would appreciate arriving as soon as is possible."

Kat sighed, and she moved slowly as she approached Starlight. "My thanks. You're right on the mark."

The man raised an eyebrow.

She cleared her throat. "I mean, you are correct."

Mouse's mouth formed a slight grin, and he took her bags from her, which he added to the horse previously ridden by Kesiad, and once again used for baggage. He then turned back to Kat and linked his hands together to form a step. She placed her foot on them, and he tossed her upwards into the saddle.

She did not feel like a thistle today but, rather, a lump of aching, tired muscle.

As they departed the grounds of the hut, one guard led the procession, while the other brought up the rear, with the baggage animal tied to the back of his saddle.

❋❋❋

They had travelled for some time, when the roadway widened enough so that Kat could move up to ride beside Mouse.

"I did not abandon you, Kat." He cleared his throat. "At the hut, I mean."

"What? I never thought for one moment that you did."

"You must have wondered where I was when the soldiers attacked."

"There wasn't much time to worry. I assumed you had gone for help."

"Before they broke through the gates, I saw how many males were attacking. There were far too many for me to fight on my own. I needed to ride immediately for help from Makinti. I knew you would be safe because you were locked in your room, and only Kesiad had the key." He shook his head. "I saw him as I was leaving, and told him to hide and never to give up the key to your room." Mouse sighed and shrugged his shoulders. "He agreed and pointed me in the best direction. Unfortunately, it appears he did not have time to hide the key or himself."

"Poor Kesiad. He tried so hard to foil them." Kat bent her head and shook it regretfully. "I believed her when she said she would spare him if I relinquished my dagger."

"Cathked made her pay for her sins."

"He certainly did." Kat shook her head, frowning. "I would never have known what a harsh leader he is. I found him quite frightening because he was so…" She shook her head again. "He was spine-chilling."

"I hope you now know how fortunate you have been in your dealings with him. I assume you realize that after your testimony against Kerdinon, he did not reassign a minder to you, nor did he expect you to continue to perform as a stable hand. His actions indicate he trusts you."

"Your goddess Caleesh must have been smiling on me. He is not an evil man, but is harsh and without compromise. I understand why his people obey him without question." She grimaced. "I don't like him, but I do respect him."

Kat was still dumbfounded how Cathked could turn from deep love of Kerdinon to such grim hatred. Then, she remembered what she'd read about ancient Japanese integrity. Only a man who committed ritual suicide, known as seppuku, could regain honor for himself and his family if he had failed in performing his duty. Perhaps in Cathked's view, Kerdinon needed to die to bring honor back to her family and to the ruler of Baklai. *Not a way of life I take comfort from.*

She, Mouse, and the two Rifellans had left the hut immediately after the noon-turn meal with Cathked and travelled until Pridden's star began its slow slide into the horizon. Kat spied the fortress at the border with relief. "At last. I am so tired, I thought we would never arrive here."

Their two guards rode up on either side of them and waved at another guard on the battlements to open the gates.

They rode over to the stable, and Kat wearily slid to the ground.

The lead guard halted her when she tried to remove her saddle. "Stop, Lady Kat. We will make sure your horses are fed and bedded down. Makinti requested we do this. He is aware how exhausted you must be." He smiled at her. "Ildiren, our apprentice healer, will guide you to your rooms, and our stable hand will carry your luggage."

Kat muttered a grateful thanks and almost collided with the healer waiting outside the stable. She and Mouse stumbled after Ildiren. The healer handed keys to them, and they unlocked their doors and entered. The apprentice from the stable followed them in with their bags.

Kat took Wink's cage and placed it on the dresser. She took off her Rifellan leather uppers, and dropped them on a chair. As she moved to shut the door, she called out to Mouse, whose door was still ajar. "See you for the morning meal." He grunted in response.

She shed her clothes, threw them on the same chair, and, weeping with weariness and sorrow, collapsed on her bed. Pulling a cover over her, she slept.

❋❋❋

The thump of boots and the clank of swords and lances wakened Kat. For a moment, she wondered what was happening. She remembered. The men on guard were changing from the night watch to the first watch of the morrow. Feeling safe and secure in her warm, cozy bed, she stretched and cracked the muscles in her spine. She opened one eye, closed it, and cuddled in among her blankets again.

She lay dozing, when a hungry chirp roused her once more. "Okay, Wink, I'm coming."

She rose, scratched an itch on her hip, and yawned. Although she needed to shower, she walked to the dresser and fed her squeaking pyrock first.

Later, clean, awake, and well-rested, she dressed herself in black loose pants and a brilliant emerald blouse. Hungry and ready for her morning meal, she put her leathers aside to request they be cleaned, and threw on her robe instead. She opened her door to ask Mouse to join her for the morning meal and was startled by his appearance at the entrance, his hand raised to knock.

"Your timing, Mouse, is impeccable."

"Makinti will be joining us for the morning meal."

"Fine, I still have a few things to tell both of you, and I assume we will also need to spend time in planning our departure from Baklai."

"Food first?"

Kat smiled, nodded, and with a lighter step than the previous day, moved ahead of him down the hallway to the dining lounge. Makinti appeared from the opposite direction as they arrived at the entrance.

They followed him to a table, and sat to order their meal from one of the apprentice servers.

"You didn't order a meal, Makinti. Have you already eaten?"

"I have. Thane Cathked had much to settle at the hut, and we arrived here late at night. He rose early this morrow, and we spent our morning's meal attending to our usual discussions on the state of forces here in Baklai." He rolled his shoulders, apparently to ease the stress of meeting with the Thane. "The Thane banished a few of Kerdinon's guards to Air Wyth, because he felt they believed in her without thought of loyalty to himself. The rest were pardoned. They assumed she was acting with the Thane's permission. And, by the way, Kat, he sent his hope that you will have a less eventful journey through Morden than you enjoyed here in Baklai."

"I hope so too."

Mouse moved a mug to make room for his meal. "We will examine my plans for our trip through Morden to assure us the safest route. I think it best we study the maps I have obtained during our noon-turn meal."

Kat glanced at him and nodded. "Before that meal, I will bring all my journals and writing up to date in my room."

When meals arrived, Kat shared more information. "I should tell both of you about the man who came to my aid after Kerdinon had trapped me."

Mouse glanced at her with one eyebrow raised. "You never mentioned another man before."

"That's why I'm telling you now. He is from Morden, and he came to my room after stealing a key. He cut my bonds and left me with a loose set of ropes I could use to pretend I was still bound. He also left me a knife, which he hid up my sleeve." Kat faced Makinti. "Did you see him, and do you know who he was?"

"No, I only saw Galdin's personal army of Mordens. I saw no others."

"His name is Ssestin."

Mouse widened his eyes and gulped. "The man from the boat?"

Makinti frowned. "You met him before?"

"Yes. What you also don't know, Mouse, is that Ssestin is indeed a member of the Assassins' Guild. Although Thane Galdin thought a number of Assassins would join Kerdinon's army, only Ssestin was on the scene."

"Only him. Why?" Mouse seemed puzzled.

"Ssestin advised me his Guild Master does not support Galdin, and they were afraid for my well-being. Apparently, they believe I am important to their challenges with their Thane. Ssestin was sent to make sure I was safe and also to pretend to Kerdinon that the Assassins had attended her gathering. She had no idea that he was the only member there. I never saw him again, and I assume he is back at his Guild."

Mouse's expressive eyebrows nearly joined his hairline. "So, the Assassins do not support their Thane? If that is true it is most interesting."

"No, they don't. I trust Ssestin is telling the truth. I believe the Assassins are concerned about what the Thane might do next."

Makinti cast a worried glance at Mouse. "This sounds as if your journey through the land of Morden might be the worst one yet." He rose. "I have duties to perform. Make all your plans to ride into Morden, and if you need anything for your journey, ask an apprentice to find me. We will help with anything you need."

They thanked him and drank one more mug of tea and headed for their own rooms, before agreeing to meet for the noon-turn meal.

❋❋❋

Kat spent the morning, packing her bag for the trip through Morden and bringing her journal and other writings up-to-date. She also sent her leathers for cleaning, and the young man who collected them promised he would return them before the evening meal. By the time she was ready to meet with Mouse, her hand ached from writing for so long. She massaged her fingers and added a soothing lotion. A knock summoned her, and when she opened the door, Mouse was waiting for her to join him for a meal.

"Perfect timing. I am feeling peckish."

He furrowed his brow.

"I'm hungry."

"An interesting word. When I hear it from you, I think of birds pecking at grains on the ground. Does this mean you are willing to eat off the ground because your hunger is so acute?"

Kat laughed. "Not at all. It means I am beginning to feel hunger pangs."

Mouse frowned slightly, cocked his head, and nodded.

They strolled the lengthy hall, Mouse with his map bag over his shoulder. Once inside the dining hall, he ushered Kat to a quiet table in the corner, large enough to spread maps on, but with only two chairs.

Kat ordered what she considered might well be her last meal of blick stew. "Will they have blick in Morden?"

"I doubt it. Baklai and Mordens do not trade much with each other. That is, except for the Mordens from the south. All Mordens do purchase horses from Baklai, but these trades are arbitrated via the Rifellans."

Mouse drew out his maps of Morden and began to point out the route he intended they should follow.

Their meals arrived, and he stopped for them to eat.

Kat was curious, and, between mouthfuls, questioned him. "How can we safely travel through Morden, without running into the Thane? I believe I should avoid him completely."

Mouse pointed on the map as he spoke. "We will initially travel northwards, with the Farralawn River on our left, and the forests, which the Mordens refer to as Doos, on our right. We will visit with various southern Mordens on our way." He folded the map over, and continued to eat. "Wait until we finish, and I will show you in better detail."

When they finished the meal, they pushed their plates aside and Mouse traced the trip on the map. "I will need to be ready to alter our plans from time to time, depending upon our experiences in Morden."

"Are you sure that's the best route?"

"I believe so, but as I said, we may have to alter our plans, depending upon what we encounter." Mouse folded his maps, and they left to return to their rooms.

As Kat unlocked her door, she swiveled back to Mouse.

"I'm going to rest up for our trip, and I'll order a light meal in my room for the evening. I'll meet you for the morning meal, with my baggage ready, and we can set out from there."

He nodded, unlocked his door, and entered his room.

❋❋❋

Kat spent the period after the noon-turn determining what to wear on her travels. She put her hand in a side pocket of her bag and pulled out the ring created for her by Garren pen Darryn, the glass blower in Glowen, and her pink crystal bracelet. She gazed at them fondly. *Why not?* As she clipped the bracelet to her wrist, and slipped the ring on her middle finger, she felt a sense of release of the violence from the past few turns. Beautiful things pushed away the dark and also lightened her mood.

After admiring her ring, she sat to review her notes. She tried to nap but decided to meditate instead and sat in a comfortable chair, wrapped in a bed cover. Mentally drifting in alpha rhythm, she relived some of her times with Liandock, and again wondered about him. She still missed her home and all the places she was familiar with, but would she be happier if she stayed with the gorgeous Metal Master? Her heart said yes, but her head told her she must return home. Her real life was back on her world. She knew she didn't really belong in any of the lands she had traveled so far. Even Liandock had told her she should return.

❋❋❋

The following morning, Kat woke early, fed Wink, and attached her cage to the back-pack. Rested, clean and dressed in her leathers, and despite the early hour, Kat paced the room, and kept double-checking her bags. At last, unable to keep still, she hoisted her bags, exited her room, and knocked on Mouse's door.

When he opened the door, clad in his usual gray robes, he grinned. "You feel the need to leave too?"

She smiled and nodded.

They trudged with their bags to the dining lounge, and, upon entering, saw Makinti at a table for four, waving at them to join him. "Mouse and Kat, I am glad I caught you before you left."

"Good morrow, Makinti, and we're glad we caught you. We will leave the baggage animal with you and would appreciate it if you would contact Haydar and ask him if he wishes to have his horse back. If he does, would you please return it to him?"

"I will."

An apprentice appeared at their table to take their orders, and Kat added karri-san to her meal.

Makinti raised a questioning glance. "Karri-san, Kat? There are few if any Rifellans in Morden."

"I suspect as much. This is merely a celebratory drink for all the Rifellans I met here in Baklai. I certainly will not need it in Morden."

"Speaking of needs, Mouse, you may have need of these." He passed a small bag to him.

Mouse peered inside. "Messenger moths."

"They have not been imprinted with any specific recipient, so you may use them to summon help from anyone."

"Thank you, Makinti. A fine parting gift."

Their meals appeared, and they ate mechanically, with little conversation. When they finished, they all rose, and Kat hugged Makinti goodbye. He and Mouse shook hands in the Rifellan manner.

Kat followed Mouse, their luggage in their hands, to the stables.

Their horses stood waiting, already saddled and bridled. They heaved their luggage onto the back of the saddles and lashed them securely in place.

Mouse hauled himself up on his horse, while a stable hand helped Kat secure her seat. She leaned forward. "Good morrow, Starlight."

Mouse chuckled at her greeting to her animal.

They set off toward the bridge over the Farralawn, clopped over the wood, and then paused in the middle. Kat glanced back at Baklai, and then, forward to Morden.

She eyed Mouse speculatively. "I understand, Mouse, that it is protocol when entering a new land to call upon the Thane or Lord as soon as possible."

He regarded her curiously. "Usually, yes."

"Under the circumstances, would we not be wiser to visit the Assassins' Guild first?"

Mouse laughed. "You might be right, but we will wait to make that decision until we enter Morden." He completed crossing the bridge and led Kat into Morden.

Kat shifted in her saddle.

Maybe we'll never have to see Galdin.

A HINT OF BOOK 6

THE ASSASSINS

The horses' hooves crushed the fleshy mass of leaves, and the scent of lemon flooded the air. The smell stirred some forgotten ancient memory, and a shiver ran up Kat's spine.

She pulled on the reins and Starlight slowed.

Mouse had led them off the Guards' Keep bridge and wheeled his horse to the left. As he did so, Kat's horse, Starlight, had balked and danced sideways as she nickered a horse-type grumble.

Mouse swiveled his head and stared at her. "Why have you stopped?"

"Starlight is upset by something." She rubbed the goosebumps on her arms. "As we stepped off the bridge, I got the creeps and felt as if I walked through a cold web of air. And the forest directly ahead of us appears dark and foreboding."

"I did mention that Morden might be a difficult land for us to traverse."

"I know, and you also mentioned our first journey should be to our left beside the Farralawn up to the northern villages. But…"

Starlight continued to move restlessly and Kat reached

down and tried to soothe her.

"But what, Kat?"

"The Assassins' Guild beckons to me."

"The Guild? Why?"

Kat turned her horse to the right and the animal settled. "Even Starlight wants to head away from the north." She shifted in the saddle. "I know you've always set our routes through each land, but I'm convinced we should meet with Ssestin and his Guild Master first, before we meet with the Southern Mordens." She held up her hand to stop Mouse's objection. "I don't know why I'm drawn to the Guild, but I'm sure it will be a mistake if we don't go there first."

"If you wish to head for the Assassins' Guild that strongly, we can cut through the Merga forest."

"That's the one directly ahead, isn't it? You mentioned it before we left Baklai." She shuddered. "I truly don't like the look of it. Can't we go around the southern part of it?"

"We can, but I am not familiar with the land on the most southern tip of Morden, and I only have a rudimentary map."

"Is that way dangerous? Are there vicious creatures?"

"I have very little knowledge about that area." He nodded toward the trees in front of them. "The Merga ahead of us has always been known as a benign area. You should know that Morden possesses virtually no resting huts, so we will have to camp at nights as the Mordens do. They use their saddles for pillows, and cut leafy branches for bedding. They wrap themselves in their robes for cover. Luckily it never gets that cold at night. Only when one camps in the forests will we be reasonably comfortable on the ground and have the shelter of leaves overhead."

"So, we have no gear to make our nights more pleasant outside of these forests?"

"No. Remember we spoke about moving with greater speed through Morden, so we had to leave all those items behind."

"Mouse, I really feel strongly about visiting the Assassins first. So, in the interests of experiencing at least some physical comfort, I'll agree to go through the forest."

"Excellent. We will ride right, and enter the Merga closer to the southern end. Before we enter it, we will stop for the noon-turn and consume our meal given to us by Makinti. Since we cannot reach the Guild before nightfall, we will stop again in the early evening at the edge of the Merga to rest for the night. We will resume our journey on the morrow."

Kat nodded, and they both rode forward between the trees. Another shiver crept down her spine.

Is this forest truly benign? My stone isn't cold, but we're not in the forest yet.

ABOUT THE AUTHOR

J. M. Tibbott is a prize-winning author, writing instructor, and editor. She has been writing since her early school years, and has continued to study literature and the English language ever since. She believes there is always something new to learn.

Her works include magazine and newspaper articles, newsletters, online blogs, and story collections. This most recent book, *The Horse Masters*, book five of The Pridden Saga, a myth/fantasy series, was published in September of 2022. Book six of the series is currently in the works.

J. M. feels strongly that the well-being of any author is maintained by belonging to a number of writer's groups. Since early 2020, her groups have morphed into virtual ones.

DRAMATIS PERSONAE

NAME	DESCRIPTION	FROM
Aenid	A hunter from Tirenna	Rifella
Afeena	Of the pen Deon pod and bond mate to Kerron	Glowen
Alderon	Second-in-command to Makinti and Rifella head of the Border Keep	Rifella
Anwen	Apprentice Healer and guide for Mouse and Kat in Shendea	Shendea
Ariang	Master Miner at Haligon	Rifella
Argelwyd	Original Lord of all Pridden	Morden
Arrogol	Praetor of Murwenna's guards bond mate of Olwyn	Rifella
Bardu	Praetor of Eduardo's guards, bond mate of Irina	Rifella
Ballinor	Leader of guards in Roothlan	Rifella
Banhadron	Refugee from Morden	Morden
Bannigus	Horse Master in Rifella	Baklai
Bannon	Caretaker of Pontis in Kaylin	Kaylin
Benden	Stable master at Geronna	Rifella
Brennan	Thane of Glowen, of the pen Taddyn pod	Glowen
Brigden	Leader of Morden travelers in Morden	Shendea
Brith	Seamstress for Eduardo's Keep	Kaylin
Bodeth	Assistant to Tythan, with the guard unit in Geronna	Rifella
Bronwyth	Head of functions for Eduardo	Shendea

NAME	DESCRIPTION	FROM
Calanta	The Hunter God of Baklai, whose mate is supposedly Caleesh (Spirit only)	Baklai
Caleesh	Goddess for Pridden (except in Morden)Spirit only	Pridden
Caleth	Healer to Thane Cathked	Shendea
Carlo	Designer/coder for Nick	Earth
Carrog	Busta, bonded to Brynn	Rifella
Casseg	Busta, bonded to Kat	Rifella
Cathked	Thane of Baklai	Baklai
Clune	Financial clerk for Eduardo	Kaylin
Colwin	Apprentice serving Kat	Shendea
Cranna	Busta, bonded to Arrogol	Rifella
Dafid	Door guard for Eduardo	Kaylin
Dayleeya	Bond mate to Rifellan guard leader Jagloran, in Glowen	Rifella
Deleth	Healer to Lord Rhognor, womb mate to Wynneth	Shendea
Derwynn	Head of Thieves Guild	Shendea
Dibron	Food stall owner in Eeglos village market place in Baklai	Baklai
Didahanus	Leader of the Grain Farm	Baklai
Drainin	Counselor to Eduardo	Morden
Ebron	Of the pen Darryn pod, a well-respected artist	Glowen
Eduardo	Lord of Kaylin, related to Mouse	Morden
Eestred	Bond mate to Makinti and warrior in her own right.	Rifella
Eeloria	Bond mate of Alderon	Rifella

NAME	DESCRIPTION	FROM
Emrys	Of the pen Godron pod and uncle to Tessia, brother to Gwindon, and is in charge of the Orenberry winery in Pridden	Glowen
Erathin	Of the pen Deon pod and bond mate to Tevalow	Glowen
Fardith	Assistant to Halfin	Shendea
Farnon	Headmaster for Dizerth	Shendea
Farth	Of the pen Peskajorie pod	Glowen
Fenneth	Healer to Murwenna	Shendea
Ferren	Apprentice to Marreth	Shendea
Flank	Burgomaster of Magwin	Shendea
Fraglan	Leader of Mating crew	Baklai
Galakis	Hunter Master for Cathked	Baklai
Galdin	Thane of Morden	Morden
Garren	Of the pen Darryn pod, and talented glass-blower	Glowen
Gaviska	Of the pen Yuwen pod, manages the pathways around Kadwee	Glowen
Gaynore	Of the pen Deon pod, chief advisor to Brennan	Glowen
Gayzella	Head of House for Cathked	Baklai
Godrith	Tapestry Master in Shendea	Shendea
Gorhelion	Of the pen Cadno pod, and Master of the shipyards.	Glowen
Grayseen	Bond mate of Galakis, who is Master Hunter	Baklai
Grendel	An honor guard of Murwenna's	Rifella

NAME	DESCRIPTION	FROM
Gritch	Thane of Morden prior to Galdin, and Galdin's male parent.	Morden
Gweer	Hut apprentice near Border Keep	Baklai
Gwinrick	Leader of Murwenna's personal guards	Rifella
Gwindon	Of the pen Godron pod, brother to Emrys and father to Tessia. He is head of the wine-makers	Glowen
Halfin	Lady of Shendea, Lord Rhognor's bond mate	Shendea
Hamrid	A servant to a Morden, rescued by Kat	Baklai
Haydar	Horse-Master for Eduardo; Mayda's father	Baklai
Hesginn	Grey Magician, Head of Magician's Guild and advisor to Lord Rhognor, and Brother to Walden	Shendea
Ildiren	Apprentice healer at the Border Keep	Shendea
Illian	Apprentice builder, Penrow's daughter	Kaylin
Irina	Member of Keep guards, Bardu's bond mate and sister to Liandock	Rifella
Istra	Serving woman at Vendi's Inn	Shendea
Ivenon	Assist apprentice for Losgayrin	Baklai
Janella	Murwenna's bond mate, sister to Tiwellan	Rifella
Jagloran	Praetor of Guards to Brennan	Rifella

NAME	DESCRIPTION	FROM
Joona	Daughter of Didahanus	Baklai
Kadnu	Bardu's second-in-command	Rifella
Kaleen	Met Kat at Ponti Inn, member of Rifellan guards	Rifella
Karen	Friend to Kat, Nick's wife	Earth
Kanorang	Of the pen Darry pod, and is a master musician	Glowen
Kat Karim	Katherine Karim - mother a red-headed Scot and Father a handdsome bronze Iranian	Earth
Kaydith	Serving woman for Kat	Shendea
Keedin	Rifellan warrior stationed at Roothlan in Shendea	Rifella
Kerryon	Of the pen Deon pod. Second-in-command to Gaynore, who is head of the Wine growers and bond mate to Afeena	Glowen
Kesiad	Guard assigned to shadow Kat	Baklai
Kitterin	Bond mate of Didahanus head of Graini Farm	Bakla
Koosela	Of the pen Yuwen pod, manages pathways around Kadwee	Glowen
Kraklin	Grey Magician, second-in-command to Hesginn	Shendea
Krogen	Leader of the pen Yuwen pod	Glowen
Kurdin	Rifellan guard in Brevista	Rifella
Kerdinon	Bond mate to Cathked, and while born in Baklai, one of her parents was from Morden	Baklai/ `Morden

NAME	DESCRIPTION	FROM
Larryna	Bond mate to the head of the Fruit Farm	Baklai
Laylin	Serving woman for Kat	Kaylin
Liandock	Metal Master of Kaylin, brother to Irina, lover to Kat	Kaylin
Lanerch	Lord of Kaylin prior to Eduardo, and adoptive father to Eduardo	Kaylin
Lilliwon	Of the pen Iselon pod, now of the pen Taddyn pod, bond mate to Thane Brennan	Glowen
Layleene	Bond mate to Healer Caleth	Rifella
Makinti	Praetor for Thane Cathked, Bardu's friend	Rifella
Manga	Of the pen Yuwen pod and manager of the Camp in Glowen	Glowen
Maregiti	Stable hand at hut leading to Border Keep	Baklai
Marreth	Healer to Thane Brennan of Glowen	Shendea
Master Keeper	Manages the village of furred stingers	Glowen
Maxwell	Cousin to Kat's ex-husband	Earth
Mayrin	Wife of Horse-Master Haydar Mayda's mother	Baklai
Mayda	Serving woman and apprentice to Wynneth, daughter to Haydar	Baklai
Mazon	Head of the Mazon Family who welcome guests in Dizerth	Shendea

NAME	DESCRIPTION	FROM
Melindar	Sister & Advisor to Murwenna	Rifella
Merrindock	Prefect of Pakanna	Rifella
Milva	Of the pen Darryn pod, bond mate to Ebron	Glowen
Morshag	Legendary horse thief of Baklai, now a curse word	Bakla
Mouse	Serves Galdin, guide for Kat in Pridden related to Eduardo	Morden
Murwenna	Lord of Rifella, bond mate to Janella	Rifella
Neerin	Assistant to Walden	Shendea
Nellabon	Bond mate to Penabon, Horse-Master	Baklai
Nick	Kat's supervisor, spouse of Karen	Earth
Nooville	Guard leader in Brevista	Rifella
Penabon	Horse-Master to Cathked	Baklai
Penrow	Master Builder of Kaylin, Illian's father	Kaylin
Pentramore	Prefect of Tirenna	Rifella
Pilar	A Tirennian hunter	Rifella
Ponsin	Leader of Glazenwyth	Shendea
Ragvenoos	Leader at the Eeglos village near the Mating arena	Baklai
Rantor	Store owner in Blain	Rifella
Rhognor	Lord of Shendea, Titular head of all Guilds and bond mate to Halfin	Shendea
Saglit	Ssarff's first second-in command	Morden
Salssin	Agent of Assassins' Guild	Morden

NAME	DESCRIPTION	FROM
Sha-hee	Androgenous beings who share a hive mind, and can take on forms of other sentient being. They can read and can erase memories if necessary They are Glowens secret.	Glowen
Sherwyn	Head of house for Eduardo	Kaylin
Seegal	Offspring to Ssestin, apprentice and will become Sseegal when he is made a full Assassin.	Morden
Skonya	Of the pen Yuwen pod, manages the flower reserve	Glowen
Souris	Waiter at hotel in Tortola	Earth
Ssarff	Leader of the Assassins' Guild	Morden
Ssayleese	Snake Goddess in Morden (Spirit only)	Morden
Ssestin	Second-in-command to Ssarff	Morden
Ssorin	Assassin in Brevista	Morden
Taddyn	First Lord in Glowen	Glowen
Tammyn	Servant to pen Godrons	Glowen
Tannis	Brings gornog meat to Rifella	Kaylin
Tessia	Of the pen Godron pod and niece to Emrys	Glowen
Tevalow	Of the pen Deon pod, lead berry grower and bond mate to Erathin	Glowen
Thontook	Master Weaver of Kaylin	Kaylin
Tiwellan	Economic advisor to Murwenna adopted brother to Janella he was born in Morden	Rifella/ Morden

NAME	DESCRIPTION	FROM
Trevalynn	Of the pen Godron pod. 2nd-in-command to Emrys pen Godron	Glowen
Troyon	Heir to the Rifellan throne, son to Murwenna	Rifella
Tythan	Head of the guards in Geronna	Rifella
Walden	White Magician, brother to Hesginn	Shendea
Wealin	Taylor in Murwenna's Keep.	Rifella
Wielder	A person who demonstrates strong Powers, including an ability to fly, do magic, etc. All the strongest wielders are Lords, although some others also demonstrate Wielder abilities	Pridden
Wolfdrang	Second-in-command to Arrogol	Rifella
Wynneth	Healer to Lord Eduardo, womb mate to Deleth	Shendea

THE GLOWEN PODS

pen Taddyn	Royalty and royal relations
pen Deon	Vineyard growers and cultivators
pen Godron	Wine makers
pen Darryn	Artists of all kinds, including musicians
pen Cadno	Shipbuilders and keepers of wharves
pen Yuwen	Growers of foodstuffs
pen Iselon	Responsible for relationships with other lands
pen Puskees	In charges of fishing

FLORA AND FAUNA OF PRIDDEN

NAME	DESCRIPTION	FROM
Blicks	Small rabbit like creature, delicious in stew	Rifella
Blud	Rare, strong, red Glowen wine, addictive	Glowen
Bonbrie	Delicious fruit similar to peach	Shendea
Boradai	Furred creature size of a kitten, who can read the minds of people and is considered sentient	Shendea
Brantor	Small, short-legged, carnivores, who hunt in packs, with massive claws and small two horns, and black lengthy teeth.	Rifella
Brynosh	Tall plants that are used for tapestries and by Rifellans for their leather armor.	Shendea
Busta	Sentient creatures who bond with Rifellans to fight the Crosa (see -- specific busta in Personae)	Rifella
Cantobean	A chocolate-like bean for a stimulating tea Rifella	Rifella
Canobwint	A tea specifically for focus and clarity. Also known as clarity tea	Morden
Cathnog	Large ferocious cat-like creature, with four huge canines, resembling a sabre toothed tiger.	Shendea

NAME	DESCRIPTION	FROM
Difoona	Flower whose scent helps keep one awake	Glowen
Drag	Largest snake in Morden, similar to a python in that it crushes its prey; Grows about ten feet in length	Morden
Eedhenna	Vicious bird resembling buzzards mixed with pterodactyl genes	Glowen
Eethnaire	A root vegetable that when combined with dried brantor products; creates a delicious and nutritious stew	Rifella
Fara tea	A tasty balancing tea made from fara root and leaves	Glowen
Fire Mouth	A hot spice that is similar to Peri-Peri sauce	Baklai
Flamewort	Perfumed flower that acts like a roofie	Kaylin
Furred Stingers	Similar to our bees and they produce Golden River, which is similar to our honey	Glowen
Flying Nips	Similar to mosquitos, they draw draw blood and leave behind a a dreadful itch	Glowen
Gondal	Two-foot-long lizards with black tongues excellent for eating.	Baklai
Gornog	Pig-like animal, size of a jaguar, grey and black, covered in stiff bristles, two sets of tufted ears, six clawed feet, and twelve-inch tusks in a warted mouth. Meat is tender,	Kaylin

NAME	DESCRIPTION	FROM
Gornogs	are also sweet and delicious, although they causes gas in those who consume much of it.	
Groonnan	A dish made from grains from Kadwee used for morning meals	Glowen
Gwindle	A tea for mind and body focus	Shendea
Haggapoe	Large carrion bird that is attracted to shiny objects. One attacks Wink But Kat scares it off.	Rifella
Hissar	Rodent-like creature 1.5 feet with the temper of a Tasmanian devil, three rows of barbed teeth, and the strength of a creature ten times its size. an is incredible fast over short distances	Baklai
Horse	Almost the same as in our world, except much larger in size. In Baklai a small horse is at least seventeen hands high.	Baklai
Hydodd	Large elk-like animal with huge horns is cantankerous and a match for the ferocity of cathnogs	Shendea
Kamelona	Small scaled creature which almost resembles a chameleon. About six inches in length, with a tail three times as long can spit toxic saliva that can swiftly cause death in its prey. One bonds with Kat and she calls it Brade	Rifella
Karri-san	Tea that blocks Rifellan pheramones	Kaylin

NAME	DESCRIPTION	FROM
Kithra	Dog-sized rodent with black eyes , Needle-sharp teeth and brown hair; travel and attack in packs. Is incredibly vicious	Kaylin
Klim	Plant that produces nut-like seeds and is cooked into journeyklim, a porridge like meal, or dried in pieces to be used for eating while traveling.	Shendea
Koska	Flowers whose scent helps with sleep	Glowen
Kossil-Kweth	Tea with calming qualities	Glowen
Liquid Sha-hee.	Huge creatures that live in the sea, but are actaully part of the Sha-hee they have enormous teeth and resemble whale sharks. Are actually benign	
Loftin	A Ponti who escorted people among the vineyards of Glowen	Kaylin
Lowen	Flowers whose scent conveys happiness	Glowen
Lowenna	Happiness tea related to the lowen flowers which are grown in Glowen	Baklai
Lymnava	A fruit which tastes much like a lemon but which resembles an avocado	Glowen
Meena	Pet hissar to the daughter of Didahanus	Baklai
Mowzers	Similar to a house cat, but larger and is feral	Baklai

NAME	DESCRIPTION	FROM
Musserel	A large vegetable that mimics the flavor of steak.	Glowen
Nerthon	Flowers whose scent conveys energy	Glowen
Orenberry	Berries from which white wine is pressed	Glowen
Panwon	Thick glue-like substance produced from the horns, claws, and hooves of brantors.	Rifella
Ponti	Resembles a horse, but with a very large head for its body size, large splayed feet, short legs, wide girth, very sure-footed in mountainous regions. Pontis grow to about seven or eight hands high. Are ungainly looking	Shendea
Prickle-fur	A blue plant with red berries and soft barbs on the leaves, is toxic to human skin, and leaves a red itching rash when touched.	Rifella
Pyrock	Tiny, furry animal, with long tail and leathery wings, can transport instantly, and locate any person anywhere on Pridden; answers only to one person during lifetime, fits in one hand; used for sending messages anywhere on Pridden.	Kaylin
Red-leaf tea	Tea that helps with nausea	Baklai
Red-line berries.	Sweet berries which taste similar to strawberries	Glowen

NAME	DESCRIPTION	FROM
Red Rash	A dangerous virus, which emerges every seven years, and, unless treated may cause excruciating pain and death	Pridden
Reekers	Small vermin (pests) that destroy the Baklai food supplies, and when touched, emit a foul smell, which is difficult to cleanse oneself of	Baklai
Repella	Keeps flying nips away	Glowen
Scented Ritual.	Flower which raises intense sexual feelings	Glowen
Sea Swimmers.	Fish from the Bay at the Mora usually either roasted over coals or presented in a stew called cassolet	Shendea/ Rifella
Shade	A huge black panther-like animal with brilliant emerald eyes that became Kat's protector in Shendea	Shendea
Skat-koska	A strong sedative used to bring about unconsciousness	Shendea
Syeth	Small but deadly poisonous snake, venom causes almost instant death but is used by Shendean Healers to produce potion to combat Red Rash	Morden
Wullawerth	Sheep-like animal with masses of fine soft hair, excellent for clothing and prized for eating.	Kaylin

GEOGRAPHICAL NAMES

NAME	DESCRIPTION	FROM
Air Wyth	The unknown lands, about which nothing is known. The area, is totally unexplored, often used for banishment of wrongdoers.	Pridden
Afon-Asgwin	River, mostly underground, beginning at the Ponti pool and travels through Morden, and also contains a number of cenotes	Morden
Aythin	Village	Glowen
Bar Braich	The right crag of Mount Diffenna	Shendea
Barthon	Trading town	Rifella
Blain	Town in south of Shendea	Shendea
Border Keep	Stronghold manned by Rifellan guards at the Morden border	Baklai
Brevista	Village	Rifella
Brondish	A Forest close to the Hellesmouth	Rifella
Burning Rock	Mountain. Volcano	Shendea
Carrog	Word for rivers in Shendea	Shendea
Carrog Kennin	River in Shendea	Shendea
Carrog Mannin	River in Shendea	Shendea
Clog Arth	Mountain separating Shendea, Morden and Rifella, and contains the tunnels from Shendea to Morden	Shendea/ Morden/ Rifella
Carrog Dunlan	River thatbisects Morden	Morden
Clog Neran	Mountain in Kaylin	Kaylin

NAME	DESCRIPTION	FROM
Clog Nordad	Mountain between Shendea and Kaylin	Shendea/ Kaylin
Carrog Pandy	River acting as border between Shendea and Rifella	Shendea/
Rifella		
Clog	Word for mountains in Kaylin Shendea, and Rifella (also sometimescalled a Mount)	Pridden
Crimson Cauldron	Therapeutic hot mud baths	Shendea
Crystal Dunes	Area containing fine crystals, located near the Hellesmouth Desert	Rifella
Dark Forest	Forest used by the Healers as a place for renewal	Kaylin
Deon House	Location of the wine-berry farm	Glowen
Dinerth Caleesh	Women's place of spiritual celebration	Baklai
Dizerth	Town	Shendea
Doo	Word for forests in Morden	Morden
Dornish	Village at the wineries	Glowen
Dowron	Word used for rivers in Glowen	Glowen
Eeglos	Village where Mating of Horses takes place	Baklai
Fangliven Ford	Entrance into Morden, with high cliffs on either side.	Morden
Farralawn	The primary river separating Baklai, Morden and Rifella	Rifella
Farratown	Town	Rifellan
Finrase	Town	Shendea
Frothan Farm	Baklai fruit farm	Baklai

NAME	DESCRIPTION	FROM
Garrenn	Village	Shendea
Geronna	Village	Rifella
Glassen Swamp	Habitat of kithras	Kaylin
Glazenwyth	Town	Shendea
Godron House	Winery location	Glowen
Grain Farm	Farm where grain is separated from the straw	Baklai
Grening Stream.	stream on Kaylin	Kaylin
Haligon	Village nears the Mines	Rifella
Hanford Forest	Rest area in Shendea	Shendea
Halfway Haven	The resting place between the final inn and Rhognor's Keep	Shendea
Heer River	River bisecting Morden	Morden
Hellesmouth Desert	Middle of Rifella	Rifella
Hewder Dowron	River through Glowen	Glowen
Hyal Sea	The sea surrounding all coastal areas of Pridden	Pridden
Jasteen	Village near the shipyards	Glowen
Kadwee	Village	Glowen
Kamerdow	Village	Glowen
Kennes-Doo	Forest next to border of Baklai	Morden
Kroakin Woods	A forest of hard woods	Shendea
Krugg	Name for mountains in	Glowen
Krugg Menyd	Mountain in Glowen	Glowen
Lake Brynwog	Lake that is habitat of kithras	Kaylin
Lake Glenaddie	Resort lake	Shendea
Lake Yuffern	A northen resort lake	Glowen
Lanfair	Village established by Liandock	Kaylin
Lan-Kloon	The equivalent of heaven	Pridden

NAME	DESCRIPTION	FROM
Losgayrin	The vegetable and spice farm	Baklai
Magwin	Town	Shendea
Marnabee	Town where outward-bound ships dock	Glowen
Merga-Doo	Merga Forest	Morden
Merrithan Forest	Southern forest in Rifella	Rifella
Mora Waters	Fjord between Shendea and Rifella	Shendea/ Rifella
Mont	Word for mountains in Morden	Morden
Mont Diffenna	Mountain where Lord Rhognor's Keep is located.	Shendea
Netht Dowron	River leading to the sea	Glowen
Nordic Pass	The pass between Kaylin and Shendea	Kaylin/ Shendea
Old Forest	Forest inhabited by gornogs	Kaylin
Old Town	The ancient city attached to the Keep where the unsavory people & criminals live	Kaylin
Orkanna Harbor	Main harbor	Rifella
Pakanna	Village where armorers live and work	Rifella
Penrow Pool	Huge whirlpool leading under the Clog Blue mountains and is suspected to become the underground river flowing through Morden	Kaylin
Pinacle Rock	A rock island off the north coast	Glowen
Ponti Inn	Inn where horses & pontis are are exchanged	Shendea

NAME	DESCRIPTION	FROM
Rashnig	Village	Rifella
Restin	Village	Rifella
Roothlan	Resort Village	Shendea
Skinya-Doo	Skinya forest	Morden
Straw Farm	The farm where the grain is grown an where straw is converted to mattresses	Baklai
Tangata	Village	Rifella
Tasik	Resort village	Glowen
Tavollen	Village	Glowen
Tirenna	Village of brantor hunters	Rifella
Torrenton Forest	Forest in northern Rifella	Rifella
Tottawanga River	River located in Rifella	Rifella
Trigoran	Large trading city	Kaylin
Tyrol River	A river flowing through Rifella	Rifella
Vendi's Inn	Inn near Rhognor's Keep	Shendea
Yuffern Dowron	The Yuffern River	Glowen

THE PRIDDEN SAGA

THE 4 PREVIOUS BOOKS

This saga consists so far, of four previous books: Be sure to order yours from Amazon.com.

The Arrival, The Pridden Saga, Book 1

New world. New creatures. Can a flawed but brilliant woman survive their bizarre social customs?

The Healers, The Pridden Saga, Book 2

Surrounded by danger. A powerful woman ignores advice and constantly falls afoul of the inhabitants of this extraordinary world

The Warriors, The Pridden Saga, Book 3

Encountering teams of powerful warriors and hordes of seductively erotic men. Can one woman survive this combination?

The Pleasure Seekers, The Pridden Saga, Book 4

Overwhelming sexual advances, highly potent alcohol and erotic blossoms. Is a femal game designer equipped to handle this?

Order yours today from Amazon.com

www.ingramcontent.com/pod-product-compliance
Lightning Source LLC
Chambersburg PA
CBHW072043190726
48294CB00005B/1378

9781739018900